Counselling in India

Sujata Sriram
Editor

Counselling in India

Reflections on the Process

Springer

Editor
Sujata Sriram
School of Human Ecology
Tata Institute of Social Sciences
Mumbai, Maharashtra
India

ISBN 978-981-10-0583-1 ISBN 978-981-10-0584-8 (eBook)
DOI 10.1007/978-981-10-0584-8

Library of Congress Control Number: 2016931297

Printed on acid-free paper

This Springer imprint is published by Springer Nature
The registered company is Springer Science+Business Media Singapore Pte Ltd.

This book is dedicated to the faculty and students, past, present and future, of the School of Human Ecology, Tata Institute of Social Sciences, Mumbai.

Acknowledgments

A work of this nature would be incomplete without acknowledging the many people who have played pivotal roles in bringing this volume to fruition. First and foremost, I would like to acknowledge the contributions of my friend and colleague, Prof. Rajani Konantambigi, Professor, School of Human Ecology, Tata Institute of Social Sciences (TISS), Mumbai. It was she who conceptualized the idea of converting the dissertations of the MA students of the then Centre for Human Ecology into publishable papers. She applied for a project for the Board of Research Studies, TISS. When the MA in Counselling programme was conceptualized, with a dissertation based on primary research as a compulsory, integral part of the programme, one of the aims was to encourage students to carry out research on aspects of counselling and counsellors in India, under the supervision of the faculty, which could be converted to published papers in journals or books on the issue. This volume is the first rendition of the research of the School of Human Ecology.

I would like to thank the Board of Research Studies (BRS), TISS, Mumbai that provided the initial funding for this project. The BRS and the Director TISS have been very supportive of this venture. Dr. Pooja Bhargava and Dr. Nandini Ravi were research assistants on the project and did the initial work of converting the dissertations into the papers that make up this volume. I would like to thank them for their contributions in producing the first drafts of the papers from the dissertations. The drafts prepared by them have subsequently gone through many edits to come to the present form, but their input has to be recognized.

All the authors who have contributed to this volume have waited patiently to see the outcome of their hard work. They have taken the time to reply to the mails sent, and answer my many questions and requests to provide details that I felt necessary for this enterprise. Many of the students whose papers are featured here are working in full-time jobs, as counsellors and therapists, and have had to perforce dig through their dissertations to examine the connect between these papers and their dissertations. All the papers have had the reference lists and citations updated, so that the material presented is current and relevant for the reader. Any errors that may be there are attributable to me, and not to the individual authors.

My faculty colleagues need to be acknowledged. Vrinda has always been supportive of this venture. Chetna and Aparna have contributed to this volume. I would like to thank them and my other colleagues for their encouragement and excitement to see the fruit of the collective hard work develop over the last year. I hope the publication of this volume will serve as an incentive to publish more of the research that is carried out by faculty and students at the School of Human Ecology.

All the anonymous participants who have taken the time to participate in the research studies featured here deserve a resounding thank you from me and from the authors of the chapters. It is their contribution that has made this volume possible; some of their voices are represented in the chapters here. I would like to thank the anonymous peer reviewers for their inputs and comments, which have helped in developing this volume into a more readable, user-friendly product.

I would like to thank Springer for giving us the opportunity to bring this volume to a larger audience of readers. I hope this will be the first of many volumes produced on the research of the School of Human Ecology, TISS.

Last, but not least, I would like to thank my family. My long-suffering husband Sriram and my mother need to be thanked for the unstinting support and encouragement given to me in order to complete this project.

Sujata Sriram

Contents

Editor and Contributors

About the Editor

Sujata Sriram is Associate Professor and Dean of the School of Human Ecology, Tata Institute of Social Sciences, Mumbai. She was awarded the Fulbright Nehru Senior Research Fellowship at the Department of Anthropology at the University of California San Diego. Sujata has a Ph.D. from the University of Delhi. Prior to her appointment at TISS, she was Reader in the Department of Child Development, Lady Irwin College, University of Delhi, Delhi. She has a background in Human Development. At TISS she worked to develop the MA in Counselling programme, and the MA Applied Psychology programmes. She teaches and supervises students from the MA Applied Psychology programme. She guides research for students in the MA, M.Phil. and Ph.D. programmes of TISS. From 2012, she has been part of a team that developed iCALL, the psychosocial helpline at TISS, Mumbai, that provides telephonic and email-based counselling services for individuals in psychosocial distress. Her research interests are diverse, and extend from psychological counselling and guidance, belief systems, development of the self and identity, religion and religious identity, cultural psychology, social networking and its impact, positive psychology and happiness, marriage and family issues, and socialization in childhood and adolescence. E-mail: sujatasriram@gmail.com

Contributors

Swarnima Bhargava is passionate about research and the practice of psychology. She believes in supporting the strengths and agency of each individual by exploring and working with their narratives. Swarnima is currently privileged to be working with children, adolescents and families at Children First, New Delhi. Swarnima has received an M.Phil. in Clinical Psychology from the Institute of Human Behaviour and Allied Sciences, Delhi as well as Masters in Counselling from the Tata Institute of Social Sciences, Mumbai. Her research interests lie in the field of psychotherapy, marital and sexual satisfaction, child and adolescent mental health, and process research. E-mail: swarnima.bhargava@gmail.com

Chetna Duggal is an Assistant Professor at the School of Human Ecology, Tata Institute of Social Sciences, Mumbai. She has completed her M.Phil. in Clinical Psychology from NIMHANS (Bangalore). She is at present pursuing a Ph.D. at TISS. Her doctoral research is on beliefs and values of psychotherapists. She teaches courses on psychotherapy and counselling and her research interests include therapist factors in psychotherapy, psychotherapy change process, psychotherapy training and supervision, intimate and couple relationships and couple therapy, child and adolescent mental health and psychotherapy. Ms. Duggal has been practicing as a psychotherapist for over 10 years, working with individuals, couples and families. E-mail: chetnaduggal@gmail.com

Aparna Joshi currently works as Assistant Professor at the School of Human Ecology, Tata Institute of Social Sciences (TISS), Mumbai. She teaches in the MA Applied Psychology programme at TISS. She has completed MA in Clinical Psychology from Mumbai University and has received further training in psychotherapy from various institutions. At present she is pursuing a Ph.D. at TISS, which involves an exploration of counsellors' journeys of working with issues of domestic violence and couple conflicts. She has been practising as a psychotherapist for the past 17 years. She has been involved in envisioning and implementing mental health service programmes in clinical, community and institutional settings and in training of different stakeholders (including government and non-government agencies) on issues of mental health and counselling. In 2012, she initiated a counselling helpline called iCALL, which provides telephonic and email-based counselling services for individuals in psychosocial distress. Her areas of interest and expertise are gender and mental health, violence against women, couple and family therapy and ethics in psychotherapy. E-mail: aparnasathe73@gmail.com

Sandhya Limaye is an Associate Professor and Chairperson of Centre for Disability Studies and Action, School of Social Work, Tata Institute of Social Sciences, Mumbai. She has almost three decades of experience in working with the disabled population. She has worked with different types of disabled people across the lifespan, especially with teenagers with disabilities and their families. Her intervention work with the disabled is at the individual and family level. She has conducted many community education programmes and workshops such as sensitisation about disability, awareness about disability among railway commuters, and inclusive education practice in regular schools. She has had the opportunity to work with different stakeholders working in the field of disability at the level of policy issues, and also for implementation of programmes. She has received many awards and fellowships, such as the Rockefeller Fellowship, Fulbright-Nehru Senior Research Fellowship and the Erasmus Mundus Fellowship. E-mail: limaye.sandhya@gmail.com

Afshan Mariam works with different groups of children across the districts of Pondicherry and Cuddalore, in Tamil Nadu, India. After completing the Master of

Arts in Counselling from TISS, she has worked with children in multiple settings. Her work includes counselling, farming and gardening, mindfulness practices as well as forum theatre. She works with children from varied backgrounds—some study in an alternative school, some are children with autism and some of them are part of a centre for street children. Living in Pondicherry, which has been a centre for Indian psychology as well as various experiments in education, she carries out independent research studies which examine the relationships between philosophy and psychology in education. E-mail: afshanmariam15@gmail.com

Sneha Anant Nikam has an MA in Counselling from the Tata Institute of Social Sciences, Mumbai. She has had an interest in Health Psychology from her undergraduate days as a psychology student in Vaze College, Mumbai. Sneha has worked as a telephone counsellor at the Vandrewala Foundation, Mumbai. Sneha is now a counsellor with "Cankids.... Kidscan", an NGO in Mumbai which works for the cause of childhood cancer. As an employee of the NGO, Sneha is placed in the paediatrics department of the Tata Memorial Hospital (TMH), as a counsellor for children and families of children suffering from cancer. E-mail: snehnikam@gmail.com

Rashmi Rangarajan received her MA degree in Counselling from the Tata Institute of Social Sciences in Mumbai. Rashmi worked as a counselling psychologist with the Latika Roy Foundation in Dehradun, from August 2013 to July 2015. She worked with children with disabilities, and their families, developed an intake tool called 'Knowing Me Better' to facilitate teacher–parent partnerships and smooth transitions for children from their homes to the early intervention centre, and also founded and facilitated support groups for caregivers and parents. E-mail: rashmir90@gmail.com

Mithila Rao completed her BA in Psychology from St. Xavier's College, Mumbai, and then an MA in Counselling from the Tata Institute of Social Sciences, Mumbai. Mithila has worked with an NGO called Arpan in Mumbai, providing psychotherapy for children who had been sexually abused, as well as to adult survivors of child sexual abuse. Research has always been a fascinating part of her life through college and work life. Mithila now works as a qualitative researcher at Quantum Consumer Solutions, a market research firm, in Mumbai. E-mail: mithila294@gmail.com

Paras Sharma has an MA in Counselling from the Tata Institute of Social Sciences, Mumbai. He has worked in the Medical Social Work wing at two major tertiary-care hospitals in Mumbai, where he was involved in providing counselling to patients and caregivers, fundraising for the socioeconomically backward, and training paramedical and administrative hospital staff. Paras is currently the Programme Coordinator at iCALL Psychosocial Helpline, a pan-India telephone and email-based counselling service, which is a field-action-project of the School of Human Ecology at TISS, Mumbai. His current work involves training and supervision of mental health professionals, as well as design and delivery of workshops/training modules for private and governmental organizations. E-mail: sharmaparas8@gmail.com

Sindhura Tammana has an MA in Counselling from the Tata Institute of Social Sciences (TISS), Mumbai. Sindhura has attended Level 1 of EMDR (Eye Movement Desensitization and Reprocessing) training. She worked with Arpan, an NGO in Mumbai that works in the area of child sexual abuse where she received the Most Creative Counsellor Award for the psychotherapeutic work she carried out. She has worked with TISS at the Centre for Human Ecology as a fieldwork supervisor for MA students. She has taught papers in psychology to degree students at K.C. College, Mumbai, and has worked at the Piramal Foundation for Education Leadership and was involved in building a Leadership Development Curriculum for internal development. Sindhura's other engagements include work with School Guru Eduserve as a Visiting Faculty in Psychology, and a brief stint as a Consulting Counsellor at Royal Girls High School, Mumbai. At present, she is part of the team at Inner Space, a counselling centre in Mumbai, where she works with adolescents and young adults. E-mail: sindhura.tammana@gmail.com

Sinduja Vummidi holds an MA degree in Counselling from the Tata Institute of Social Sciences, Mumbai. She graduated in Psychology from Madras University. She is presently working as a researcher at the Cognitive Measurement Lab at Illumine Knowledge Resources Pvt. Ltd., Mumbai. She works on designing and building of cognitive tests and diagnostic tools. As part of her work, she has participated in building and administering measurement tools for financial services professionals, school and university students, career seekers, candidates for recruitment and others. Her areas of focus include mind-set assessment, cognitive state mapping, modes of engagement and measuring of ideals. She had previously worked with People First, a coaching and training company, where she mentored a team of coaches in conducting transformation workshops. E-mail: sindhuja1188@gmail.com

List of Tables

Chapter 1
Counselling in India: An Introduction to the Volume

Sujata Sriram

Abstract This volume titled 'Counselling in India: Reflections on the Process', brings together empirical research on practising therapists and counsellors in India. The experiences of being therapists and counsellors in India are illustrated, with an emphasis on the process of therapy and counselling. In India, the stigma related to mental illness and going to a mental health practitioner persists, compounding the task of the counsellor. The discourse on counselling, as practiced in diverse contexts, such as hospitals, schools, private practice, family courts and helplines, have been summed up. Challenges confronted at the initial stage of joining the profession as novice counsellors, the motivational factors that contribute to entering the profession, the synergies between the personal and the professional self of the therapist have been discussed. The use of the creative arts such as music, art and intermodal methods in therapy have been considered. Counsellor training and implications of the gaps therein have been deliberated.

Keywords Counselling · Counselling process · Novice counsellors · Motivating factors · Creative arts therapy · Counselling training · Helpline counselling · Marriage counselling

> 'Would you tell me, please, which way I ought to go from here?'
>
> 'That depends a good deal on where you want to get to,' said the Cat.
>
> 'I don't much care where-' said Alice.
>
> 'Then it doesn't matter which way you go,' said the Cat.
>
> '–so long as I get SOMEWHERE,' Alice added as an explanation.
>
> 'Oh, you're sure to do that,' said the Cat, 'if you only walk long enough.'
>
> (Lewis Carroll, *Alice in Wonderland*)

S. Sriram (✉)
School of Human Ecology, Tata Institute of Social Sciences, Mumbai, India
e-mail: sujatasriram@gmail.com

S. Sriram (ed.), *Counselling in India*, DOI 10.1007/978-981-10-0584-8_1

This volume brings together papers that reflect common issues and concerns, pertaining to the development of counselling as a profession in India. The papers have been drawn from primary research carried out with counsellors and therapists working in varied settings across different cities in India, such as Delhi, Mumbai, Chennai and Bengaluru. To channel Lewis Carroll and Alice, the journey of counsellors in India is much like stepping through the looking glass. Counsellors and psychotherapists in India still tread on paths not widely travelled.

While there have been rapid strides made in the development of counselling in India, concerns have emerged alongside. Education for the training of counsellors is available in many colleges and universities in the country (Arulmani 2007). However, it is a harsh reality that the number of professionally qualified counsellors and therapists in India are barely adequate to serve the needs of the population (Bhola et al. 2012; Manickam 2010; Laungani 2004). While there has been a proliferation of professional training programmes and courses for counsellor education in India, there is no standard curriculum followed. The need for licensing and regulation of the profession has been expressed by practitioners and academics in the field; however, there have been limited efforts to regulate the profession. There has been limited research in India related to the field of counselling psychology and the effects of counselling and therapy on issues and individuals. The existing research is scattered and rarely disseminated to academics and practitioners in the field (Bhola et al. 2012; Manickam 2010).

While interest in psychotherapy has been there for many years, research in the field began in real earnest only in the middle of the twentieth century. Psychotherapy research can be broadly divided into two main streams: outcome and process research. The difference between process and outcome research have been identified by researchers (Orlinsky et al. 2015; Hill and Corbett 1993). Psychotherapy outcome research consists of studies related to the effectiveness and impact of therapy of the client or patient, often after the conclusion of the therapy. Psychotherapy process research in contrast, examines what happens during the psychotherapy sessions, the interactions between the client and the therapist. The process can be determined by various aspects such as the issues brought by the clients for therapy, the therapeutic model or approach that the therapist uses with the client, their skills, expertise and the nature of the therapeutic alliance they develop with the clients. The therapeutic process can additionally be affected by contextual factors such as the social and economic climate prevailing, the various stressors that individuals face and the nature of the delivery of mental health services. Process studies require attention to be paid to the locations of the enquiry, the details of what to study and how to investigate the same, along with the duration for which the analysis is to be carried on for.

1.1 Psychotherapy and Counselling in India

The founder of the Indian Psychoanalytic Society, Girindrasekar Bose is considered to have begun the practice of Western psychotherapy in the Indian subcontinent. In an important project, in 1976, Varma and Ghosh attempted to compile objective information on the nature and extent of psychotherapy practiced in the country. Their survey revealed that Indian psychiatrists practiced psychotherapy, but to a limited extent, which was different from Western models. Varma (1982) advocates that in countries like India, it would be necessary to carry out an analysis between psychotherapy and faith healing, in order to develop an objective understanding of both, and if possible to incorporate some of the latter into the former, especially for simple neuroses (Varma 1982). Further studies have shown that insufficient attention has been given to the aspects of teaching and learning of psychotherapeutic techniques to psychiatrists during training (Bhola et al. 2012; Raguram 2001).

Schoonover et al. (2014) in a study on perceptions of traditional healing for mental illness in rural Gujarat found that traditional healers were the first line of service providers sought. Despite recognizing that doctors were more effective in treating mental illness as compared to traditional healers, there was tremendous faith reposed on the traditional healers, indicating the degree to which they were integrated into the local community. The findings indicate the necessity for collaboration between medical practitioners and faith healers for the treatment of mental illness.

Until recently in India, specialized services of counselling offered by trained professionals did not exist; however, forms of counselling were available within social relationships, such as the '*guru-shishya parampara*' (teacher–disciple tradition) wherein the guru (teacher) had the onus of moulding the lives of the students, and by general practitioners, indigenous doctors and lay therapists (Bhola et al. 2012; Varma 1982). The changes that have swept across India over the centuries have gradually eroded such relationships (Arulmani 2007). It is against the background of social and economic changes in the Indian context, that counselling needs have emerged. Economic reforms over the past three decades have transformed lifestyles, and enhanced the pace of change. There are increasing numbers of individuals and families who require professional assistance to deal with changes in personal and professional spheres of their lives, often due to the inability of existing systems such as the family to provide supportive interventions. The role of counsellors and counselling services becomes more necessary and relevant in these situations and contexts.

Despite the economic progress made by India, it has been seen that about 80 per cent of those who need mental health care are outside the purview of treatment. Community healthcare services in India are scarce, and mental health service providers are unevenly distributed (Kumar 2011; Thara and Patel 2010). The problem of service delivery is compounded by negative attitudes and lack of knowledge among the population, which prevents the timely seeking of help. Mental health literacy is one of the aims of the National Mental Health Programme (NMHP) through public awareness with information, education and communication material. One of the added tasks of the NMHP is the reduction of stigma and discrimination meted out to persons with mental illness in both rural and urban areas. Enhancing mental health literacy of people will contribute to better access to services and provide a more conducive environment for individuals with mental illness and their families. Data from India indicate that mental health education needs are yet to be met (Gaiha et al. 2014).

Western approaches to psychology form the basis of most available counselling services and models for training in the discipline in India. These approaches are not always based on the Indian cultural context, wherein relationships are given importance over individual notions of the self. Kapur et al. (1996, p. vi.) cite the importance for theoretical constructs suitable to Indian social reality, without which the entire process of learning and practice of psychotherapy would appear abstruse. At times therapists grieve that Indian patients are unsuitable for psychotherapy. The level of awareness of the social reality is in direct proportion to the depth of the understanding, of training and practice of psychotherapy. In the absence of a consolidated Indian model of psychotherapy, it is important that therapists do not blindly follow Western models.

Much of the training done for counsellors in India draws from Western models and therapies. There are few attempts to consider how to contextualize these Western models to Indian contemporary reality. The need to develop indigenous models of therapy has been expressed often; however, the development of such contextual models has been slow (Arulmani 2007; Kapur et al. 1996; Varma 1982).

Counsellors in India today work in multiple settings. Professional counsellors can be found in hospitals, schools and educational institutions, family courts, non-governmental organizations working with women and children, workplace sites, helplines, de-addiction centres, in private practice, to name just a few of the settings. Counsellors in India are drawn from multiple disciplines, ranging from social workers, to psychologists and psychiatrists. Some of the intricacies involved in the regulation of the field relates to the diversity in issues and contexts within which counsellors function in India in the context of the twenty-first century (Bhola et al. 2012; Manickam 2010).

Counselling[1] in the Indian context is slowly gaining recognition; albeit in the metropolitan cities and urban areas. While the need for counsellors and counselling services is felt in all parts of the country, the profession is yet to establish itself in the hinterland. Counselling needs in India have arisen from the rapid pace of change in the social, cultural and economic environments with which individuals and families come into contact. The processes of urbanization and modernization have resulted in an increase in the momentum of change, which have in turn placed a burden of expectations, demands and roles on the individual. Alongside, the traditional support systems such as the family, peer group and school have shrunk

[1]The terms psychotherapy and counselling have been used interchangeably in this chapter and in this volume.

over time, and have not been able to sustain in enabling individuals in times of crisis. The increase in individual and family vulnerability has necessitated the development of professional counsellors in order to facilitate the process of coping with the myriad vicissitudes of everyday life. Gaiha et al. (2014) indicate the crucial role played by counsellors and teachers in India as important sources of information on mental health. In their study, counsellors and teachers emerged as key players, with 'the power to influence and inspire health seeking behaviour' (p. 154).

The papers in this volume address a multiplicity of issues that surround the counselling profession in India, drawing from narratives of counsellors with varying amounts of experience in the field. The papers have been developed from research studies carried out by the faculty and students from the School of Human Ecology in the Tata Institute of Social Sciences. Apart from counsellors who use Western models of counselling and psychotherapy, the experiences of counsellors using creative arts in therapy have been explored. Issues in counselling education has been captured through the perceptions of trainers of counselling programmes. The process of therapy as followed in marriage counselling in the family courts, in telephone counselling on a helpline and in a school have been examined in papers in this volume. Issues arising with respect to values and beliefs of therapists and the motivation that compels counsellors to take up the profession have been scrutinized in some of the papers.

1.2 The Papers in This Volume

The volume begins with a paper by Bhargava and Sriram titled 'Counsellor Characteristics and the Counselling Experience'. This is an exploratory study that looks at how counsellors and therapists working in Delhi and Mumbai view their counselling experience. Eight counsellors working in varied settings were interviewed, and their voices, views and experiences about working in the field of counselling and psychotherapy have been obtained. It was found that counsellors were intrinsically motivated to help others and develop within the profession. Efforts were made to locate themselves within the sociocultural milieu of the clients. The participants used resources such as supportive networks of professionals, as well as methods such as meditation and exercise as means of self-care. Data revealed the need for self-work by the counsellors in their search for new skills to enhance their professional credibility. The shift from the biomedical to the biopsychosocial model was emphasized by the participants, which was in keeping with the changes taking place in the field of mental health.

The paper by Duggal and Rao titled 'Challenges Experienced by Novice Counsellors' uses a mixed methods approach to examine how novice counsellors negotiate their entry into the field. Duggal and Rao use Rønnestad and Skovholt's (2003) phase model of counsellor development. Novice counsellors represent the first few years after graduation and entry into the field. This is a crucial phase in the development of counsellors, wherein disillusionment and feeling of insecurity and inadequacy can contribute to counsellor burnout and attrition. Data obtained from counsellors indicated that novice counsellors experienced challenges on personal and professional dimensions. Many novice counsellors expressed feelings of inadequacy, uncertainty and incompetence about handling clients and issues. There was the felt challenge of applying skills and techniques learnt in theory in practice. Caseload burdens coupled by inadequate supervision often caused by being the lone counsellor in a setting posed challenges to the novice counsellors. The participants spoke of learning on the job about how to adapt skills in order to work with different client groups. Self-care methods such as seeking supervision have been mentioned. The need to regulate the profession was another feature that emerged.

Vummidi and Limaye's paper titled 'Synergies between Personal and Professional Lives of Counsellors' uses a qualitative method to study how the counselling process affects the personal and professional development of counsellors working in Chennai. Data from the study showed that counsellors integrated their personal and professional lives; this helped in the positive view held about the profession. The counsellors acquired mastery over their skills on the job. New skills and techniques were acquired as a means of professional development; alongside counsellors developed the ability to contextualize the skills for use with clients from differing backgrounds. Over time, the participants became more self-reflective about their practice, and developed their own eclectic models of working with clients. Despite encountering multiple challenges, all counsellors expressed satisfaction, fulfilment and a sense of purpose in the profession that had been chosen, and had a commitment to help the profession grow.

Duggal and Sriram's paper titled 'Beginning the Journey: What Motivates Therapists to Join the Profession?' attempts an examination of what leads therapists and counsellors to join the profession. A qualitative dominant mixed methods study was formulated to examine factors that led individuals to become therapists. An interest in the human mind, in healing and reading and in working with children, led therapists to enter the helping profession. Personal qualities such as being a people's person and being a patient listener facilitated the choice. Experiencing life changing events and personal distress, receiving professional help, or adopting certain roles within the family were mentioned as facilitating factors. Personal needs and the role of destiny and chance were also identified as contributing elements. Different therapists took different routes in their journey towards pursuing the profession of counselling and psychotherapy. Awareness of factors that contribute to entering the arena through self-reflective practice in training and supervision helps in the long-term engagement with the profession.

Rangarajan and Duggal's paper titled 'Exploration of Therapists' Personal and Professional Values' offers insights into the interplay of values for experienced therapists. A mixed methods study was carried out with eight therapists working in Dehradun and Delhi, with varying therapeutic orientations and work settings. Quantitative data were collected using the Portrait Value Questionnaire (Schwartz et al. 2001) and in-depth interviews provided the qualitative data. Therapist values have been found to substantially affect the progress and outcome of therapy; and therapists cannot avoid communicating their values to their clients. Values have also been found to affect therapists' choice of the profession, and though it is possible to speak about personal values as being distinct from professional values, in actuality, effective practice requires an amalgamation of personal and the professional values. The findings of the study suggested the integration of personal and professional values. The four value priorities of the participants were benevolence (care and compassion), honesty, self-direction (growth and respect), and universalism (equality and justice). The main sources of their values were reported as family, training, clients, religion and spirituality.

The paper by Sriram and Nikam titled 'Training in Counselling: Current Status and Trainer's Perspectives' captures trainers' perspectives on counselling in Mumbai, using a qualitative dominant embedded mixed methods study. Data revealed that there were three formats available for counsellor training—short-term, diploma and degree programmes. The purpose of each of these programmes varied; the short-term programmes were seen as skill-building and market driven courses to augment skill sets, and were mainly offered by private institutes. The diploma and degree programmes were of longer duration and were offered by colleges and universities. There was no standard curriculum followed by the various programmes, which led to considerable discrepancy in content and pedagogy. The number of students admitted for the programmes had steadily increased over the years. A marked gender disparity was seen in the admission of students across programmes, with women dominating the men. While all trainers acknowledged the importance of field experience for students, there was inadequate supervision and rigour emphasized for the same. Trainers bemoaned the fact that untrained individuals were allowed to enter the field, and expressed the need to regulate the profession. The need to develop counsellors who could work in languages other than English was emphasized.

The paper by Mariam and Joshi titled 'Exploring Expressions: Therapist's Use of the Creative Arts in Therapy' is an exploratory qualitative study that looks at therapists' experience of using the creative arts. Participants for the study were ten therapists from Chennai, Bengaluru and Mumbai who used creative art forms such as visual art, dance, drama, music and expressive/intermodal approach as therapeutic modes on issues of mental health. The therapists included in the study used the creative arts to gain deeper insight into the problems, which helped in the attainment of the therapeutic goals. The needs of the client were assessed through both formal and informal means, which helped in the formulation of therapeutic goals. These therapeutic goals can be defined by the client, or by the therapists understanding of the needs of the client. While intervention strategies used by creative art therapists vary, the phases of warm up, theme building and closure can be seen. Creative art therapies are seen as alternate therapies that complement existing practices.

'The Role of a School Counsellor' by Tamanna is a first person narrative account of the travails of a beginning counsellor who works in a school setting. The multiple roles that are occupied by a school counsellor have been illustrated by the author. An effectual school counsellor has far more to do than working with children in individual and group settings. The school counsellor can be a lynchpin for ensuring the success of school mental health programmes as defined by

Kapur (2011). The difference in beliefs and values between the counsellor and the teachers, administrators and parents has implications on the development of the role of the counsellor itself. School counsellors face the challenge of validating the profession of counselling by making the various stakeholders aware about the need, the nature and the methods of counselling. Often the methods used by the school counsellors were considered as inappropriate by teachers and administrators, necessitating negotiation, followed by teacher and parent training.

Sriram and Duggal's paper titled 'Marital Counselling in India: Perspectives from Family Court Counsellors' explores the process of marriage counselling as practiced by counsellors in the Family Courts in India. The Family Courts Act (1984) in India requires all couples filing for divorce to seek counselling by trained marriage counsellors. The interventions of the marriage counsellors in the family courts were intended to ensure that women received a fair hearing, and their rights were upheld in the judicial system which tended to favour the interests of men. While the Family Courts Act, 1984, recommends that suitable trained and qualified marriage counsellors be appointed to provide the necessary therapeutic inputs, in practice, most states in India have not done so. Even in states where there are counsellors in places, procedures and rules have not been laid down. States that have employed trained counsellors and social workers provide a modicum of counselling for families who come for divorce. Unless the issues involve aspects of custody or maintenance, there is little done by way of counselling for couples and families to deal with the aftermath of divorce.

While most of the papers in this volume examine counselling in the face to face mode, the paper by Sriram, Joshi and Sharma titled 'Telephone Counselling in India: Lessons from iCALL' offers insights into the process of counselling using a distance mode. Bringing in the experience of running a helpline offering counselling by telephone and email on varied psychosocial issues, the paper examines how the therapeutic alliance develops in a distance mode. Unlike face to face counselling, counsellors using the telephone draw on paralingual cues in order to develop empathy and offer assistance. Telephone counselling offers valuable alternatives in countries such as India, where the delivery of mental health services are strapped by the shortage of professionals and other resources. Surveys of counselling provided by the distance mode indicate that they are efficacious in dealing with a wide variety of mental health issues. Counselling helplines run by professionals can provide a valuable adjunct to existing mental health services. The paper offers an understanding about issues involved in the setting up, training needs required for counsellors, and ethical issues involved in telephone counselling.

1.3 On the Methods Used

Most of the studies included in this volume use qualitative approaches and methods for obtaining data, and are exemplars of small sample research. In these studies, random sampling is rarely used as a sampling procedure, with a preference for purposive, purposeful and convenience samples. The few studies that use a mixed methods approach use a qualitative dominant approach. Psychology in its drive to become a science has been predominantly focused on studies using random sampling and more quantitative approaches for obtaining data. Orlinsky (2008) writes that over the years, psychotherapy research has appropriated the methods of 'normal science, meaning that research by and large has become devoted to incrementally and systematically working out the details of a general 'paradigm' that is widely accepted and largely unquestioned' (p. 4). In the same essay, Orlinsky comments that a dependence on the paradigms of the natural sciences 'represents a risky premature closure in understanding the actual nature of psychotherapy and the people who engage in it' (Orlinsky 2008, p. 6).

Bhola et al. (2012) reflect on the difficulty in using random sampling in collecting data on psychotherapists in India. Their own study, carried out with a relatively large sample of 250 therapists was not randomly drawn, and cannot be considered to be illustrative of psychotherapists in India. According to them 'the population of 'psychotherapists' spans multiple professions and is a 'fuzzy category' with poorly defined boundaries, making meaningful random sampling virtually impossible' (Bhola et al. 2012, p. 12).

Gordon (2000) writes about the importance of qualitative methodology in psychotherapy research. He writes that the reductionist quantitative research methods fail to engage with the complexity of personal experience and do not take account of context and human agency in their attempt to provide simplistic cause and effect explanations. According to McLeod (2001), qualitative methods have an inherent appeal for counsellors and therapists;

> Many of the techniques and skills used in qualitative research are similar to those used in therapy: eliciting people's stories, sensitive listening, building up an understanding, checking it out. The knowledge generated by qualitative research—holistic, nuanced, personal, contextualised, incomplete—is a knowing that is familiar to therapists. (p. viii)

The field of psychotherapy has been dominated by 'verificationist research' with an emphasis on establishing legitimacy through research designs which are experimental and related to hypothesis testing. Over time, this perspective has begun to change, to include a methodological pluralism, including qualitative and mixed methods approaches. The main advantages of quantitative methods relate to their ability to deal with large samples, to investigate relationships and interactions between variables, and to establish cause–effect relationships between variables (Lutz and Hill 2009; McLeod 2001). Qualitative research methods on the other hand, play an important role in helping understand how the world is constructed and the meaning that individuals draw from the variety of experiences encountered by them. Qualitative research depends on words, narratives and clinical judgment. The philosophical stance of knowledge being local and contextual permeates qualitative research, contributing to variety of ways in collecting and analysing data.

One of the major criticisms to qualitative research relates to the problem of generalizing findings. In quantitative research, generalizability of findings refers to the possibility of extending the findings from the sample to the population at large.

Given the nature of qualitative research, the samples tend to be small, theoretical samples, with care being taken in their selection. Researchers and readers of qualitative research make the connection between the findings of the qualitative studies and their local level behaviour and practice. This is known as transferability in qualitative research (Jenson 2008). Yin (2011) refers to the process of analytical generalization to overcome the problem of statistical generalization that comes from quantitative research.

Transferability and analytical generalization allows the findings from one study to be extended to other situations and contexts, beyond the scope of the context of the original study. In order to increase transferability, researchers can use the technique of 'thick descriptions', which provide the reader with details about the context, the participants who took part in the study, the research design, and the details about the researcher's entry into and engagement in the field. Additionally, purposeful sampling of participants is done, wherein respondents are selected because they best represent the research design and the strengths and limitations of the study (Patton 2002).

Apart from qualitative approaches, some of the studies in this volume use mixed methods approaches, wherein efforts are made to combine the strengths of both quantitative and qualitative approaches. Both quantitative and qualitative data are collected and analysed. Cresswell identifies three ways of mixing methods; 'by merging, connecting, or by embedding' (Cresswell 2008, p. 527). The mixing of methods can take place at different places in the research process, during data collection, during analysis of data or during interpretation. Mixing methods in research 'provide both quantitative information about magnitude and frequency as well as qualitative information from individual perspectives from participants and the context in which they were commenting on the research problem' (Cresswell 2008, p. 527).

The ten papers in this volume bring together current issues of relevance to the development of the profession of counselling in India. They are a valuable addition to the sparse research available on the process of counselling and psychotherapy in India today.

References

Arulmani, G. (2007). Counselling psychology in India: At the confluence of two traditions. *Applied Psychology: An International Issue, 56*(1), 69–82.

Bhola, P., Kumaria, S., & Orlinsky, D. E. (2012, July 5). Looking within: Self-perceived professional strengths and weaknesses among psychotherapists in India. *Asia Pacific Journal of Counselling and Psychotherapy*, 1–14. doi:10.1080/21507686.2012.703957.

Cresswell, J. W. (2008). Mixed Methods Research. In L. M. Given (Ed.), *The Sage Handbook of Qualitative Research Methods* (Vol. 1 and 2, pp. 526–529). Thousand Oaks, CA: Sage.

Gaiha, S. M., Sunil, G. A., Kumar, R., & Menon, S. (2014). Enhancing mental health literacy in India to reduce stigma: The fountainhead to improve health-seeking behaviour. *Journal of Public Mental Health, 13*(3), 146–158. doi:10.1108/JPMH-06-2013-0043.

Gordon, N. S. (2000). Researching Psychotherapy, the Importance of the Client's View: A Methodological Challenge. *The Qualitative Report,* (Vol. 4, nos. 3 and 4). Retrieved November 4, 2015, from (http://www.nova.edu/ssss/QR/QR4-3/gordon.html).

Hill, C., & Corbett, M. (1993). A perspective on the history of process and outcome research in counselling psychology. *Journal of Counseling Psychology, 40*(1), 3–24.

Jenson, D. (2008). Transferability. In L. M. Given & L. M. Given (Eds.), *The sage encyclopaedia of qualitative research (Vols. 1 and 2)* (p. 886). Thousand Oaks, CA: Sage.

Kapur, M. (2011). *Counselling Children with Psychological Problems.* New Delhi.

Kapur, M., Shamasundar, C., & Bhatti, R. (1996). *Psychotherapy training in India.* Bangalore: NIMHANS.

Kumar, A. (2011). Mental health services in rural India: Challenges and prospects. *Health, 3*(12), 757–761. doi:10.4236/health.2011.312126.

Laungani, P. (2004). *Asian perspectives in counselling and psychotherapy.* New York: Brunner-Routledge.

Lutz, W., & Hill, C. E. (2009). Quantitative and qualitative methods for psychotherapy research: Introduction to special section. *Psychotherapy Research, 19*(4), 369–373. doi:10.1080/10503300902948053.

Manickam, L. (2010). Psychotherapy in India. *Indian Journal of Psychiatry,* 366–370. doi:10.4103/0019-5545.69270.

McLeod, J. (2001). *Qualitative research in counselling and psychotherapy.* London: Sage Publications.

Orlinsky, D. (2008). Comments on the State of Psychotherapy Research (As I See It). *Existenzanalyse,* 81–83. Retrieved November 4, 2015, from http://www.existential-analysis.org/fileadmin/4editors/dokumente/GLE-Int/Forschung/Comment_on_the_State.pdf.

Orlinsky, D., Heinonen, E., & Hartmann, A. (2015). Psychotherapy Process Research. In J. Wright, *International Encyclopedia of Social and Behavioral Sciences (2nd Edition)* (pp. 515–520). Elsevier. doi:10.1016/B978-0-08-097086-8.21083-0.

Patton, M. Q. (2002). *Qualitative research and evaluation methods* (3rd ed.). Thousand Oaks, CA: Sage.

Raguram, R. (2001). Aspects of supervisory process: A personal account. In M. Kapur, C. Shamasundar, & R. S. Bhatti (Eds.), *Psychotherapy training in India* (2nd ed., pp. 71–79). Bangalore: NIMHANS.

Ronnestad, M. H., & Skovholt, T. M. (2003). The journey of the counsellor and therapist: Research findings and perspectives on career development. *Journal of Career Development, 30*(1), 5–44. doi:10.1177/089484530303000106.

Schoonover, J., Lipkin, S., Javid, M., Rosen, A., Solanki, M., Shah, S., & Katz, C. L. (2014). Perceptions of traditional healing for mental illness in rural Gujarat. *Annals of Global Health, 80*, 96–102. doi:10.1016/j.aogh.2014.04.013.

Schwartz, S. H., Melech, G., Lehmann, A., Burgess, S., Harris, M., & Owens, V. (2001). Extending the crosscultural validity of the theory of basic human values with a different method of measurement. *Journal of Cross-Cultural Psychology, 32*, 519–542.

Thara, R., & Patel, V. (2010). Role of non-governmental organizations in mental health in India. *Indian Journal of Psychiatry, 52*(1), 389–395.

Varma, V. K. (1982). Present state of psychotherapy in India. *Indian Journal of Psychiatry, 24*(3), 209–226.

Varma, V., & Ghosh, A. (1976). Psychotherapy as practised by the Indian psychiatrists. *Indian Journal of Psychiatry, 18*, 177–186.

Yin, R. K. (2011). *Qualitative research from start to finish.* New York: The Guilford Press.

Chapter 2
Counsellor Characteristics and the Counselling Experience

Swarnima Bhargava and Sujata Sriram

Abstract A qualitative study on counsellors' characteristics and experiences was carried out with counsellors practicing in Delhi and Mumbai. In-depth interviews were conducted to collect data from eight counsellors (two male, six female) coming from different educational backgrounds such as clinical psychology, psychiatry and social work. The participants worked in varied settings—schools, hospitals and private practice. Analysis of the data suggested that counsellors were highly motivated individuals committed to helping and to the process of growth. Participants attempted to locate their practice in contextual socio-cultural real ity of their clients and to interact with them in culturally sensitive ways. In the course of their work, practitioners encountered and overcame obstacles arising from the workplace, professional relationships, nature of clientele, and the nature of the counselling process itself and ethical dilemmas regarding confidentiality, and involuntary medication. Participants demonstrated resilient behaviours and self-care coping strategies such as engaging with a supportive social network, meditation and exercise.

Keywords Counsellor characteristics · Counsellor experiences · Motivation · Impact on personal life · Effect on professional life

In the context of the twenty first century, counselling has evolved from advice giving to a profession encompassing different themes, emphases, practices and schools of thought (Belkin 1985). In many parts of the world, professionalization has helped in defining the role of counsellors and has given an identity to counselling separate from social work and other related disciplines that aim to fill the same position in the market.

Swarnima Bhargava (✉)
Children First, New Delhi, India
e-mail: swarnima.bhargava@gmail.com

S. Sriram
School of Human Ecology, TISS, Mumbai, India

S. Sriram (ed.), *Counselling in India*, DOI 10.1007/978-981-10-0584-8_2

2.1 The Role of the Counsellor

In 1997, the American Counselling Association (ACA) adopted the following definition of professional counselling: 'The application of mental health, psychological, or human development principles, through cognitive, affective, behavioural or systemic intervention strategies, that address wellness, personal growth, or career development, as well as pathology' (as cited in Marini and Stebnicki 2009, p. 16). This definition establishes guidelines for the official ACA role of counselling and seems to endorse a professional that works with the normal population as well as with those with pathology.

Counsellors help clients in reaching 'their optimal level of psychosocial functioning through resolving negative patterns, prevention, rehabilitation, and improving quality of life' (Hershenson and Power 1987, as cited in Marini and Stebnicki 2009, p. 16). Counsellors work in varied settings like schools, hospitals, corporate settings and so forth, and their role also varies depending upon the setting in which they practice (Marini and Stebnicki 2009).

2.2 Counsellor Experiences in the Field

The personal attributes of a counsellor affect not only the work with clients but also personal and professional development (Rogers 1961). It has been suggested that the most important element in counselling is the 'personhood' of the counsellor (Gibson and Mitchell 1999) and that the most powerful impact on the client may be that of observing what the counsellor is or does. Several researches have been undertaken to explore counsellor characteristics and experiences. The selfhood of the counsellor has been conceptualized and researched as 'inner conversation' (Rober 2002, 2005).

Several research studies have explored the experiences of counsellors in their work. Hill and O'Grady (1985) have studied therapist intentions. Llewelyn (1988) studied the therapist's view of helpful and unhelpful events in therapy. Melton et al. (2005) mapped the inner emotional experiences of therapists in training. The most comprehensive research on therapist within-session experiences is that of Orlinsky and Howard (1977), using the therapy session report. They provide a composite portrait of the process of psychotherapy from the subjective perspectives of clients and therapists through descriptions of 11 dimensions of client experience of therapy sessions and 11 dimensions of therapist experience.

Numerous authors have highlighted the significance of counsellors' experiences of the therapeutic relationship to their growth and development (e.g. Orlinsky 2001; Skovholt and Ronnestad 1992; Goldfried 2001). Research on counsellor development suggests a close link between how counsellors manage challenges in the therapeutic relationship and their experiences of either growth or stagnation in their professional development (Ronnestad and Skovholt 2003).

In a study focusing on therapist development by Skovholt and Ronnestad (1992), 100 therapists and counsellors ranging from the first year of graduate school to 40 years beyond graduate school were interviewed. The goal of this study was to generate knowledge pertaining to issues of therapist development such as challenges, emotional reactions, attitudes towards work, influential factors in development, learning method, perceptions of role and working style, conceptual ideas used and measures of success and satisfaction. One hundred therapists and counsellors were divided by education and experience into five groups. Skovholt and Ronnestad (1992) used a 23-item questionnaire based on their written work and previous research on the topic, their own experience as supervisors and teachers in graduate programs and the literature on professional development. The following six phases were described: the lay helper, the beginning student, the advanced student, the novice professional, the experienced professional and the senior professional.

In addition to the phase model, Ronnestad and Skovholt's analysis found 14 themes of counsellor development. They noted that counsellor development is a complex process requiring continuous reflection. They also stated that much like the client–counsellor relationship's strong influence on treatment outcomes, research findings support 'a close and reciprocal relationship between how counsellors/therapists handle challenges and difficulties in the client relationship and experiences of professional growth or stagnation' (2003, p. 40). They also noted that interpersonal experiences in the personal life and the professional are significant sources of influence for professional development.

Another large-scale international study of psychotherapists (Orlinsky and Ronnestad 2005) provides information about a variety of professional experiences. Nearly, 5,000 psychotherapists from four countries and three continents participated. Findings suggested three broad dimensions of therapist difficulties: self-doubt, the frustrating case and negative reactions to clients.

Research regarding counsellor experiences also shows polarity, and on the positive end is research about the personal satisfaction and transformative growth that counsellors gain from their work (for example Sussman 1992; Burton and Associates 1972). Other literature focuses on the potential for experiences of extreme stress and the possibility of therapist burnout (for example Figley 2002; Sussman 1995). Smith et al. (2007) explored therapists' reactions in difficult sessions. It was seen that therapist reactions to difficult sessions had certain features in common such as feelings of shock, anxiety, a sense of being overwhelmed, somatic feelings and the need to talk about their experience. The findings highlighted the importance of sharing difficult experiences with colleagues as a supportive factor.

2.3 Counselling in India

In an effort to better understand the experiences of counsellors in India, we must examine the cultural context where they practice. A growing need for counselling services is being recognized in India, especially in the urban context. While the need for counselling in rural parts of the country is not deniable, it must be recognized that counselling in India is a phenomenon more easily available in urban, metropolitan areas, still to spread into the hinterlands. The past decade has seen the birth of counselling programs for various developmental stages across the life span as well as counselling for specific issues and contexts. Many universities in India currently offer training in psychology, with a focus on psychotherapy and counselling. However, not much pertinent research on counselling and psychotherapy has been done in India. Research suggests that the number of professionally qualified counsellors is far less than would adequately meet the needs of the population (Manickam 2010; Laungani 1994). The paucity of research that adapts Western counselling practices to the Indian context results in educational institutes teaching counselling from material that is located in another culture that is either the mainstream American or British tradition.

The fact that there is no common curriculum for counselling or psychotherapy training in India compounds the problem of lack of regulation of the profession. There is no central accrediting body or policy of licensure available to regulate counselling as a profession. Ethical standards and practices are not regulated by any governing body. There is no check upon private practitioners or their qualifications. Professionalization of counselling has yet to be established in India although organizations such as the Rehabilitation Council of India (RCI) and the Counsellor Association of India (CAI) indicate a step in that direction. The RCI is the only statutory council in India that documents details of all qualified professionals who operate and deliver training and educational programs for the disabled, disadvantaged and special education requirement communities. Although not regulatory in nature, CAI is another association of counsellors in India. It provides a forum for counsellors working in different settings to share their knowledge and expertise with each other.

In India, counsellors are employed in settings such as hospitals, schools, colleges, workplaces, private counselling centres and in private practice. Dissimilarity is encountered in the work profile of counsellors depending upon the setting in which the practitioner is placed. Additionally, counsellors belong to varied educational traditions such as social work, psychology, clinical psychology and psychiatry. The shared practice and knowledge domains of counsellors and other helping professions, coupled with the diversity within the counselling profession has, on the one hand, produced a rich, comprehensive and inclusive field; yet, on the other hand, it has contributed to a disjointed identity that lacks clear roles and functions (Bhola et al. 2012). Regardless of training, affiliations and credentials, social workers, psychologists and counsellors often share the same clientele, apply a common theoretical framework and compete for the same jobs, in which they are hired to perform the same tasks and hold the same responsibilities. To remain competitive, counsellors need to be perceived as different from other helping professionals and equally, if not more, effective in carrying out counselling services.

The lack of concise and comprehensive information available on the experience of counsellors in India, and the process of counselling, creates an acute need for research on this subject.

2.4 Studying Counsellor Characteristics and Experiences

The paper draws from a research study that attempted to form a comprehensive picture of personal and professional characteristics of counsellors and how they shaped their experiences through their narratives.

Presently, metropolitan cities are more amenable to counselling services (Laungani 2004); hence, it was decided to interview counsellors in two major metropolitan cities—Delhi and Mumbai. The sample consisted of individuals who had a postgraduate degree in fields such as psychology, clinical psychology, social work, psychiatry and so forth. Two participants were pursuing their Ph.D. during the course of this study. Counsellors with a minimum of 5 years of work experience were interviewed, as it was felt that they would have adequate experience in the field and would be likely to persist in the field in future.

Participants were chosen from diverse settings, ranging from schools, NGOs, government organizations, hospitals and private centres, with the purpose of acquiring a global picture of counselling, as it is understood in India. The profession of counselling is largely women-dominated in India, with few men entering the field (Laungani 2004). An effort was made to include both genders in the sample, in order to explore the experience of men in counselling. The sample consisted of eight participants (two male and six female), ranging in age from 27 to 66 years.

Respondents were contacted telephonically and provided information about the study and their informed consent was sought. They were assured of ethical considerations such as anonymity, confidentiality and so forth. The names of all participants have been changed to protect their identity. Sample details are given in Table 2.1.

Table 2.1 Details of the sample

S. no.	Gender	Work exp. (years)	Educational qualification	Nature of setting	Location
1	F	5	M.A. in clinical psychology	Child guidance centre, public school	New Delhi
2	F	12	Ph.D.	Public school, Private practice	New Delhi
3	M	30	M.D. psychiatry	Private practice, corporate health centre	Mumbai
4	M	13	M.A. in clinical psychology	Counselling centre	Mumbai
5	F	32	Ph.D.	Private practice, NGO	New Delhi
6	F	10	M.A. in social work	Corporate health centre	Mumbai
7	F	12	M.A. in social work	Private practice, family court	Mumbai
8	F	14	M. Phil	Super specialty hospital	Mumbai

Gender F Female; *M* Male. *Work Exp.* Work experience of participants

The participants were co-constructors of the understanding of the counselling process. An interview guide was developed, with open-ended and nondirective questions and probes to encourage participants to elaborate on their responses. Items were listed based on experience with the theory and practice of counselling such as details about training, work setting, nature of work, type of clients, work satisfaction, etc. The interview guide ensured that the same basic lines of inquiry were pursued with each person interviewed while allowing conversation to flow freely within the time available. A face-to-face interview was conducted with each participant ranging in duration from 1.5 to 3.5 h in their work setting, home or both. The conversations were audio recorded, with consensus of the participants, to retain an accurate summary of the conversation, including elements of tonality and emphasis with minimal intrusion in the interview situation. The interviews were transcribed, and the transcripts were analysed, using the grounded theory method to reduce, analyse and interpret the data generated. The text was coded into manageable categories on a variety of levels. Categories started out from descriptive level and moved onto the analytical level as analysis progressed. An effort was made while labelling categories to utilize words or phrases used by the participants in the study. Throughout the process, memos were written that contributed to elaborating the codes by identifying their properties, the conditions under which the code arose, and comparisons with specific data and other codes. Themes within and across participants were identified (Willig 2008).

2.5 The Self of the Counsellor

Wosket (2002) observed that some aspects of the counsellor's self unavoidably becomes accessible to the client to a greater or lesser degree. Further Wosket (2002) states that counsellors'

> *Use* of self is evident in the way that they *extend* aspects of their personality with the intention of influencing the client. Use of self involves the operationalisation [*sic*] of personal characteristics so that they impact on the client in such a way as to become potentially significant determinants of the therapeutic process. (p. 11, italics in original)

It was important to explore the particular aspects of self, both personal and professional, that counsellors brought to bear in their work and to study the subsequent impact on their experiences.

2.6 Counsellor Characteristics

In order to develop a profile of individuals who were drawn to counselling, the professional and personal characteristics of the counsellors were examined. The participants had varying levels of experience, based on number of years of practise in the field. According to the model suggested by Ronnestad and Skovholt (1992), the participant who had 5 years of experience could be conceived of as falling within the 'Competent stage'. Five participants had 10–15 years of experience and can be categorized as 'Proficient'. Two participants fell in the 'Expert Stage', with over 30 years of counselling experience.

2.6.1 Professional Characteristics

Professional characteristics refer to details that helped locate the counsellor in the context of educational background, training, work experience, designation, nature of setting and remuneration. Professional characteristics help in establishing a picture of the professional identity of counsellors and of the value associated with the counselling profession in the market.

Educational Background and Training

The eight participants belonged to diverse educational backgrounds such as social work, clinical psychology and psychiatry. Despite this, all participants had shared that the classroom training they received was inadequate to meet the needs of the profession. They gave credit to on the job learning contributing to their growth as skilled professionals. Experiential learning is a common influential theme found in counsellor identity research (Auxier et al. 2003; Furr and Carroll 2003; Nelson and Jackson 2003). Participants demonstrated an enthusiasm for learning and a motivation to acquire new skills. Raina[1] had expressed that an M.A. in Social Work was insufficient to prepare for the counselling profession. She suggested that one also needed additional training in various popular therapeutic approaches.

In its Code of Ethics, the American Counselling Association (ACA 2005) cited the need for continuing education for counsellors. Staying true to this credo, some participants had acquired certificates in cognitive behaviour therapy (CBT), rational emotive behaviour therapy (REBT), transactional analysis, emotion freedom technique, Reiki and Yoga. Two of the participants had Ph.D. degrees, and two participants were in the process of acquiring their Ph.D., while one had an M.D. in Psychiatry, two others had an M.A. in Clinical Psychology and two others had an M.A. in Social Work.

Designation

Participants reported mixed feelings about their designation. Raina had noted that for clients the title '*doctor*' was important. Kunal, Manjeet and Rashmi had stated that the scope of their work was broader than indicated by their designation,

[1]All names of participants used here are fictitious.

which was counsellor. Megha had advocated for a more specific designation and preferred to '*introduce* (herself) *as a medical counsellor for paediatric oncology*'. She had determined it to be a matter of professional ethics and professional pride: '*we have specialized ourselves for something and we should be proud of this*' indicating that she strongly associated her designation as being an expression of her professional identity.

Remuneration

Participants reported that while counselling as a service was increasingly gaining recognition in the market and despite the apparent paucity of qualified practitioners in India (Manickam 2010; Laungani 2004), practitioners were not being compensated in a like manner. Most were not fully satisfied with the remuneration they received. It was also observed that a corporate setting provided better remuneration as compared to other settings. It was seen that counsellors with more work experience were better able to set the terms for their services in terms of fee, clientele and work hours.

Approach to Counselling

The participants practiced an eclectic model of counselling that had been empirically driven with its components based on the nature of the client's problem. Their approach tended toward flexibility and client responsiveness and pragmatism, rather than being theory bound. The participants had refined their approach in the light of experience, perceived client need and their own personal characteristics and preferences. It was observed that an orientation to wellness did not dominate their discourse. Participants defined their practice in terms of problem solving, thus representing the 'freedom from' approach (Laungani 2004) where the focus was on 'treating' the person and helping him to be free from, rid oneself of, escape from, overcome, treat, cure, get better and so forth.

The participants revealed they had a personal preference for therapeutic approaches such as cognitive behaviour therapy (CBT) and rational emotive behaviour therapy (REBT) due to their time-efficient nature. In keeping with this preference, participants had a collaborative approach to their practice and acknowledged it as a factor in determining the outcome of the counselling process. All participants had received training in these approaches through various modalities such as postgraduate training, or a workshop, or on the job. Other approaches used by the participants were transactional analysis, narrative therapy, play, art and psychodynamic techniques; family therapy, behaviour therapy and person-centred approach. Only Rajesh had explicitly professed to follow a purely person-centred approach for a brief time; however, it was seen that most participants' approach had been coloured by Rogerian values of empathy, being non-judgmental, client autonomy and so forth. All participants identified Yoga and meditation as indigenous approaches to counselling and had incorporated techniques of Yoga in their practice as relaxation training for clients.

Therapists selected techniques and theories because of who they were as persons: therapy strategies are manifestations of the therapist's personality. McConnaughy asserts that 'The therapist as a person is the instrument of primary influence in the therapy enterprise' (McConnaughy 1987, p. 304). This brings our attention to a detailed examination of personal characteristics of counsellors.

2.6.2 Personal Characteristics

Personal characteristics refer to qualities that the participants attribute to themselves that help in exploring the inner world of the individual. Personality characteristics of the counsellor have an important bearing on therapeutic outcomes (Garfield and Bergin 1986; Barnlund and Araki 1985). Wosket (2002) has suggested a natural correlation between the personal characteristics of the counsellor and the way their style and approach develops. The participants had ascribed several attributes to themselves during the course of the interview and believed that most of their personal attributes contributed to their effectiveness as a counsellor. The participants had delineated certain personal attributes such as being a good listener, being patient and accepting; as contributing to their effectiveness as a counsellor.

Motivation

Sussman (1992) suggested that there are certain common motivations behind the pursuit of the profession. These include desires to be idealized, to provide nurturance, to be in a dominant position and to achieve intimacy. In order to construct a more adept picture about the nature of counsellors, an examination of the motivation that drove counsellors to join and sustain in the profession was vital. Most of the participants had expressed a desire to help people and to work closely with them. Many were drawn towards psychotherapy as a career because of their own personal difficulties, in keeping with past research (Dryden and Spurling 1989). Prachi and Megha had accounted for their motivation to observing significant others deal with disability and terminal illness. Wosket (2002) suggests that counsellors are willing to deal with clients' loss, grief and anguish as a way of rehearsing their own losses; thus, the 'wounded healer' (Jung 1951) may be attempting to prevent further injury.

Additionally, role models served as inspiration to the participants. Rajesh and Raina gave credit to a college teacher for having kindled their interest in counselling. Henry et al. (1973) found that over 60 % of psychologists were primarily influenced in the counselling profession by teachers. Megha believed that supervisor feedback helped her grow and sustain in the field despite the sensitive and emotionally exhausting nature of her work in paediatric palliative counselling. She also credited a family member (grandfather) as a role model who inspired her to join the field of counselling. Over two-thirds of those surveyed by Henry, Sims and Spray indicated that their initial interest in the field was due to the influence of family members who served as role models, who overtly encouraged the career choice, or enthusiastically supported the future therapist's personal choice.

It was particularly interesting to discover that Rajesh, a psychiatrist, turned to the counselling profession after he had found himself dissatisfied with the profession of psychiatry. He felt that psychiatry did not consider the social interactions between doctor and patient as a valid concern, having an impact upon the healing process. He then turned to counselling and therapy as a means to bridge this gap. It is significant to note that despite primarily being identified as a psychiatrist, Rajesh goes beyond the biomedical model of mental health to include psychosocial elements as well.

There is also an element of circumstantiality and chance in participants' entry to the profession. Rashmi professed that counselling alone was not sufficiently satisfying for her and that she entered the field '*as a last resort*'. Though Manjeet had entered the profession '*by chance*', she enjoyed working with children and accounted for it to keep her motivated and engaged in the field.

The participants had expressed several needs and their manifestations in the course of their narrative—to help, for achievement, learning, respect, approval and belongingness. Burton and Associates (1972, p. 2) expressed the view that 'psychotherapy succeeds best when the therapist himself participates deeply in the process as a human being. When some of his growth needs are met, the therapy prospers; when they are not met, the therapy languishes'. All participants had expressed the need to help people and Prachi regards altruism as an essential value that counsellors should possess. The need for achievement and for learning has been inferred from the career trajectory of the counsellors. The participants had acquired certification in several therapeutic modalities and two were pursuing their Ph.D. studies.

The participants were very driven individuals and took initiative in their career. Megha systematically specialized in the field of palliative and paediatric counselling across her academic and professional career. She also '*pioneered in setting up the first paediatric palliative centre in India*'. Manjeet had been negotiating with the school administration to provide students with more time available to access one-on-one counselling sessions. Raina had been undergoing supervised practice and therapy in an effort to better herself as a professional. There is some evidence that personal therapy enhances the subsequent professional effectiveness of counsellors by giving a reliable basis for the confident and appropriate 'use of self' (Baldwin 2009) in relationships with clients. Personal therapy has also been positively associated with the ability to display empathy, warmth and genuineness, and his or her increased emphasis on the personal relationship in therapy (Wogan and Norcross 1985).

Values

Packard believes that all individuals behave in accordance with a set of values, whether these have been thought out and made explicit or not. Therefore, it is impossible for a counsellor to maintain a position of neutrality (Packard 2009). Values have been defined as broad preferences concerning appropriate courses of action that counsellors should take. Participants had been asked about values that a counsellor brings to the process and about the values that they believe guide the profession such as rights of a client. The resulting responses have, thus, been categorized into two types—personal/cultural and professional values.

Personal/Cultural Values

In order to be able to relate to clients who hold different values and cultures from their own, counsellors need to develop sensitivity to value differences, a very important issue in the counselling process (Kelly and Strupp 1992). Participants had considered altruism and respect for individuality as overarching values that defined their practice.

Participants had demonstrated sensitivity to value differences and attempted to resist imposing their own value system on the client. For example, Megha did not believe in gender discrimination but deliberately refrained from expressing this to a client who held a different view to avoid alienating the client and affecting the counselling process. Kunal experienced a conflict of values with certain clients who he defined as '*typical masculine husbands who think women are beggars or their servants who are here to serve them*'. He found it difficult to work objectively with such clients, and noted himself experiencing anger during the counselling process. According to Propst (1996), counsellors' sensitivity to clients' values can be decisive to the success of the therapy, since the counsellors' competence in communicating within the clients' value framework influences the outcome for the clients. This opinion has been supported by Bell (1996) and Wosket (2002).

Professional Values

The participants were asked about the values they believed were an essential part of the process of counselling. All agreed that confidentiality and being nonjudgmental were the most important professional values. Nondirective behaviour, empathy and respecting the client were other popular responses. Client autonomy was regarded as the central goal of counselling by all participants. Equality between the client and counsellor had also been emphasized. Raina deliberately made use of the term 'client' to establish equality. Most participants viewed their role as service providers and believed values such as providing maximum benefit to clients and not over-charging clients should govern the counselling process. Kunal emphatically stated that as counsellors—'*you need to give the client value* *for money... Not give the client s****'. The participants advocated collaboration and taking client feedback regarding the process and outcome of counselling.

Updating one's skills had been explicitly advocated by Raina who had trained in a different therapeutic modality every year since she had begun practicing. The importance of competence is echoed by Sommers-Flanagan (2012) when they state that the practitioner must have the knowledge to perform whatever service the profession offers. Other participants also shared this value as demonstrated by their pursuit of further training and updating their skills. Closely related to competence is an important ethical concept—informed consent—that refers to clients' rights to know about and consent to the ways the counsellor intends to work with them. Raina explicitly discussed the value of informed consent and the client's right to refuse to participate in the process of counselling.

Biases

Counsellors are not without their 'shadow' side, which reflect their vulnerabilities and blind spots. The narratives revealed biases that participants held against certain types of clients and issues. Rashmi indicated a bias against clients of high SES, and claimed that they tended to be '*suspicious*' and preoccupied with confidentiality. She had opinions regarding sharing information pertaining to therapeutic modality: 'We usually don't discuss such details with the clients. They don't understand all these therapies and all.' This bias seems to be stemming from the traditional hierarchical doctor–patient relationship in which doctors are seen to wield expert power (French and Raven 1959); and by behaving like doctors, counsellors may be attempting to gain respect and public recognition for their work. Allying themselves with a more powerful group may also be an attempt at defining professional identity.

Rashmi shared an anecdote about a gay client who came for counselling with problems at work. The anecdote revealed how a counsellor's unacknowledged bias could impact the counselling process.

> It was a very difficult case for me. It was transgender. Gay. It was a little away from my regular normal cases. That was challenging. I worked with him and I heard that he is doing well now. But his original problem has not been solved. He just wanted one session. He knows about it for a long time…about his problem but he also doesn't want to come out. He doesn't want to talk about it or about any other option. He wanted to live within his own limitations. Then better for him. See I am very realistic. If he wants to be like this, let him be like this. When there are no options for them, I tell them straight away. If at one needs to be radical then one has to be. (Rashmi)

The manner and tone of voice in which the client was refereed to—'*a gay*'—was seen as pejorative. The participant's stance reflected that the client's homosexuality was inherently abnormal. Further, she conceptualized it as problematic and as a '*limitation*'. Besides, she did not refer the client to another counsellor who may have been better equipped to help him. Neither did the counsellor explore her role in influencing the outcome of this particular encounter.

Surprisingly, a bias against the 'wounded healer' was also seen in the narrative of a participant. According to Guggenbühl-Craig (1971), in the therapeutic encounter, there is the healer-physician and the wounded patient. In order to promote healing, the physician tries to activate the patient's own healing powers. And yet, the healer-physician has wounds too and this experience of being wounded is what makes them equals. Kunal expressed a bias against counsellors who admitted to having personal problems and found solace in the process of counselling. Kunal felt that such individuals jeopardized the profession. Acknowledging a fellow counsellor's vulnerability may be seen as threatening, as it may necessitate the confrontation of personal vulnerability, which goes against the image of the counsellor as healer, expert and problem-solver.

Stressors and Coping Style

Participants also shared experiences of stress with the researcher. 'Stress' was conceptualized as an *impact* of certain aspects of the job, as a *result* for example in burn out, and as an *experienced state* which could be understood by reflection. The participants reported encountering problems related to time, workplace politics, excessive workload, emotional depletion and excessive paperwork. Megha, Raina and Prachi had confessed to burn out due to personal losses and tiredness, depression and reluctance to go to work. They had taken time off from work and turned to their support system of family and friends to help them cope.

Participants were asked how they coped with stress and emotional distress that the counselling process can sometimes bring up. '*Switch on/switch off*' mechanism was a particular favourite of all participants. They used this term to describe a mechanism that they have developed with experience, which allowed them to distinguish between their personal and professional lives. Participants shelved feelings and thoughts in the counselling room that 'contained' them until they were ready to revisit them. Containment refers to a space where the individual's feelings can be borne and thought about; it can be used to understand the role that the physical setting of the counsellor's room serves (Bion 1970). Within the counselling situation, participants used humour and detachment to maintain objectivity. Participants also deliberately cultivated an optimistic perspective regarding client drop-out by attributing them to clients' feeling better and ceasing to require counselling. Rashmi credited her training with making it easier to deal with the emotional problems that clients shared by responding with empathy rather than sympathy.

Participants also turned to distractions such as television, watching movies and cooking as ways of relaxing. Exercise, meditation and prayer were used as means of coping. Physical exercise is a major self-care strategy for many counsellors, not only for its physical benefits and its contrast with the sedentary nature of their work but also for its psychological benefits (Hays 2002) as cited in (Pope and Vasquez 2007).

In terms of coping it has been noted that psychologists find a variety of coping methods useful namely, talking, socializing and connecting with family. It seems that social support is of great importance (Worden 2009; Doka 2002). The participants in the study also turned to their social network for support in helping them to cope with work stress. Discussions with one's colleagues, supervisor, mentor and spouse also helped them to cope. For example, Megha's work with terminally ill clients, especially children, generated stress, as it was a high-affect situation that made large demands upon her but denied her a chance to affect the outcome. She narrated an incident in which she had been called into work at the request of a dying child.

> I just opened the door, he looked at me and he said, 'aunty' and he died…after that at least eight days I couldn't sleep. I used to remember his face and those eyes. After that I cried and cried in front of Madam. She never said that don't cry. And she said that 'you should look at this from another perspective; that while dying that child thought of you so you really became that important for him and so you could give him a peaceful death. And secondly you could give him smiles for three months, so it's ok.' So you know that was a good help for me to deal with my own emotional and psychological issues. That day I came home and I actually told my husband that that was my last visit to hospital and after that I cannot go. He was really very supportive. And after a while I started going back. (Megha)

The tremendous loss that one sometimes experiences as a counsellor and the strength it takes to sustain in the profession are aptly demonstrated in Megha's account.

2.6.3 The Narrative Experience of Being a Counsellor

'The inescapable fact of the matter is that the therapist is a person, however much he may strive to make himself an instrument of his patient's treatment' (Orlinsky and Howard 1977, p. 567). In an effort to explore the personhood of the counsellors, the researcher encouraged them to share their feelings, thoughts, learning, triumphs and hardships on the journey of being a counsellor, from when they entered the profession till the present. Each practitioner had a markedly different approach to counselling as evidenced by their narratives. Factors such as educational background, workplace and length of work experience all played a strong role in shaping each participant's growth in the profession.

Participants acknowledged relationships with other mental health professionals as agents that shaped their professional identities. Important interactions included receiving feedback from supervisors, and hearing the viewpoints and experiences of other practitioners. In addition, participants indicated that experiences with clients contoured their understanding of the role of a professional counsellor. Several had made changes in their process of counselling in order to better meet client needs, moving from an academically derived process to an empirically derived approach. For example, keeping in mind client comfort, Raina had modified the initial interview to focus on the problem that the client presents with, rather than following the traditional approach of history taking. Shruti, newest to the field, had attributed learning on the job chiefly to client feedback and supervisor feedback. Counsellors had also evaluated their professional efficacy based on client feedback. Research conducted by Skovholt and Ronnestad (1992) has indicated that clients' feedback to therapists is a primary contributor to the evolving professional self.

Schein (1980) proposed that as a person's career and life unfold, there is a gradual clarification of self-image around needs and motives, and talents and values (Schein 1980, as cited in Palmer and Bor 2008). The participants also observed changes in themselves over the years and felt that they had grown in the profession, and experience had shaped them to greater patience, acceptance, objectivity, confidence and assertiveness. The participants claimed greater expertise in areas of 'detecting the client's problem' (Manjeet), 'greater sensitivity to the nuances in client's behaviour' (Raina) and a 'greater comfort level with issues related to sexuality' (Megha). Counsellors shared that their work enabled them to enjoy more meaningful personal relationships.

Participants revealed some perils of the profession. Kunal and Raina shared that people informally approached them for counselling, much to their discomfort and annoyance. Raina had evolved a strategy for dealing with the awkwardness—'to come to my office to discuss it in detail and that this is not the right place'. Working with children who had faced sexual abuse and incest, Manjeet confessed that it had made her a more '*hyper*' mother and more vigilant about the adults interacting with her children lest they be sexual predators. She considered this the 'fallout of the profession where one is exposed to the dirty side of the world'. Wosket (2002) writes that foremost among their own losses that an experienced counsellor will undergo is the forfeiture of innocence and naivety. This is particularly true for counsellors who work to any extent with clients who have been abused, where they will need to 'contain material that will be of a deeply disturbing nature' and 'make contact at a deep level whilst remaining intact themselves' (Walker 1992, p. 197, as cited in Wosket 2002).

2.6.4 Satisfaction

Participants shared that they found the process of counselling satisfying. For Manjeet the evidence of a client's will to change was a reward in itself. She found it touching that some clients showed gratitude by praying for her. Shruti was satisfied when she 'feels that I have made a difference with them. It gives me … satisfaction that I have done some good during my day'. Working with paediatric palliative care, Megha often came across death and grief; however, she obtained satisfaction in being with 'children and seeing them grow and lead lives. Helping family members cope better'. Prachi had 32 years of experience working as a counsellor and she credited sustaining in the field to the rewarding power of being able to 'manage to make positive changes to a person's life. That's probably why I've stayed at this for so long'.

2.7 The Totality of Being a Counsellor in India

The aim of the research was to study the characteristics and experiences of counsellors working in metropolitan cities of Delhi and Mumbai in India. Data was collected from detailed in-depth interviews carried out with eight counsellors working in varied settings. Participants from varied educational backgrounds, with differences in their training and career trajectories, had been selected. The participants had belonged to fields such as psychiatry, clinical psychology and social work. Work experience for the participants had ranged from 2 to 32 years.

Laungani (2004) has written extensively on the subject of counselling as practiced in Asia. According to him, in the market and in the eyes of the public, ambiguity persists regarding the appropriate credentials and role of a counsellor. Bhola et al. (2012) refer to the fact that the category of 'counsellor' in India was a 'fuzzy one', lacking clarity due to the overlap of additional roles played by the individuals concerned. India is yet to jump on the bandwagon of counsellor professionalization. However, movements in this direction have begun as indicated by the emergence of groups such as the Counsellor Association of India and the Rehabilitation Council of India. The participants in this study had endeavoured to resolve this dilemma by defining their practice and their role within the workplace and the domain of their practice. They had identified themselves as service providers and used the term 'client' to represent help seekers as consumers. Participants were particular about the designation that identified them and cleverly juxtaposed it with that of doctors to gain awareness and respect from clients.

The participants' relationships with other mental health professionals impacted their professional identities. Important interactions included receiving feedback from supervisors, and discussing the viewpoints and experiences of other practitioners. In addition, experiences with clients had helped them to improve their efficacy as skilled professionals. Participants altered their approach to the counselling process, moving from an academically derived process to an empirically derived approach. Counsellors emphasized collaboration during the process of counselling beginning with goal setting to termination. The participants took feedback from the client regarding the process and outcome of counselling. They had credited client feedback on par with feedback from their supervisors as sources of learning to be skilled professionals.

The participants conceptualized a client's problems in terms of the bio-psychosocial model as contrasted with the biomedical model, as they believed it to be a broader, more pervasive approach. Participants shared their preference for some therapeutic approaches such as cognitive behaviour therapy and rational emotive behaviour therapy as they found them to be time efficient.

The participants commented on their personal development over the years and felt that they had grown in the profession and became more patient, accepting, objective, confident and assertive. Participants were drawn to counselling for a multitude of reasons, chief among them being the desire to work closely with people and to help others. Some had chosen this career because of their own personal difficulties. Role models had tremendous impact on counsellors' decision to join and continue in this profession.

Burton (1972) expressed the view that 'psychotherapy succeeds best when the therapist himself participates deeply in the process as a human being. When some of his growth needs are met, the therapy prospers; when they are not met, the therapy languishes' (as cited in Wosket 2002, p. 50). The participants expressed 'growth needs' that had been fulfilled by their work—to help, for achievement, learning, respect, approval and belongingness. The needs for achievement and for learning had shaped the career trajectory of the counsellors. The participants demonstrated an enthusiasm for learning and motivation to acquire new skills. They had trained beyond the classroom and had credited on the job learning as contributing to their growth as skilled professionals. Experiential learning is a common influential theme found in counsellor identity research (Auxier et al. 2003; Furr and Carroll 2003; Nelson and Jackson 2003). The participants had refined and developed their approach in the light of experience, perceived client need and their own personal characteristics and preferences. In line with the Code of Ethics of the American Counselling Association, the participants showed a need for continuing education. There was a close engagement with academia and motivation to grow as professionals. In addition to enhancing themselves professionally, the practitioners effected change in their field such as by increasing accessibility to counselling services in a secondary setting.

The participants exhibited certain qualities that have been associated with successful outcomes like warmth, interest in people, curiosity and so forth. They demonstrated sensitivity to the client values and awareness of situations where a conflict of value systems arises and they had reported dealing with it by relying on their training such as responding with empathy. Participants identified and practiced values such as client's right to confidentiality and respect, being non-judgemental and nondirective and responding empathically to clients. The participants had based their approach on the values of altruism and respect for individuality. These values are primarily Judaeo-Christian and have shaped the development of counselling in the West. In India, the approach traditionally has been to respect family and community and for collective goals to take precedence over goals of the individual. A melding of values is reflected in the counselling approach. Client autonomy has been held by all participants as the overarching goal of counselling. The focus of the participants had been on problem solving and it represented the 'freedom from' approach (Laungani 2004) where the focus is on 'treating' the person and helping him to be free from, rid oneself of, escape from, overcome, treat, cure, get better and so forth.

'Counsellor' and 'client' were social roles, and the ways in which participants made sense of the aims and work of counselling were shaped by the culture within which they lived (Cheung 2008). The participants' approach had been shaped by the values of the profession and by the Indian socio-cultural context and reflected a culture-specific construction of counselling. Counsellors had made use of religion and spirituality to inform the rituals that were a part of their practice, as a therapeutic tool and as a means of coping. All participants had identified Yoga and meditation as indigenous approaches to counselling. They utilized techniques of Yoga in their practice as part of relaxation training.

Cultural contexts shaped the participants' approach and they demonstrated sensitivity to the value differences between themselves and their clients. They were not immune to vulnerabilities and to making mistakes. However, they acknowledged their mistakes and treated them as a source of learning. The participants had encountered ethical dilemmas in practice in the areas of confidentiality, involuntary medication and clinical trials. The participants reported encountering problems related to time, organizational politics, excessive workload, emotional depletion and excessive paperwork. Some had also confessed to experiencing burn out due to personal losses. They deliberately cultivated self-care strategies (Pope and Vasquez 2007) to foster resilience and to cope with stressors. Setting aside adequate time and opportunity for exercise, recreation, meditation, prayer and other spiritual or religious practices had comprised an important aspect of self-care for most counsellors. Social support was valued by all participants, as were relationships with other professionals and with clients (and sometimes their families).

Wosket (2002) suggests that as counsellors we may develop an inflated sense of self-importance as a means of protecting ourselves. It hints at a broader discourse that may prevail in the field of counselling. By acknowledging a fellow counsellor's vulnerability, one may also have to face up to one's own vulnerability as a person which goes against the image of the counsellor as healer, expert and problem-solver.

We see that counsellors have evolved as individuals and professionals within the field of counselling and locate their practice in the socio-cultural realities of their context. They are motivated individuals who are on the constant look out to better themselves and their practice. To that end they had engaged in evolving a client-responsive approach and going for further training, asking clients and supervisors for feedback, networking with other professionals. Counsellors in urban India defined their own professional identity and worth as juxtaposed with others in the field who presumptuously aspire to the title *counsellor*.

There are a number of implications and suggestions for future research. The limited transferability of the current findings may be addressed in several ways. First, additional interviews would help to determine whether the experiences and concerns shared by counsellors working in metropolitan cities in India find expression in other cities. Interviews with counsellors reflecting a wider range of ages, educational backgrounds, gender, socioeconomic status and backgrounds would be useful. Second, efforts toward developing quantitative methods for assessing various aspects of the counsellor's experience would be useful. The development of instruments that measure counsellors' characteristics such as salient identities, conceptions of the role of counsellor and definitions of the counselling process would provide tools that may be useful in practice and training. Process research could be used to reduce the limitation of retrospective data. For example, counsellors' perceptions of their needs, as well as their satisfaction and beliefs about self-efficacy with the counselling relationship may be assessed through the course of counselling one client.

Finally, greater efforts should be taken in the direction of professionalization of counselling. Various stakeholders such as educational institutions, the CAI and the RCI, currently practising counsellors and others should work toward forming a regulatory body that lays down rules regarding eligibility, training, credentials, continuing education and supervision, and forms a culturally relevant code of ethics to ensure accountability in practice.

Acknowledgments The authors would like to thank all the participants who took part in the study.

References

Auxier, C. R., Hughes, F. R., & Kline, W. B. (2003). Identity development in counselors-in-training. *Counselor Education and Supervision, 43*, 25–38. doi:10.1002/j.1556-6978.2003.tb01827.x.

Baldwin, M. (2009). *The use of self in therapy*. New York: Haworth.

Barnlund, D. C., & Araki, S. (1985). Intercultural encounters: the management of compliments by Japanese and Americans. *Journal of Cross-Cultural Psychology, 16*, 9–26. doi:10.1177/0022002185016001002.

Belkin, G. S. (1985). *Introduction to counseling* (3rd ed.). Iowa: WM. C. Brown Publishers.

Bell, E. (1996). *Counselling in further and higher education*. London: Open University Press.

Bhola, P., Kumaria, S., & Orlinsky, D. E. (2012, July 5). Looking within: Self-perceived professional strengths and weaknesses among psychotherapists in India. *Asia Pacific Journal of Counselling and Psychotherapy*, 1–14. doi:10.1080/21507686.2012.703957.

Bion, W. R. (1970). *Attention and interpretation*. London: Tavistock Publications.

Burton, A., & Associates. (1972). *Twelve therapists: how they live and actualise themselves*. San Francisco: Jossey-Bass.

Cheung, F. M. (2008). Deconstructing counseling in a cultural context. *The Counseling Psychologist, 28*(123), 123–132. doi:10.1177/001100000028100.

Doka, K. J. (2002). *Disenfranchised grief: New directions, challenges, and strategies for practice*. Champaign, Ill: Research Press.

Dryden, W., & Spurling, L. (1989). *On becoming a psychotherapist*. London: Routledge.

Figley, C. R. (2002). Compassion fatigue: psychotherapists' chronic lack of self care. *Journal of Clinical Psychology, 58*(11), 1433–1441. doi:10.1002/jclp.10090.

French, J. R. P., & Raven, B. (1959). The bases of social power. In D. Cartwright & A. Zander (Eds.), *Group dynamics*. New York: Harper and Row.

Furr, S. R., & Carroll, J. J. (2003). Influence of critical incidents in student counselor development. *Journal of Counseling and Development, 81*(3), 483–489. doi:10.1002/j.1556-6678.2003.tb00275.x.

Garfield, S. L., & Bergin, A. E. (1986). *Handbook of psychotherapy and behaviour change* (3rd ed.). New York: Wiley.

Gibson, R. L., & Mitchell, M. H. (1999). *Introduction to counselling and guidance*. London: Prentice Hall.

Goldfried, M. H. (Ed.). (2001). *How therapists change: personal and professional reflections*. Washington, DC: American Psychological Association.

Guggenbühl-Craig, A. (1971). *Power in the helping professions*. Dallas: Springer.

Hays, K. F. (2002). *Move Your Body, Tone Your Mind: The Workout Therapy Workbook: a Scientifically Proven Program to Help You Ease Anxiety, Lift Depression, Manage Stress, and Enjoy Your Body.* New Harbinger Publications.

Hershenson, D. B., & Power, P. W. (1987). *Mental health counseling: theory and practice*. New York: Pergamon Press.

Henry, W., Sims, J. H., & Spray, S. (1973). *Public and private lives of psychotherapists*. San Francisco: Jossey-Bass.
Hill, C. E., & O'Grady, K. E. (1985). List of therapist intentions illustrated in a case study and with therapists of varying theoretical orientations. *Journal of Counseling Psychology, 32*, 8. doi:10.1080/09515070.2012.716192.
Jung, C. G. (1951). *Aion: Researches into the Phenomenology of the Self (Collected Works Vol. 9 Part 2)*. Princeton, N.J.: Bollingen.
Kelly, T. A., & Strupp, H. H. (1992). Patient and therapist values in psychotherapy: perceived changes, assimilation, similarity, and outcome. *Journal of Consulting and Clinical Psychology, 60*(1), 34–40. doi:10.1037/0022-006X.60.1.34.
Laungani, P. (1994). Cultural differences in stress: India and England. *Counselling Psychology Review, 9*(4), 25–37. doi:10.1007/BF01857886.
Laungani, P. (2004). *Asian perspectives in counselling and psychotherapy*. New York: Brunner-Routledge.
Llewelyn, S. (1988). Psychological therapy as viewed by clients and therapists. *British Journal of Clinical Psychology, 27*, 223–238. doi:10.1111/j.2044-8260.1988.tb00779.x.
Manickam, L. (2010). Psychotherapy in India. *Indian Journal of Psychiatry*, 366–370. doi:10.4103/0019-5545.69270.
Marini, I., & Stebnicki, M. A. (2009). *The professional counselor's desk reference*. New York: Springer.
McConnaughy, E. A. (1987). The person of the therapist in psychotherapeutic practice. *Psychotherapy, 24*(3), 303–314. doi:10.1037/h0085720.
Melton, J. L., Nofzinger-Collins, D., Wynne, M. E., & Sussman, M. (2005). Exploring the affective inner experiences of therapists in training: The qualitative interaction between session experience and session content. *Counselor Education and Supervision, 45*, 82–96. doi:10.1002/j.1556-6978.2005.tb00132.x.
Nelson, K. W., & Jackson, S. A. (2003). Professional counselor identity development: A qualitative study of hispanic student interns. *Counselor Education and Supervision, 43*(1), 2–14. doi:10.1002/j.1556-6978.2003.tb01825.x.
Orlinsky, D. E., & Howard, K. I. (1977). The therapists' experience of psychotherapy. In A. S. Gurman & A. M. Razin (Eds.), *Effective psychotherapy: A handbook of research*. Oxford, England: Pergamon Press.
Orlinsky, D. E., & Ronnestad, M. H. (2005). Research implications: Ongoing and future studies. In D. E. Orlinsky & M. H. Ronnestad. *How psychotherapists develop: A study of therapeutic work and professional growth* (pp. 203–208). Washington, DC: American Psychological Association (APA). doi: 10.1177/0011000009333986.
Orlinsky, D. E., Ronnestad, M. H. Willutzki, U., Wiseman, H., Botermans, J-F., & Collaborative Research Network, CRN. (2001). The prevalence and parameters of personal therapy in Europe and elsewhere. In J. D. Geller, J. C. Norcross, & D. E. Orlinsky (Eds.). *The psychotherapist's own psychotherapy: Patient and clinician perspectives* (pp. 177–191). New York: Oxford University Press.
Packard, T. (2009). The 2008 Leona Tyler Award address: Core values that distinguish counseling psychology: personal and professional perspectives. *The Counseling Psychologist, 37*, 610–624. doi:10.1177/0011000009333986.
Palmer, S., & Bor, R. (2008). *The practitioner's handbook: A guide for counsellors, psychotherapists and counselling psychologists*. London: Sage.
Pope, K. S., & Vasquez, M. J. T. (2007). *Ethics in psychotherapy and counseling*. San Francisco: Wiley.
Propst, L. R. (1996). Cognitive-Behaviour therapy and the religious person. In E. P. Shafranske (Ed.), *Religion and the clinical practice of psychology*. Washington: American Psychological Association.
Rober, P. (2002). Constructive hypothesizing, dialogic understanding, and the therapist's inner conversation: Some ideas of knowing and not-knowing in the family therapy session. *Journal of Marital and Family Therapy, 28*, 467–478. doi:10.1111/j.1752-0606.2002.tb00371.x.

Rober, P. (2005). Family therapy as a dialogue of living persons: a perspective inspired by Bakhtin, Volosinov and Shotter. *Journal of Marital and Family Therapy, 31*, 385–397. doi:10.1111/j.1752-0606.2005.tb01578.x.
Rogers, C. (1961). *On becoming a person: A therapist's view of psychotherapy*. London: Constable.
Ronnestad, M. H., & Skovholt, T. M. (2003). The journey of the counselor and therapist: Research findings and perspectives on professional development. *Journal of Career Development, 30*(1), 5–44. doi:10.1177/089484530303000102.
Schein, E. H. (2008). Organizational Psychology. In Palmer, S., & Bor, R. (Eds.). *The practitioner's handbook: A guide for counsellors, psychotherapists and counselling psychologists.* (pp.197). London: Sage.
Skovolt, T. M., & Ronnestad, M. H. (1992). *The evolving professional self: Stages and themes in therapist and counselor development*. Chichester, England: Wiley.
Smith, A. J. M., Klein, W. C. H. R., & Hutschemaekers, G. J. M. (2007). Therapist reactions in self-experienced difficult situations: An exploration. *Counselling and Psychotherapy Research. Special Issue on Supervision, 7*(1), 34–41. doi:10.1080/14733140601140865.
Sommers-Flanagan, J., & Sommers-Flanagan, R. (2012). *Counseling and psychotherapy theories in context and practice: skills, strategies, and techniques*. Hoboken, NJ: Wiley.
Sussman, M. B. (1992). *A curious calling: Unconscious motivations for practicing psychotherapy*. Lanham, MD: Jason Aronson.
Sussman, M. B. (1995). *A perilous calling: The hazards of psychotherapy practice*. New York: Wiley.
Walker, M. (1992) *Surviving Secrets: The Experience of Abuse for the Child, the Adult and the Helper.* Buckingham: Open University Press.
Willig, C. (2008). *Introducing qualitative research in psychology*. London: Open University Press.
Wogan, M., & Norcross, J. C. (1985). Dimensions of therapeutic skills and techniques: Empirical identification, therapist correlates, and predictive utility. Psychotherapy: Theory, Research, Practice, Training, *22*(1), 63–74. http://dx.doi.org/10.1037/h0088528.
Worden, J. W. (2009). *Grief counseling and grief therapy: A handbook for the mental health practitioner (Fourth edition.)*. New York, NY: Springer Pub. Co.
Wosket, V. (2002). *Therapeutic use of self.* London: Taylor and Francis.

Chapter 3
Challenges Experienced by Novice Counsellors

Chetna Duggal and Mithila Rao

Abstract Existing literature emphasizes the initial years in the profession as crucial to counsellor growth and development. A mixed methods study was conceptualized to explore the challenges experienced by novice counsellors in India. Thirty novice counsellors filled the Development of Psychotherapists Common Core Questionnaire (DPCCQ) and in-depth interviews were conducted with six of the counsellors. The data from both methods was triangulated in the interpretation phase of the research. Results revealed that novice counsellors experienced challenges in the following areas—in the session, challenges related to the organization, and to counselling as a profession. The participants employed multiple coping strategies with the most important being seeking supervision. Implications for professional training, supervision, and licensing are discussed. Further research on therapist growth and development is recommended.

Keywords Novice counsellors · Challenges · Counselling in india

Counselling and psychotherapy are emerging professions in India. A substantial number of counsellors and psychotherapists have entered the professional field in the last couple of years. However, there is not much known about counsellor experiences in their early years of practice. As compared to trends worldwide, research on counsellors and therapists is still in its nascent phase in India and there is scant documentation of counsellor experiences and professional development.

Chetna Duggal (✉)
School of Human Ecology, Tata Institute of Social Sciences, Mumbai, India
e-mail: chetnaduggal@gmail.com

Mithila Rao
Quantum Consumer Solutions, Mumbai, India

S. Sriram (ed.), *Counselling in India*, DOI 10.1007/978-981-10-0584-8_3

3.1 Psychotherapy Research

In the past 50 years, interest in psychotherapy research has increased substantially across the globe. Psychotherapy research has focused on outcome—'changes that happen as the result of the process of psychotherapy' and process—'what happens in psychotherapy sessions in terms of therapist behaviours, client behaviours and the interaction between therapists and clients' (Hill and Corbett 1993, p. 3). Most research in counselling and psychotherapy started in the 1950s and 1960s and focused on the outcomes of psychotherapy. The effectiveness of therapy being proven, around the 1980s psychotherapy research began investigating process variables to study specific therapeutic processes. Research findings indicated that the client–therapist relationship was a strong predictor of therapeutic outcome (Lambert and Barley 2001). In the recent years, the therapist's self as an instrument which helps form a strong therapeutic alliance and helps therapeutic change is increasingly receiving attention (Reupert 2006). Wampold (2007) speaks of how, 'There is increasing evidence that it is the therapist and not the treatment per se that is responsible for therapeutic change' (p. 868). However, further research is needed on therapist factors, especially on the experiences of psychotherapy trainees and novices (Hill et al. 2007).

3.2 Novice Counsellors

Therapists and counsellors go through different phases of professional development, each with their own unique experiences and challenges. There have been different approaches proposed to look at development of counsellors and one of the most widely cited and accepted models of counsellor development is the phase model of counsellor development proposed by Rønnestad and Skovholt (2003). They studied 100 counsellors and therapists ranging in experience from the first year of graduate school to 40 years beyond graduate school and proposed the following six phases: the Lay helper; the Beginning student; the Advanced student; the Novice professional; the Experienced professional; and the Senior professional.

The data presented here focuses on novice counsellors, which is understood as a phase during the first few years of practice after graduation. Rønnestad and Skovholt (2003) found that novices may experience unexpected challenges when they begin practice, leading them to become disillusioned with their training and themselves, with accompanying feelings of inadequacy and insecurity. At this stage, novice counsellors need guidance and support and look for the same in mentors. The novice counsellors' development is enhanced by the exploration of the self and the professional environment, where the novice tries to deal with the challenges and disillusionment by exploring and expanding the skills, limitations, values, attitudes and interests.

3.3 Challenges During the Novice Counsellor Phase

Struggles of the novice counsellor form a theme that predominantly runs through the body of literature available on novice counsellors and psychotherapists. These challenges are important to look at as they inevitably influence the novice's development, either by hampering or furthering growth.

Feelings of doubt and uncertainty about one's competence and skills are reported by psychotherapists and counsellors at all levels of experience and development, however, novices are plagued more often by these feelings (Thériault et al. 2009). Feelings of incompetence (FOI) are 'the emotions and thoughts that arise when therapists' beliefs in their abilities, judgements, and/or effectiveness in their role as therapists are reduced or challenged internally' (Thériault et al. 2009, p. 106). Pressure to be a good therapist, difficulties in managing their reactions to clients, stepping out of the psychotherapists' role to do something 'unprofessional', and using counselling skills have been reported as challenges experienced by trainee and novice counsellors (Hill et al. 2007).

According to Skovholt and Rønnestad (2003), novices' stress is exacerbated by the ambiguity of professional work. The human condition itself presents so many ambiguities that the novice does not feel equipped to deal with them. Another important challenge that the novice faces is the lack of an adequate conceptual map to make sense of their experience. The novice has to replace their existing map of the lay helper with the professional map of helping their clients which may turn out to be a very challenging task. Skovholt and Rønnestad (2003) also emphasize the novices' glamourized expectations from the field and their work being a source of stress. Many novices enter the field with idealized expectations of making a difference in someone's life or being in a noble helping profession. This leads them to have high and overly optimistic expectations from themselves which are not always met. The novice's professional self-worth is closely related to client improvement and takes a hit when the expected results are not seen.

Once faced with these challenges, novice counsellors may feel 'stuck' and immobilized during sessions and these FOIs may spill over beyond the session and affect their self-esteem and have a detrimental effect on the therapeutic process and consequently on the therapeutic outcome (Thériault et al. 2009). Due to the demands that are made of novice counsellors, not all of which they are able to negotiate well, they may fall victim to a lot of stress, to the extent that there is a possibility of burnout (Briggs 2007). Research does suggest that inexperienced professionals are at a higher risk of burn out due to their inability to deal with the demands of their profession. Novices may also have difficulties in regulating their emotional boundaries leading to client's emotions spilling over to their personal lives. The novice's practitioner self is fragile and under-developed and does not have the capacity to absorb and process input from clients without defensively protecting the self. This makes them highly vulnerable to being emotionally reactive as well as to counter transference (Skovholt and Rønnestad 2003).

There are many factors that influence the professional development of the novice counsellor, and the novice finds ways of coping with the challenges posed by this phase of professional development. Supervisors have been found to have a very important role in the novice counsellor's professional development and are the second most important influence after direct client contact (Orlinsky et al. 2001; Bischoff et al. 2002). Positive supervisory feedback boosted and increased confidence and helped novice counsellors develop a trust in their skills as a therapist (Bischoff et al. 2002). The lack of a mentor or a supervisor could lead to immense distress for the novice, and so could the presence of a mentor who does not fulfil the novices' intense need for encouragement and guidance. This distress has been referred to 'orphan distress' or 'novice neglect' (Skovholt and Rønnestad 2003, p. 55).

Another important influence on the development of novice counsellors that emerged in Bischoff et al.'s (2002) analysis was contact with peers. Peer interaction helped novices reduce their feelings of incompetence and resulting anxiety by normalizing the experience of these feelings. Another important way in which peers influenced each other's professional development was through a mutual learning from each other's experiences. Providing advice or suggestions to peers was also a boost for novice counsellors' confidence as they then saw themselves as a valued resource for their peers.

Experiences in one's personal life also seem to influence the counsellors' functioning and development. Rønnestad and Skovholt (2003) in their discussion of themes relating to psychotherapist development suggest that personal life of psychotherapists influences the therapists' selection of work role, theoretical orientation, challenges as well as coping particularly in the first few months of practice.

3.4 Novice Counsellors in India

The literature on the challenges experienced by novice counsellors, and the coping strategies employed by them to deal with the challenges experienced, in the context of India, is scarce. This paper attempts to draw out the experiences of novice counsellors in India, using a concurrent mixed methods design where qualitative data and quantitative data were collected simultaneously (Creswell et al. 2003), and the data were analysed separately with integration taking place at the interpretation stage (Hanson et al. 2005).

For the quantitative part of the study, the Development of Psychotherapists Common Core Questionnaire (DPCCQ) developed by the Society for Psychotherapy Research (SPR) collaborative network led by Orlinsky, was obtained and used with permission. The DPCCQ is a 'set of self-administered research instruments that would describe participating therapists in adequate detail, include data for direct and indirect assessments of development and survey factors that seemed most likely to facilitate or hinder development' (Orlinsky et al. 1999, p. 133). For the study, the items on current practice characteristics, challenges and coping were included. An in-depth interview guide was developed by the researchers to obtain qualitative data for the study.

The sample consisted of novice counsellors, currently practicing in Mumbai, with three to eighteen months of clinical experience, with a post-graduate degree or diploma in counselling or counselling psychology. Thirty participants were selected from five different post-graduate programs which provide formal training in counselling in Mumbai, for the quantitative study and six of them were interviewed to obtain qualitative data.

The quantitative data was analysed using descriptive statistics. Qualitative data obtained through the electronically recorded interviews was transcribed, coded and analysed using thematic analysis. The results from the quantitative and qualitative data were subsequently triangulated at the interpretation phase.

3.5 Counsellor Profile and Practice Characteristics

The 30 participants included 27 women and three men. All the participants had a post-graduate qualification in counselling or counselling psychology, in the form of a degree, or a post-graduate diploma. The mean age of the participants in the study was 24 years. Only one of the 30 counsellors who participated in the study was married. The counsellors had been practicing for an average of 6.5 months and the clinical experience of the counsellors in the sample ranged from 3 to 18 months.

All the participants were affiliated to an organization. Three counsellors also had a private practice apart from their attachment to an organization. Twenty of the novice counsellors were employed in schools, five were working in adult mental health service settings, three counsellors were working in health care services and two were involved in a rehabilitation setting and a family therapy service unit respectively.

While the counsellors were attached to different organizations, in various areas of counselling, they had different designations. Sixteen participants were working under the designation of 'Counsellor', nine used the designation of 'Counselling Psychologist', two counsellors had the designation of 'Co-ordinator' and one of the counsellors was working under the designation of 'Social Worker'.

The average number of clients seen from the time that the counsellors began practicing was 34. Currently, the novice counsellors had an average of around 10 h per week of direct clinical contact in their practice. In terms of treatment modalities, the most commonly and frequently used modality was individual counselling. Twenty-nine out of the thirty counsellors in the sample handled individual cases. Family counselling was used by ten counsellors. The group counselling modality was also used by ten counsellors in the sample. Couple counselling cases were seen only by one counsellor.

The participants were asked the question 'Who are your supervisors?' and were allowed to choose multiple options. Twenty-one participants reported that they were supervised by their seniors at the workplace. Eight novices received supervision from peers, eight from mentors and three consulted past professors from their training for supervision. The average supervision time that the counsellors received was 1.10 h per week. The sample consulted around one to two supervisors on their cases.

3.6 Challenges Encountered

In the DPCCQ participants were asked to rate nineteen difficulties that they may have faced in their work since starting practice, on a scale of 0–5, where 0 stood for Not at all and 5 for Very often. It was seen that only one difficulty received a rating that was above 2 (Occasionally), i.e. lacking in confidence that you can have a beneficial effect on a client, which received a mean rating of 2.04 (SD = 1.19) (see Table 3.1). The novice counsellors also felt unsure how best to deal effectively with a client, which received a mean rating of 1.74 (SD = 1.01). These difficulties fall into the category of Professional Self Doubt (Orlinsky and Ronnestad 2005). Research on novices suggests that these 'feelings of incompetence' or

Table 3.1 Difficulties faced by novice counsellors in therapeutic practice as rated on the DPCCQ

DPCCQ item	Mean	SD
Lacking in confidence that you can have a beneficial effect on a client	2.04	1.19
Unsure how best to deal effectively with a client	1.74	1.01
Troubled by ethical issues that have arisen in your work with a client	1.74	1.11
Distressed by your powerlessness to affect a client's tragic life situation	1.54	1.28
Angered by factors in a client's life that prevent a beneficial outcome	1.54	1.33
Demoralized by your inability to find ways to help a client	1.50	1.17
Irritated with a client who is actively blocking your efforts	1.47	1.07
Unable to generate sufficient momentum to move therapy with a client in a constructive direction	1.44	1.01
Conflicted about how to reconcile obligations to a client and equivalent obligations to others	1.37	0.96
Frustrated with a client for wasting your time	1.30	1.29
In danger of losing control of the therapeutic situation to a client	1.24	0.97
Unable to comprehend the essence of a client's problems	1.20	1.03
Uneasy that your personal values make it difficult to maintain an appropriate attitude towards a client	1.17	1.12
Frustrated by the limited relevance of your therapeutic theories and techniques to the problems presented by a client	1.10	0.80
Bogged down with a client in a relationship that seems to go nowhere	1.10	1.21
Unable to have much real empathy for a client's experiences	1.00	1.02
Unable to withstand a client's emotional neediness	0.94	0.83
Afraid that you are doing more harm than good in treating a client	0.94	1.11
Unable to find something to like or respect in a client	0.80	1.03

feelings of self-doubt and uncertainty about one's own competence are reported very often by novice therapists (Thériault and Gazzola 2007).

Two other difficulties which received a relatively high rating were being troubled by ethical issues that have arisen in your work with a client; (1.74, SD = 1.11) and feeling distressed by your powerlessness to affect a client's tragic life situation" (1.54, SD = 1.28). The mean ratings for 18 out of 19 of the items were below 1.75, suggesting that the novices experienced these difficulties occasionally or even rarely. Banerjee and Basu (2012, unpublished) used the DPCCQ in their study and their findings showed that the psychotherapists found that one of the biggest difficulties they faced was "feeling distressed by powerlessness to affect a client's tragic life situation".

The items that received the lowest ratings were the inability to withstand a client's emotional neediness, fear that they were doing more harm than good in treating a client and an inability to find something to like or respect in a client. These three items received ratings below 1, suggesting that the participants never or rarely faced these difficulties.

As part of the section on challenges, the counsellors also answered the question 'In the last few days, outside of sessions, how often have you found yourself…' followed by five options that dealt with preoccupation with the clients issues outside of work. The item 'thinking about how best to help resolve a client's problems' received the highest mean rating of 3.20 (SD = 0.96), where 3 stood for moderately preoccupied. The ratings for three of the other items, remembering the feelings expressed by a client, reflecting on your own feelings towards a client and imagining a conversation with a client of yours, were above 2.50. It can be said that the counsellors would remain preoccupied with therapeutic issues occasionally to moderately. For a novice counsellor regulation of emotional involvement and boundaries can be a difficult task. This preoccupation is an "off-duty penetration of one's own emotional boundaries" (Skovholt and Rønnestad 2003, p. 49). These findings may suggest that novices may at times find it difficult to regulate their emotional involvement and boundaries with their client to a certain extent.

The interviews were expected to give a better understanding of the kind of challenges faced by novice counsellors in the Indian context. In the data that emerged from the six interviews conducted, it was seen that the challenges the novice counsellors had faced fell broadly into three categories. The challenges that the novices faced included those that were related to the organization they were attached to, challenges related to their practice, and those that stemmed from the profession as a whole. Finally, the feelings of incompetence experienced by the novice counsellors as well as the counsellors' attributions for the challenges are also discussed.

3.6.1 *Organization Related Challenges*

The first category of challenges was related to the organization that the counsellors worked in. Challenges related to the organization were mentioned by all the counsellors and this category had the largest number of challenges as well.

Being the Lone Counsellor

Three of the six counsellors felt that the biggest challenge for them was the fact that they were the only counsellors working in the organization. They felt lost, as they had no one to share their experiences with. The presence of peers can be an important aspect for the novice's development as peers help them normalize their experiences. This theme was also seen when the novices spoke about their peers as being important influences on their work. Without anyone to share their experiences with, these counsellors found it hard to make sense of their experiences and to normalize them. Shared experiences with peers can also provide validation of one's experience, which some of the counsellors were missing. One of the counsellors said that she felt lonely at her workplace, as she did not have anyone to talk to or to discuss her cases with.

> Sometimes you feel lonely… I always prefer to be around people. In this area, you don't have that. You're always working alone. …you don't have the time to share what you are going through or how would you like to work. Sometimes you need a support. And you don't get it at times. So at times I've felt that it's getting to me. (Richa, 23 years)

High Workload

Another challenge faced by the counsellors was high workload. Three of the counsellors spoke about the heavy workload and the large number of cases that they were working with. Since they did not have another counsellor working with them, the entire caseload fell upon them. In one of the cases, the counsellor, employed in a hospital, had another counsellor as a colleague; yet found that the workload was so high that he feared he would burnout very soon. According to this counsellor, the threat of burnout arises not only out of the workload but the work routine that one has to follow once one starts working,

> In terms of volume it does test your skill. It's not so much the difficulty of each case but the volume. And the fact that you are working on a nine to six basis, day in and day out…I mean there are so many factors before you start your day that could tie you down. And then you have the whole day ahead of you, you have the rest of the week ahead of you. The biggest factor that doesn't really sink (in) till you start working full time is burnout. And it's not just burnout in terms of your work load that is too heavy or the cases are too stressful. Just the whole routine of working. And that is one thing that you don't really anticipate unless you get into a setting. (Rahul, 23 years)

Lack of Supervision

The other challenge mentioned by two of the counsellors was lack of supervision. They reported that due to unavailability of supervisors, they could not discuss their cases or get a sense of direction when they felt lost. According to Skovholt and

Rønnestad (2003, p. 55) the lack of a supervisor can leave a novice with 'orphan distress'. Novices use the experience and expertise of their supervisors as an anchor for their own development and lack of supervision could make navigating the unknown waters of practice very difficult and distressing.

> It's difficult to know if what I'm doing was right. There's no one to discuss it with. I just go with my own judgement and it might not, you know, be the best. I have to do my own thing, there's no such guidance like we had in college and that's difficult because there is no help that you get from teachers or anything. (Aditi, 24 years)

Another counsellor had a supervisor but she was dissatisfied with the kind of supervision she received. She rarely received feedback or guidance from the supervisor, and when she did, she found it to be extremely negative and critical, leading her to become quickly disillusioned with her supervision experience. A supervisor who is not present or is overly critical can make the novices' experience as confusing as not having a supervisor at all (Skovholt and Rønnestad 2003). The quality of the supervision and not just the presence of a supervisor is important.

The importance of support in the work setting from other professionals was expressed by one of the counsellors.

> Another thing is that when I don't have the answer myself, going to my colleague or going to the Head of the Department and asking them what to do... Getting feedback from your supervisor and your peers helps a lot. And I think it would be a very difficult job to do if I didn't have a colleague in this setting. And it would be an equally difficult job to do if there was no Head of the Department. I think jobs like this would require a supervisor. If there is just one counsellor in a hospital setting the job is very difficult to do. (Rahul, 23 years)

Other Challenges

Two of the counsellors found the newness of the setting to be challenging as they did not know what to expect from the setting, neither did they have a template of how things work or what should be done in that particular setting. One of the other challenges related to the organization faced by the counsellors was inadequate monetary reimbursement. The counsellor felt that she did not receive the kind of pay that she deserved even though the hours and efforts she put in were equivalent to other better-paid professions. One of the counsellors felt that the infrastructure was not up to the mark which made work difficult. The structure and hierarchy in the organization, where counselling and counsellors were close to the bottom, was also a challenge for one of the counsellors.

These challenges although stemming from the organization are also related to the state of the profession in India. Counselling is a growing and developing profession in the country and counsellors are struggling to make a place for themselves in the professional sphere. This is discussed in more detail in the section on challenges related to the profession.

3.6.2 Practice-Related Challenges

Another set of challenges that the participants spoke about was related to their practice. The most often cited practice-related challenge was 'feelings of incompetence'. The other challenges that the novices faced had to do with the clients that they dealt with, their skills and their own selves.

Feelings of Incompetence

Literature on novice counsellors suggests that feelings of incompetence or feelings of inadequacy, uncertainty and doubt about one's competence and effectiveness are a central feature of the novice counsellors' development experience. The counsellors were asked the question 'Was there any time when you felt unsure of yourself or lacking in confidence while dealing with your clients?' in the interview. All of the counsellors interviewed had experienced these feelings of incompetence at different points in time. The challenges posed by the organization, clients, their own self and the profession led many of these novices to question and doubt their skills, competence and effectiveness. One of the counsellors spoke about feelings of uncertainty in dealing with terminally ill patients,

> So I really feel unsure about these particular cases… This patient has completely lost all kind of hope—I'm never going to be okay again. Dealing with these cases, you always feel whether or not your meeting them is making any difference to them. …at that point in time when you are in the room and you are trying to be there for them, you are not sure whether your being there is making any kind of difference because the patient is just crying the whole time. You don't know what to do. (Rahul, 23 years)

These results were also reflected in the data from the DPCCQ, where participants reported feelings of professional self-doubt. They lacked in confidence about having a beneficial effect on their clients, and felt unsure of how best to deal effectively with a client. In the interview, these feelings of incompetence were expressed in terms of not knowing what to do or feeling stuck and being unable to move ahead in therapy. The counsellors also expressed feelings of being uncertain or unsure about their skills. The counsellors often expressed these feelings with 'what if' questions.

> Some points of time you tend to feel that, when you've got a really difficult case and somewhere you feel that you won't be able to do it… What if I lack? Or what if the client asks me something and I'm not able to deal with it? (Diya, 24 years)

These results are in line with other research that looks at novice counsellors' experiences. For example, Thériault et al. (2009) found that the novice counsellors in their study experienced these feelings of incompetence. These feelings created a lot of stress for the novices, which often spilled over outside of sessions and these feelings had a negative influence on the therapeutic process.

Clients

Participants found that dealing with certain client groups or certain types of clients was difficult for them. Clinical cases were reported as challenging for four of the counsellors interviewed. Three of the counsellors found it difficult to work with children, while two of them mentioned that they could not work with individuals with issues of addiction.

> I get a bit weak when I have a case with drug addicts. For me it becomes a bit difficult. …I get this uncomfortable feeling when a drug addict is sitting in front of me. It disturbs me. (Diya, 24 years)

The *client attributes* or qualities that were difficult to deal with for the novices were reluctant clients who were either rigid or disinterested in the process of counselling. Demanding or aggressive clients were also challenging for two of the counsellors. The counsellors did not feel adequately equipped enough to deal with these groups of clients.

Skills

The novices also felt that there were certain skills that they found challenging and difficult to use. An important aspect to this challenge was application and adapting these skills. Three of the counsellors found that the skills they had learnt to use with certain client populations during their training had to be modified and adapted if they were to be used with a different client group. For instance, one of the counsellors found that the skills she had learnt to use with adults were hard to use with children. A novice also found it challenging to apply the skills and techniques she had learnt in theory to practice. It was also difficult for the counsellors to decide which approach to take with a client or which technique or skill to employ at a particular time. Skovholt and Rønnestad (2003) attribute this to the novices' lack of an adequate conceptual map. What novices have learnt in theory are broad guidelines that can be applied to a large number of client characteristics and situations but not the particular client or situation the novice is currently facing.

While the novice counsellors felt that they were comfortable and competent with relationship building skills they reported specific challenges in using skills in termination and confrontation.

Self

Two of the novices spoke about challenges of separating their own beliefs from what was ethically right for the client and keeping their own attitudes and beliefs aside while helping the client do what was best for them. Another counsellor reported that many of her clients felt that as she was young she would not have the experience to understand what they were talking about. She found it difficult to get the clients to relate to her.

3.6.3 Profession Related Challenges

There were certain profession-related challenges that were identified by the novice counsellors who took part in the study.

Status of the Profession

The novice counsellors spoke about the status of the profession in terms of their setting, as well as in society, as being a challenge that they encountered once they entered the field. In the words of one of the counsellors, counselling is a 'fighting profession' in India. In their work settings, two of the counsellors found that their department was not always taken seriously. Counselling was not seen as an essential service or department. This at times created doubts about their roles and the importance of their role in the organization.

> In India itself, we are a fighting kind of a profession right now… We are trying to make a place for us. So being sure of what our position is… But there is that bit of sensitivity still there that people are not going to take you as seriously as a doctor… We are still fighting to make our space over here. So I am not exactly sure whether we are looked at as a very essential part of the setting. So sometimes when you start feeling cynical, sometimes that thought comes to mind that if you are not here for a whole week it's not like patients are going to… or their recovery is going to be hampered. (Rahul, 23 years)

Social Reality

In terms of the society, the novices spoke about the detrimental effects of the negative attitude of the society towards counselling and the stigma associated with seeking professional help which discouraged individuals from seeking help from a counsellor. Four of the participants in the study said that they felt that the profession was not understood by society and lay people. The novices found this distressing at times, yet there was also a sense of acceptance that this is how things are, and there was a need to make a difference by creating more awareness about the profession. One of the counsellors expressed her annoyance with the layman's conception of what counselling is,

> People are like 'Ok so you know to read minds? You know what this means? Can you tell me what I'm thinking?' You know those types. …people also expect you to be very perfect. You can't have mood swings or you can't throw tantrums or you can't act like a kid. A psychologist is one who is a good observer and all that, quiet and not opening her mouth unless and until they have an observation to make. When I don't do things according to it, they are like are you a psychologist or what? So people have a lot of stereotypes about psychologists. I don't know where they come from. Maybe from movies they see a psychologist sitting in a quiet place and talking in a certain way. People think we are very calm and quiet people but you know we have other sides too. (Richa, 23 years)

Counsellors spoke about the client environment as being a barrier to successful outcomes of counselling. This was seen as a hindrance to their effectiveness. Similar results were seen in the quantitative part of the study as well as in the findings of Banerjee and Basu (2012, unpublished) where feeling distressed by powerlessness to affect a client's tragic life situation was one of the highest rated difficulties faced by the novice counsellors. The counsellors found that at times despite their best efforts to work with the client, they were not able to bring about a successful therapy outcome because the client's environment was such that it prevented any positive change. One of the school counsellors spoke about this,

> In isolation if I have to teach a child social skills, I can't do that. I need to do it in a group setting. I need to tell the teacher that 'make sure that the child mingles'. I need to tell the parent that you make him involved. So in certain cases you feel that all the guardians that are there in the child's life, all the people that are there need to put a consistent effort. We try our level best but… the child is ultimately going to the society… I could say it's there in the setting, in the school setting but we can't control the society. So sometimes the effectiveness may also get hampered. We can't control. (Naina, 23 years)

Here, the participant acknowledged that while certain environments, such as that of the school and classroom could be controlled, the similar controls could not be extended out to the context of the home, or of wider society. There are other issues such as limited resources and the lack of accessibility to counselling resources to the masses. Another environmental factor is the reality that many people in India cannot afford to go to a counsellor, limiting the access of the profession to a particular social class.

Role Ambiguity

The challenge of role ambiguity has been elaborated upon in the section on the novice counsellors' professional role. The role of the counsellor was not clearly defined in many settings and overlapped with other professional roles, like social worker.

While the data from the DPCCQ helped identify challenges faced by the novice counsellors during the sessions with their clients, the in-depth interviews threw light on multiple other challenges that the counsellors were negotiating in their professional work.

3.6.4 Attributions

The participants were also asked to talk about what they attributed their challenges and feelings of incompetence to. All the participants reported in the interviews that their lack of experience and exposure was a major contributor to the challenges that they faced with respect to their skills and clients. They expressed disappointment with their training because the skills that they had acquired from their training did not seem to be sufficient when it came to practice. They felt that their training did not provide them with enough exposure or equip them with enough skills to deal with certain kinds of issues and client groups.

Skovholt and Rønnestad (2003) found similar themes in their review of work on counsellor development. They suggest that at this stage in of being a novice, counsellors tend to feel a sense of disillusionment towards their training which they find to have been inadequate.

3.7 Coping

To understand the coping strategies novice counsellors used in dealing with the challenges and difficulties they had faced, participants were asked the question 'When in difficulty how often do you…?' and were given 22 options that listed out coping strategies. The respondents had to rate these coping strategies on a scale of 0–5 (where 0 = Not at all and 5 = Very often), in order to determine how often they used them. The results on DPCCQ suggested that the coping strategies that the counsellors used most often were discussing the problem which poses a challenge with a colleague and consultation about a challenging case with a more experienced counsellor/therapist. Both these items received a mean rating of 3.27 (SD = 1.14 and 1.01) where three stood for 'moderate' (refer to Table 3.2). Counsellors often postponed the work of therapy to take care of a client's more pressing needs. This item received a mean rating of 3.17 (SD = 5.56).

The lowest ratings were received by the items 'criticizing a client for causing you trouble' or 'showing your frustration to the client'. The mean ratings for these items were below 1 which stood for rarely. The novices never or rarely criticized their clients or showed their frustration to their clients. It can be said that the novice counsellors used positive coping strategies rather than those that can be detrimental to themselves or to the client, while maintaining a professional stance towards the client.

Banerjee and Basu (2012, unpublished), in their study, found that the highest rated coping strategy used by psychotherapists was trying to see the problem from a different perspective, which had a mean rating of 3 (SD = 1.02). The psychotherapists also consult relevant literature, reviewed their problems privately and discussed the problem with a colleague. The strategies used by novices related more to their professional others like colleagues and seniors, while more experienced therapists use strategies that related more to themselves like referring to literature or reviewing the problem themselves. This could be because novices are more likely to require support from external sources as their therapeutic self is in its nascent stages of development. This was also seen in the novice's need for support and guidance from supervisors as well as peers.

In the qualitative interview participants were asked about how they had coped with the challenges they faced since starting practice. The participants' coping strategies could be categorized as those related to themselves and those related to others, including both professional others and significant others.

Table 3.2 Coping strategies used by novice counsellors in the DPCCQ

Coping strategies	Mean ratings	SD
Discussing the problem with a colleague	3.27	1.14
Consulting about the case with a more experienced counsellor/ therapist	3.27	1.01
Postponing the work of therapy so as to take care of a client's more immediate needs	3.17	5.56
Trying to see the problem from a different perspective	3.00	1.02
Consulting relevant articles or books	2.84	1.37
Reviewing privately with yourself how the problem has arisen	2.67	1.21
Giving yourself permission to experience difficult or disturbing feelings	2.44	1.28
Modifying your therapeutic stance or approach with a client	2.44	1.14
Seeing whether you and your client can together deal with the difficulty	2.17	1.34
Involving another professional or agency in the case	2.10	1.35
Signing up for a conference or workshop that might bear on the problem	2.04	1.40
Inviting collaboration from a client's friends or relatives	2.04	1.33
Hoping that things will improve eventually	1.97	1.47
Seeking some form of alternative satisfaction away from therapy	1.90	1.21
Stepping out of the counsellor/therapist role in order to take some urgent action on a client's behalf	1.80	1.13
Making changes in your therapeutic contract with a client	1.77	0.86
Exploring the possibility of referring the client on to another therapist	1.74	1.20
Sharing your experience of the difficulty with your client	1.40	1.04
Seriously considering terminating therapy	1.20	1.24
Avoid dealing with the problem for the present	1.04	1.16
Criticizing a client for causing you trouble	0.54	0.94
Showing your frustration to the client	0.54	1.04

3.7.1 Coping Strategies Related to Others

The results from the DPCCQ were reflected in the interview data. The novices consulted and asked for help from professional others, i.e. supervisors and colleagues. As seen in the quantitative data seeking help from other professionals, both supervisors and colleagues received the highest mean ratings. Novices got support from their professional others in the form of guidance with difficult cases and coping with challenges faced in the organization.

The participants looked at their supervisors as a guide and a teacher. Case discussions and mock sessions with the supervisor and his/her inputs were considered valuable, especially in cases where they felt stuck or unsure of how to move ahead. The supervisor also helped them deal with other issues apart from therapy or counselling that came up at the work place. The supervisor was seen as someone who had experience in the profession and had navigated the same waters.

> I would always go and discuss it with the senior psychologist. Even if it was a minor thing or something… So they've really helped me out with my cases, and whatever issues I had regarding psychology. And even if I didn't understand the meaning of a word or if I'm not understanding a disorder correctly, or if I'm not understanding some therapy, they would explain. (Diya, 24 years)

In line with the findings of the current study, a number of research studies report that for novices, supervision is the most important and enduring source of influence and is vital for their professional development (Bischoff et al. 2002; Orlinsky and Rønnestad 2005; Bernard and Goodyear 2009). Orlinsky and Rønnestad (2005), in a study of 4000 novice counsellors, found that supervision was rated as the most important factor influencing their development.

Many of the counsellors in the study were working with other counsellors who were also novices. Discussing cases with their peers was also reported as helpful as it provided clarity on issues and gave new perspectives. Brainstorming about cases, sharing the lessons and challenges helped counsellors learn from each other's experiences. It also made them realize that many of the issues they found difficult to deal with and the feeling of being stuck were experienced by their peers as well. Peers helped and influenced novice counsellors' development by providing support, helping them deal with their work stresses and adapt to the work environment. This helped develop a sense of camaraderie with their peers and colleagues who were also at the same stage of development and were facing similar challenges. Bischoff et al. (2002) also found that peers were an important source of influence on novice therapists because they helped novices make sense of their internal experience.

> And of course working with my colleague also helps because there is a support from somebody who is doing the same job and comes from the same training and knows what it is. (Rahul, 23 years)

Participants found that support from significant others also helped them deal with their difficulties. Two of the novices mentioned that their families were their support systems, while one of the counsellors mentioned her intimate partner. Novices utilized their significant others as support systems in terms of sharing their difficulties with them and getting encouragement from them.

3.7.2 Coping Strategies Related to the Self

Two of the participants mentioned that they tried to deal with their problems and challenges themselves. They utilized strategies like using positive self-talk and keeping themselves motivated despite failures or roadblocks. One of the counsellors spoke about the importance of having faith in yourself and your skills in order to cope with your difficulties.

> I said you just don't allow yourself to think that if one case has gone badly it's not good and you are never going to be able to deal with it again. So it's just that having faith in yourself. Having faith that if it's not going well sometimes, it's not that all the other cases are going to be like that. Telling yourself that is quite important. And I think when I've done that it has helped. (Rahul, 23 years)

Self-related strategies also included reading books, consulting research journals or articles and watching movies or documentaries.

It was seen that novice counsellors utilized a range of coping strategies to deal with the challenges they faced. These strategies involved seeking help from their peers and supervisors, as well, as utilizing internal and external resources.

3.8 The Experience of Being Novice Counsellors

While the counselling profession in India is growing, novice counsellors entering the field experience multiple challenges which act as hurdles in the path of professional growth and development. Counsellors develop various coping strategies to deal with the situations arising out of the encounters with the field. The multiple challenges experienced by novice counsellors were not only limited to competencies and skills, but also included challenges that stem from the setting and organization that they are attached to and related to the state of the profession of counselling in India.

The within session challenges that are related to clients directly impact the therapeutic process and outcome and have been the focus of a lot of research worldwide and have been included in standardized measures such as the DPCCQ. However, the context in which the counsellor is operating impinges on the counsellor's functioning and effectiveness and the challenges that are posed by the larger context need to be factored in when understanding the novice phase of professional development. The narratives of the novice counsellors highlighted that the challenges when trainees begin practice in India are distinctive and different from those that might be faced by novice counsellors in other parts of the world. Problems related to working with under privileged groups, working with clients who cannot afford counselling services, and the lack of awareness about mental health concerns and services in the country were unique to low income economies such as India.

The participant novice counsellors gave detailed and comprehensive accounts of their experiences. Along with sharing the challenges they experienced, their narratives also brought forward their commitment to the profession which came out in the notion that the counsellors had made a choice to be in this profession, they had committed to this profession and they would continue in it despite the challenges.

3.9 Implications

The challenges faced by novice counsellors have implications for training, supervision and the overall development of the profession. The need for a professional regulatory body for counsellors has been mooted. Novice counsellors have reported that dealing with clinical cases or serious psychological disorders was very challenging. Developing competencies and skills to work with such cases during the post-graduation level training, and encouraging students to complete their professional training before entering practice may be crucial. Research suggests that personal therapy can have a substantial influence on the novice counsellor's development. However, the novices in the study did not have an opportunity to undergo personal therapy; and training programs in India could mandate personal therapy as part of their curriculum to facilitate self-awareness and self-exploration. Novice counsellors have to deal with a high workload with multiple demands at their workplace soon as they begin practicing and feel a great need for continued support through supervision. Supervision has been seen as an important aspect in the novice counsellors' growth and development and therefore having trained supervisors who could provide formal supervision is needed.

Apart from the need for intensive experiential skill-based learning along with continued supervision, a need for a professional regulatory body that represents counsellors in India that would address issues of licensing, training, ethical codes was also emphasized. This study focused on the unique experiences of novice counsellors; however, research on the experiences of counsellors during other phases of development is also required to track the development of a professional from being a novice to a master.

Acknowledgments The authors would like to acknowledge all the participant counsellors for making time and sharing their experiences for the project.

References

Banerjee, P., & Basu, J. (2012). *Psychotherapists' views on themselves and the therapeutic change process.* Paper presented at the National Annual Conference of the Indian Association of Clinical Psychologists, Pune, India. Unpublished.

Bernard, J. M., & Goodyear, R. K. (2009). *Fundamentals of clinical supervision.* Upper Saddle River, NJ: Pearson Education Inc.

Bischoff, R. J., Barton, M., Thober, J., & Hawley, R. (2002). Events and experiences impacting the development of clinical self-confidence: A study of first year client contact. *Journal of Marital and Family Therapy, 28*(3), 371–382. doi:10.1111/j.1752-0606.2002.tb01193.x.

Briggs, D. (2007). *Burnout in Novice Counsellors: A Handbook to Reduce its Occurrence.* Unpublished. Retrieved from http://dtpr.lib.athabascau.ca/.

Creswell, J. W., Plano Clark, V. L., Gutmann, M. L., & Hanson, W. E. (2003). Advanced mixed methods research designs. In A. Teddlie & C. Tashakkori (Eds.), *Handbook of Mixed Methods in Social and Behavioral Research* (pp. 209–240). CA: Sage.

Hanson, W., Creswell, J., Plano Clark, V., & Creswell, J. (2005). Mixed methods research designs in counselling psychology. *Faculty Publications, Department of Psychology,* paper 373. doi:10.1037/0022-0167.52.2.224.

Hill, C. E., & Corbett, M. (1993). A perspective on the history of process and outcome research in counselling psychology. *Journal of Counselling Psychology, 40*(1), 3–24. doi:10.1037/0022-0167.40.1.3.

Hill, C. E., Sullivan, C., Knox, S., & Schossler, L. Z. (2007). Becoming psychotherapists: Experience of novice trainees in a beginning graduate class. *Psychotherapy: Theory, Research, Practice, Training, 44*(4), 1–27. doi:10.1037/0033-3204.44.4.434.

Lambert, M. J., & Barley, D. E. (2001). Research summary on the therapeutic relationship and psychotherapy outcome. *Psychotherapy: Theory, Research, Practice, Training, 38*(4), 357–361. doi:10.1037/0033-3204.38.4.357.

Orlinsky, D. E., & Rønnestad, M. H. (2005). *How psychotherapists develop: A study of therapeutic work and professional growth.* Washington, DC: American Psychological Association.

Orlinsky, D. E., et al. (1999). Development of psychotherapists: Concepts, questions, and methods of a collaborative international study. *Psychotherapy Research, 9*, 127–153. doi:10.1080/10503309912331332651.

Orlinsky, D. E., Botermans, J.-F., & Rønnestad, M. H. (2001). Towards an empirically-grounded model of psychotherapy training: Five thousand therapists rate influences on their development. *Australian Psychologist, 36*, 139–148. doi:10.1080/00050060108259646.

Reupert, A. (2006). The counsellor's self in therapy: An inevitable presence. *International Journal for the Advancement of Counseling, 28*(1), 95–105. doi:10.1007/s10447-005-9001-2.

Rønnestad, M. H., & Skovholt, T. M. (2003). The journey of the counsellor and therapist: Research findings and perspectives on professional development. *Journal of Career Development, 30*, 5–44. doi:10.1177/089484530303000102.

Skovholt, T. M., & Rønnestad, M. H. (2003). Struggles of the novice counsellor and therapist. *Journal of Career Development, 30*(1), 45–58. doi:10.1177/089484530303000103.

Thériault, A., & Gazzola, N. (2007). What are the sources of feelings of incompetence in experienced therapists? *Counselling Psychology Quarterly, 19*(4), 313–330. doi:10.1080/09515070601090113.

Thériault, A., Gazzola, N., & Richardson, B. (2009). Feelings of incompetence in novice therapists: Consequences, coping and correctives. *Canadian Journal of Counselling*, *43*(2), 105–209. Retrieved from http://cjc-rcc.ucalgary.ca/cjc/index.php/rcc/index.

Wampold, B. E. (2007). Psychotherapy: The humanistic (and effective) treatment. *American Psychologist, 62*(8), 857–873. doi:10.1037/0003-066X.62.8.85.

[illegible]

Chapter 4
Synergies Between Personal and Professional Lives of Counsellors

Sinduja Vummidi and Sandhya Limaye

Abstract This paper draws on a qualitative study to explore the effect of the counselling process on the personal and professional lives of counsellors and therapists. The paper reports the findings in the voices of ten practising counsellors (seven women and three men) from the metropolitan city of Chennai, India. In-depth interviews were conducted for collecting data and a phenomenological approach was used for the analysis of the data. The findings and discussion give insights into the effect of the counselling process on the counsellor's personal self, health and family and on the professional life, professional development and identity of the participant counsellors. It was found that counsellors were on their journey of actualization, striving to achieve an ideal, continuously learning experientially, and engaging with the counselling process even after a client leaves the session. It was concluded that counsellors combined their personal and professional lives, which helped them see the profession in a more positive light as compared to keeping them distinctly separate.

Keywords Counselling process · Impact on counsellor · Effect on personal life · Effect on professional life

Counselling is a facilitating or enabling relationship between a client and a counsellor that 'focuses on a person's growth, adjustment, problem-solving and decision-making needs' (Gibson and Mitchell 2003, p. 164). Counselling has been seen as progressive movement towards the resolution of an issue which requires

---

Sinduja Vummidi (✉)
Illumine Knowledge Resources (Pvt.) Ltd., Mumbai, India
e-mail: sindhuja1188@gmail.com

Sandhya Limaye
Centre for Disability Studies and Action, School of Social Work, TISS, Mumbai, India

S. Sriram (ed.), *Counselling in India*, DOI 10.1007/978-981-10-0584-8_4

a solution (Gibson and Mitchell 2003). Counselling addresses lifestyle maladjustments, developmental transitions, difficulties in coping with stress, trauma, addiction, marital disharmony, parent–child conflicts, sexual abuse, loss and grief. It is also used to aid clients to build problem-solving capabilities, decision-making capabilities, promote self-acceptance, actualization, bring about shifts in thoughts, perspectives and beliefs which are healthier and more beneficial for the client which can be dealt with at the conscious level.

4.1 The Counselling Process

The counselling process is a sequence of stages that the counsellor and client engage in for resolving the problem the client comes with. There are many factors which influence the process and its outcome. These include counsellor variables (counsellor's training, experience, frequency of supervision, values, promotion of core conditions like empathy, unconditional positive regard, relationship attitudes, intervention style, theory and approach followed), client variables (attending sessions regularly, motivation and willingness, past positive interpersonal relationships), cultural variables (attitudes and stereotypes towards bisexuals, transgender, gay, lesbian communities) and the therapeutic relationship or counsellor–client relationship (transference, counter-transference, the level of emotional attachment, trust, boundaries maintained). The therapeutic relationship has been found to play a key role throughout the process of counselling and the outcome of the process as well (Kottler 2003).

In the entire process of going through counselling with so many clients with a variety of problems, counsellors themselves go through many changes. This calls for understanding the process. The effect of the counselling process on an individual's personality has been widely studied as the profession of counselling is strongly driven by the individual's self. Fortin and Chevrier (2003) aimed to show that the counselling process was related to learning. They found that there were similarities between the underlying cognitive behaviours of the various stages of the counselling process and Kolb's experiential learning model (1984).

4.1.1 The Effectiveness of the Counsellor

The effectiveness of a counsellor has been attributed to an individual's perception about their own competence. Theriault and Gazzola (2010) found that feelings of incompetence varied in intensity and nature among novice therapists and were mainly there because the therapists were procedural, bound to micro-outcomes, uncertain of their profession or doubted their self and their identity. Other studies on the relationship between experience and perceived mastery by Orlinsky et al. (1999) showed that 83 % of novice psychotherapists with 0–1.33 years of experience perceived low mastery compared to 70 % of them with 1.33–3.15 years of experience. However, among therapists who had 3.15–5 years of experience only 52 % perceived low mastery. Thus, developing expertise in counselling and therapy takes time and experience. Jennings et al. (2003) add that it also requires additional factors such as emotional and relational characteristics, openness to change, cultural competence and comfort with ambiguity to do so.

While there are many such studies indicating that mastery comes only with experience, there are many more studies which indicate the crucial role of personal characteristics and developing the self in excelling as a therapist or a counsellor. Skovholt and Starkey (2010) found that practitioners understood client's pain and suffering if they knew and understood suffering on a personal level. Jenson (2007) found that lives of therapists were connected to their everyday psychotherapeutic practice. He also concluded that sometimes their family and cultural backgrounds contribute to them becoming therapists. Corey (2009) has spoken about assessing counsellor motivations for pursuing the profession, self-exploration on values, attitudes, needs and life experiences. Corey (2009, p. 20) suggested that the 'healer' (or counsellor) must undergo personal therapy in order to heal their own psychological wounds which would enhance their ability to deal with the 'stresses associated with clinical work'.

4.1.2 The Personal and Professional Development of the Counsellor

Ronnestad and Skovholt (2003) show consistently that interpersonal experiences in the personal life domain (early family life and adult personal life) and the professional life domain (interacting with clients, professional elders, and peers) are significant sources of influence for professional development. They go on to say that stagnation will ensue if the counsellor or therapist engages in the 'distortive process' (also called 'premature closure') and the ability and willingness to continually reflect upon professional experiences in general, and difficulties and challenges in particular are prerequisites for optimal development.

This ability and willingness to self-reflect as being crucial for professional development has been identified in other studies as well. Skovholt et al. (2004) found that deep acceptance and understanding of the self, genuine humbleness, a high level of self-awareness and an intense will to grow and learn are crucial for excelling as a practitioner. There can be several factors which can limit the understanding of a professional in his/her development path. These blocks (Skovholt et al. 1997) can either be the need to go beyond the cognitive realm to the working alliance for the fundamental construct in the domain; the need to realize that the novice-to-expert path takes a long time; the inappropriate use of a short experience differential in comparative studies of novices and experts; the importance of reflection for development; or the need for professors, in order to be experts, to also be practitioners in the domain.

While being aware that one's practice and one's intervention methods aids professional development, studies like the one by Williams (2003) found that moment-to-moment self-awareness during the counselling session was distracting and led to poorer outcome. Skovholt and Starkey (2010) found that three aspects—practitioner experience, personal life and academic research—are vital for the professional development of the practitioner. An investigation of the experiences of five trainees in a pre-practicum course in their counselling psychology doctoral programme in a study by Hill et al. (2007) revealed that the major challenges in the experience of becoming a therapist were self-criticism, managing reactions to clients, learning and using the helping skills, and session management. The gains were primarily in the areas of learning and using the helping skills, becoming less self-critical, and being able to connect with clients.

Since years of experience and capacity to self-reflect seem to play a significant role in professional development and mastery, the question arises of how much does training and supervision help. Richard and Marquez (2005) found that a diverse group of HIV/AIDS counsellors in Zimbabwe felt that they received minimal support and supervision and were undertrained. Although the participants acknowledged they have had negative psychological experiences when counselling HIV/AIDS clients, they also expressed feelings of satisfaction and fulfilment in their work. Brown (2002) found that licensed counsellors and psychologists compared to non-counsellor-trained career practitioners viewed that their degree programme had adequately prepared them to provide career counselling emphasizing theory and giving attention to personal and career issues and were more likely to consider professional development activities as important to their career counselling effectiveness.

Ortlepp and Friedman (2002) explored the experiences of non-professional trauma counsellors in the workplace. They found that on an average the counsellors did not experience symptoms of secondary trauma stress (STS) that required treatment and experienced significant role satisfaction. However, changes in cognition about world view were found to be present 6 weeks after their last trauma-counselling incident. Factors related to the nature of the trauma-counselling task and counsellors' exposure to work and nonwork-related trauma were not significantly associated with counsellors' STS or role satisfaction scores. Programme coordination, self-efficacy, stakeholder commitment, sense of coherence and perceived social support were significantly related to counsellors' experiences of STS and role satisfaction. Etherington (2001, p. 263) said, 'Counsellors might find themselves being used as a repository for the negative and/or positive feelings patients have towards other team members as representatives of parental figures (counter-transference)'. Corey (2009, p. 34) added that 'professional burnout' is an inevitable condition associated with helping professions that can lead to ineffectiveness in outcome and negative effect on counsellor–client relationship. Paine (1982, as cited in Latha 2004) found that burnout stress syndrome (BOSS) was a consequence of work stress, poor coping skills and personal frustration which can adversely affect the mental health professional's personal and social lives and his/her organization. This and many other studies showed that counsellors are likely to be influenced by their work-related experiences in both, their personal and professional lives including their own physical health. 'Self-monitoring', 'self-care' and 'self-awareness' can help counsellors/therapists be more attuned to their choices, thoughts (Corey 2009, p. 34), emotions, lifestyles, etc. 'enabling them to survive without burning out through the experience of holding and sharing the pain, fear and despair of clients' (McLeod 2003, p. 501). It has also been found that regular supervision and access to personal therapy effectively supported and contributed to all five aspects (physically, behaviourally, emotionally, socially and cognitively) of taking care of the 'Therapeutic Self' (Dryden and Reeves 2008, p. 289).

4.1.3 The Synergy of the Personal and the Professional Life

The personal life of a counsellor is different from the professional being. The personal life is where counsellors engage with their family members, experience and perform other roles such as parent, spouse, son or daughter, friend, sibling, neighbour and so on. As a performer of other roles, counsellors, just like any other individual, are expected to engage in other activities such as cooking, child care, recreation, socializing, pursue self-interests and so on. However, counsellors meet numerous clients everyday who bring with them their experiences of life and its problems which may influence the counsellors' personal lives. Research has repeatedly shown that counselling is a profession where the 'personal self' of an individual cannot be fully bifurcated from the 'professional identity' of being a counsellor. Knowing the impact such experiences might have on the personal lives of counsellors will help them in coping better with influences of their profession on their personal lives.

There are numerous difficulties and challenges throughout the counselling process faced by a therapist. Their interactions and experiences with clients may not only improve their professional practice but also affect their thinking, their way of being and their physical health. Training, introspection, self-awareness and self-care are crucial for a counsellor's mental and physical health.

Professional practice of the counsellor revolves around the counsellor's role of 'being a counsellor'. It is that part of life where the counsellor engages in activities that propel his or her development as a counsellor, where he or she reflects on his or her own practice, the skills used and improves on them. Listening, planning and dealing with each client gives counsellors unique experiences and something new to learn from every time. Just like many other professions, counselling is one where the number of years of experience plays a role in mastery of skills and techniques. Thus, each counsellor's professional growth will not only be unique but also at different stages of development.

There is an abundance of research from the developed world on counsellors' and clients' experiences of counselling and psychotherapy, its process, effectiveness and outcomes. However, since professional counselling is itself new in India, there is a dearth of research on the counselling process in India. In the current scheme of things, data about counsellors' experience of the process is of immense importance in understanding the contextual issues faced by counsellors and therapists in India.

4.2 Studying the Synergy of the Personal and the Professional

The study intended to explore and understand the effect of the counselling process on the personal life and current professional practice of the counsellor. In-depth, face-to-face interviews were conducted with ten practising counsellors in Chennai, Tamil Nadu using an interview schedule. Purposive sampling was used to identify the sample of counsellors or psychotherapists who had a minimum of 3 years of continuous experience as a counsellor, or as a psychotherapist, and had some form of prior training in psychology or counselling. The interviews were audio-recorded with the consent of the participant and then transcribed. Descriptive analysis was conducted to bring all the findings together based on similarities and differences within the sample of counsellors. A phenomenological approach was employed for data analysis.

The ten counsellors who took part in the study included seven women and three men. Interviews were conducted with one male workplace counsellor, three female school counsellors who were also private practitioners, one female marital counsellor who also had a private practice, one male and two female counsellors who worked in a hospital setting, one full-time female private practitioner and one part-time male private practitioner. The number of years of experience in current practice ranged from 3.5 to 26 years. The age of the counsellors ranged from 29 to 65 years. Four of the counsellors began their profession after the age of 40.

4.3 The Personal Life of Counsellors

The impact of the profession on the personal life of the counsellors has been broadly classified into three: the impact on the self, on health and on the family.

4.3.1 Impact on the Self

Counsellors go through a process of change themselves by being a practitioner in the counselling process. The influence of such experiences with clients and of being a counsellor has a tremendous impact on the way a counsellor looks at himself or herself as a person, and at the world (Ortlepp and Friedman 2002). Most counsellors felt that they had changed greatly and for the better. Madhuri[1] a school consultant and private practitioner described the influence of the counselling process on her life over her 26 years of counselling practice,

> The counselling process has given me a better understanding of personal relationships. Somewhere deep down it has helped me become aware of my own limitations and what I can do about many of them, if not all of them; I think self-improvement. They have taught me to accept people however they are, the way they are [even] outside the professional practice. It has taught me to value people more than ever. (Madhuri)

While many of the counsellors expressed similar influences as described by Madhuri, some of the others felt that they had become wiser, accepted themselves better and complained less about life. Most counsellors said that they became 'more patient' and that their 'frustration-tolerance levels' had increased. Prabhu, a part-time private practitioner (for children and adolescents) and a part-time professor, added 'My tolerance level has increased; I am more adjusted…'.

Vineeth, a full-time consultant, reported being able to understand himself better over his 6.5 years of practice, and has begun combining philosophy and psychology to understand himself and people better. Lakshmi, a school consultant and a private practitioner, stated '… I have changed tremendously… there has been lots of self-growth…' These also correspond to some of the qualities for excelling as practitioners given by Skovholt et al. (2004). '… I look at things differently…' and '…my outlook has changed…' were some of the expressions that indicated that the counsellors began to see the world differently.

For a few of the respondents, being a counsellor had helped them work on their own issues and selves. For instance, Rajesh, a workplace consultant with a tendency to procrastinate, had made it a point to be more organized so that he felt confident when he dealt with a client who had the same tendency. Madhuri had learnt not to be the perfectionist that she used to be. She decided to 'do well all the time and do my best where and when it really matters'.

Latha, a marital counsellor and private practitioner, had begun to '*respond rather than react*' to her husband. For Suhasini, a full-time private practitioner, the analytical skills that she had mastered over her 18 years of practice had helped her see her own problems more objectively and hence resolve them with ease.

It appeared that practising counselling can be self-changing and self-evolving; but it was found that being a counsellor had its disadvantages and could lead to negative impacts for some counsellors too. Aruna, a counsellor practicing in a hospital, found herself to be preoccupied by observing and analysing couples and people wherever she went, even if she was dining with her family in a restaurant! She also reported becoming quieter and more withdrawn from social events over her 6 years of practice.

Renu, another counsellor working in a hospital, reported '… people say that I behave and speak more maturely than my age. I feel bad and get worried

---

[1]All names of participants are fictitious to maintain confidentiality.

sometimes …'. Latha often found herself caught between her unhealthy patterns of behaviour which she was aware of and what 'psychology' preaches; she often battled with her own resistance to let go of some of her unhealthy patterns since she was in such a profession. Despite the personal struggles and dissonance, almost all counsellors agreed that the positive aspects outweighed the negative ones. '… This profession has totally enriched my life ….' said Aruna.

It appeared that because of going over the counselling process many times over, counsellors begin 'fixing themselves' over time in order to be as genuine as they could be with their clients. Some had consciously worked on their own lives to become consistent and 'better' individuals. This also corresponds to Roger's concept of congruence (Rogers 1957, as cited in Ronnestad and Skovholt 2003, p. 27) where the therapist discards 'values, perceptions and methods which do not match the personality and self of the therapist' in order to be 'more consistent to the counsellor/therapist's professional self-concept'. As the counselling process largely followed the Rogerian perspective (McLeod 2003, p. 156), the skills taught and practiced in the profession such as being non-judgmental, active listening, responding empathetically and providing respect (Egan 1994), seemed to have become a part of their personal self. These skills began to transcend the counselling setup and appeared to generalize to the other significant people in their lives. From their responses, it also appeared that counsellors changed their perspectives towards themselves and towards others by being more accepting of others, more patient and tolerant with near and dear ones and less critical of their own lives.

Practising counselling had made them feel more responsible for their own lives. Thus, it could be inferred that almost all counsellors had engaged in a process of changing themselves consciously or unconsciously thereby indicating that counsellors may have a tendency to evolve or self-actualize rather than have what Rogers calls 'static self-concepts' (McLeod 2003). It can also be inferred that most counsellors (except one) preferred to combine or integrate their personal life and professional life rather than keep them exclusive of each other. This corroborates with Ronnestad and Skovholt's (2003) finding that recognizing and integrating one's personal life (self-perceptions such as values, attitudes, interests) and one's professional life made the counsellor/therapist 'feel more at ease in their work' because they were then able to 'apply their professional competence in an authentic way'.

4.3.2 Influence on Health

Etherington (2001, p. 263) wrote that counsellors working in health settings may become 'overwhelmed or suffer burnout' as they usually deal with 'more powerful emotions, trauma and rapid turnover of clients' apart from having to deal with 'frequent process endings and pressures of the organization' that they worked in. In the present study, one of the counsellors, Aruna, reported that she felt low at times, suffered from sleeplessness and headaches. She said, '… Morning to afternoon

I am not hearing anything positive. Except when a problem is resolved, on an average I am hearing only negative things'.

Four out of ten counsellors in this study expressed that they felt emotionally fatigued especially when they were over worked and saw more than six clients in a day. Three such counsellors eventually ended up with some physical ailment such as hyperthyroidism, back pain and chest pain which then served as signals for them to change their way of working. Vineeth reported

> When I was in the Medical College and Research Institute, I was seeing 10–12 clients a day…it was too much, lunch time which was supposed to be one hour, I got to take only 30 min. More than that, I was physically present but mentally elsewhere. I eventually got back pain after three-four months. (Vineeth)

Some of the respondents experienced feelings of lethargy and tiredness, which was attributed to excessive travelling to various settings for their counselling sessions. Apart from physiological signals of fatigue, which signalled her to slow down, Suhasini also became aware that she was losing patience with clients and was showing disregard to what they were saying, and she knew she had to rejuvenate herself. Some counsellors began to take preventive measures before they got emotionally fatigued or allowed severe illnesses to set in. They have learnt to prevent it after burning their fingers a couple of times. Lakshmi said

> I have learnt to dissociate myself from challenging cases in the last 1–1.5 years. It was not easy. I take a weekend break with my family often, where we just drive off for two days… I used to do all my filing, notes and recordings (documentation) on Sundays. Now, this door [the counselling room] is not opened on Sundays, it is a complete shutdown. (Lakshmi)

Similarly, Renu added

> Earlier I used to take the cases back home, keep thinking about them and planning what to do next and reflecting on whatever happened at work. Now I completely shut off [my mind], the minute I step out of this place. (Renu)

Renu and Suhasini also engaged themselves in yoga, and practiced relaxation techniques such as meditation and breathing exercises to take care of their health. Prabhu, a part-time private practitioner, and Anita, a part-time school consultant and private practitioner, both of whom saw fewer clients in a day expressed the absence of any health problems.

It, thus, appeared that counselling was not similar to a '9 a.m. to 5 p.m.' job where there were fixed timings to work after which one could forget job-related matters and engage with other responsibilities or leisure activities. On the contrary, it appeared to be a process that continued, sometimes unconsciously, even after clients had left and sessions were over. It gave the impression that counsellors needed to spend extra time to work on challenging cases and to think over or consult others for opinions in order to plan future sessions. Thus, work spilled over into their personal lives, sometimes taking over their sleep and adversely affecting their health. It was probably an unconscious process, or a lack of ability to emotionally disengage or work stress that contributed to some of the more serious ailments that counsellors reported of. Work-related stress causing adverse effect on health has also been discussed in Latha (2004). However, in this sample of counsellors, some of them had realized the effect of extended transference and took serious and conscious measures to protect themselves from this consequence. This coincides with Hunter and Schofield's (2006) study where they found that 'all [participant] counsellors accepted a significant level of responsibility for self-care, both to enhance their effectiveness as counsellors as well as to prevent burnout or vicarious traumatization'. p. 134

4.3.3 Influence on the Family

By tradition, Indian women are socialised to be home makers and by working, they often play a dual role of home maker and a wage earner. 'Combining these two roles—work and home—successfully is not an easy task. Not only does it require skill but also physical and psychological acceptance besides some sacrifices and adjustment to the changes brought about by this combination' (Hemalatha and Suryanarayana 1983, p. 153).

Most (four out of five) of the women counsellors who were married reported that they were able to manage the balance between work life and home life much better than other women they knew. Lakshmi recounted '… I am a much better mother and wife because of counselling. I understand my partner better and where he is coming from'. Out of the three men, Rajesh said that his relationship with his wife was always good and continued to be good, whereas Vineeth said that his wife appreciated that he listened to her, unlike other men she knew or had heard of. He also felt that he had connected better with his family emotionally after entering the field of counselling. Prabhu denied any change in his family life due to the influences of his profession.

Almost all (four out of the five) counsellors who had children expressed that they had been able to raise their children in a more responsible way and have also been able to correct a few upbringing mistakes that they had made in the past when raising them. According to Rajesh, 'Life is full of problems. I am able to teach my children how to face it. If they have to travel by bus [public transport] let them. It will help them in future'.

Despite having had a degree in teaching, Suhasini had been a home maker for many years while her husband was alive. Her family and relatives were respectful of the way she had handled her life personally and professionally after the loss of her husband. Although Latha felt proud that she was contributing to the family income, she expressed that she had cancelled her personal commitments at times to accommodate some of her clients.

4.3.4 Professional Roles Versus Personal Roles

On the positive side, most counsellors opined that they had fulfilled their roles as parent or spouse better. On the negative side, many of the married women counsellors faced role conflicts between their professional and the personal roles.

For many of the woman counsellors, the professional identity of a counsellor sometimes took precedence over the other roles of parent or spouse. Latha joked 'My husband often asks me, is the psychologist talking, or my wife?' Such role conflicts could often throw some counsellors off balance. For instance, Aruna recounted being expected to be perfect in all aspects by her family members and friends. She said

> I have become a quiet person over the years. I used to be social but now as more and more people know that I am a counsellor they discuss their problems with me all the time; whether I am in my son's school, travelling in the train or at a public function. I stopped going down to the building for my walk also now. Nobody talks to me about the gossip in the building or about movies and actors. My friends and relatives think that I have to be the perfect wife and perfect mother. I cannot look angry or upset; I am always supposed to be cheerful. (Aruna)

While counsellors consciously or unconsciously found changes in themselves by being in the profession, the family members found it difficult to accept these changes; especially for those who began their profession after many years into their marriage. It appeared that married women counsellors (three out of five) were often responding from their professional roles more often than from their personal ones, thereby causing role conflicts in their own lives. This resonates with Hemalatha and Suryanarayana's (1983) study which reported that married working women do face 'role conflicts between the various roles played by women including mother, wife and earner'. While the married male counsellors expressed positive influences on their family, none of the three male counsellors expressed any such role ambiguity in their family life which indicated that they probably had a clearer demarcation between their personal and professional lives.

Most counsellors also had a strong need to practice what they preached; whether it was with changing themselves, raising their children, or accepting their spouse; indicating their own willingness to change or perfect themselves. While some counsellors appeared to be willing to strive towards a 'highly congruent' (Ronnestad and Skovholt 2003) self, others wanted to be accepted for who they were and preferred switching roles from being themselves to being the counsellor as and when required. Skovholt and Starkey (2010, p. 129) refer to Sue (2005) when they say 'integration of the practitioner's personal and professional lives is essential because then the work becomes an expression of one's total being' and the current study showed that some counsellors are in the process of achieving this integration.

4.4 Current Professional Practice

4.4.1 Professional Development

Most counsellors expressed having improved their skills and techniques over the years. 'Practitioners need to understand how humans are put together, what tears a person down, and how to heal that. That partially comes from a book but the bulk of it comes from being with it and learning from that presence' (Skovholt and Starkey 2010, p. 127). Aruna reiterated '... I learnt it all on the job. I learn every day. Learning to deal with the variety of clients and their problems does not happen overnight'. Apart from improving and honing skills and techniques, counsellors had also incorporated new approaches to their practice. For instance, Rajesh said that he had included lifestyle suggestions and spiritual exercises in his practice; Madhuri had learnt to schedule her appointments in such a way that she did not get overwhelmed or tired at the end of the day. For instance, if she had to use a deep therapeutic exercise in one session, she scheduled a session with a lighter issue next or kept a longer break before the next session.

McLeod (2003, p. 39) stated that 'Counselling is an activity that is inextricably bound up with the culture of Western Industrial societies, and is therefore not necessarily relevant to problems experienced by members of other cultural groups'. If so, how do Indian counsellors use these approaches? It was found that the sample of counsellors also invented and experimented with newer techniques and approaches that they believed in. For instance, Anita reported including energy science in her process wherein she suggested to her clients that they take a salt-water bath to remove negativity from their bodies (a practice followed in Reiki).

Counsellors also learnt from their mistakes and experiences with various clients and various client problems; they, hence, contextualized their therapy practices and approaches to suit their clientele. For instance, Suhasini, having studied and worked in the U.S.A., had realized over the years that clients in India functioned differently; so she deleted a line from her contract sheet[2] which had asked clients to pay the session's fees even if they missed their appointment. She also stated that through experience she had learnt to recognize what kind of questions or statements triggered an argument or a volatile situation between couples during her marital counselling sessions and hence avoided those. Similarly, Madhuri had found out that she could not rely entirely on psychological assessments done by various psychologists, but needed to complement those with her own observations and judgement. She said,

> Indians are culturally vocal people, they prefer talking rather than writing. So they don't like doing tests and questionnaires. On the contrary, when you are talking to them, you can observe so many things such as their body language, tone and expression which will give so much more insight and understanding compared to a written test report. (Madhuri)

This corroborates with Kolb's experiential learning model (1984). For instance, counsellors first experienced an unexpected outcome such as an intense argument between couples with marital disharmony during the session (concrete experience). They then reflected on their practice, looked for anything that they could have done differently in the session or with the client (observation and experience); they then formed abstract concepts of the possible reasons, ways to re-establish what was lost or how they could have prevented what had happened

[2]The counselling contract outlines the confidentiality and boundaries that a counsellor offers.

(forming abstract concepts) and finally applied their new ways of dealing with the similar issue with another client having a problem of similar nature (testing in new situations). This is perhaps the process of how experience taught counsellors to create new techniques and ways to deal with newer problems or difficulties faced by them in the counselling process (Smith 2001; Fortin and Chevrier 2003).

Most counsellors viewed failure as an opportunity to learn. They also viewed every single day with their client as a new learning experience. This *learning mode* observed in counsellors was seen from several responses of counsellors, 'Every client teaches you something so valuable', 'every day is a new learning experience' and 'I will learn until I die'. Such openness to learning has also been found to be an important prerequisite for optimal functioning of a therapist by Ronnestad and Skovholt (2001 as cited in Skovholt and Starkey 2010). It has also been evidenced in Skovholt et al. (2004).

4.4.2 Professional Identity

A counsellor's job is not restricted to dealing with clients alone but also networking with other professionals and maintaining a good rapport with them. Thus, over the years of practice, counsellors develop a professional identity for themselves.

Vineeth through his experiences in the profession had become more confident to talk to and deal with senior faculty and had shed his fear of people in authority. He had also earned the confidence and appreciation of many psychiatrists with whom he had worked with. Prabhu and Madhuri who worked really hard to set up their private practices felt proud of the confidence that other professionals and clients had in them when more clients were being referred to them. Madhuri said

> There is a certain amount of recognition, appreciation and respect for my work. I know that I have established myself and I am pretty confident of my credibility. That comes from my clients because every client has come by referral; I don't advertise or anything; only through word-of-mouth… It makes me feel good, feel successful. (Madhuri)

Such confidence and credibility increases motivation in counsellors to deal with more difficult clients and challenging problems. Aruna also had found herself earning the confidence of her colleagues in the hospital she worked in. She said

> Earlier doctors used to say 'what is she going to do? How can talking and listening to a patient help?' Today, they come to me and say 'this patient might be depressed since the operation, can you talk? Can you look it up and see what is wrong?' (Aruna)

According to Prabhu, 'it really takes a lot of effort and time to establish that even non-medical intervention can be equally efficient just as medical intervention…'. Rajesh who began counselling at the age of forty, found himself becoming more passionate, intrinsically motivated and always looked forward to meeting clients and engaging himself in the counselling process more. The level of credibility, competence and trust that counsellors have earned reflect on their expertise.

This professional identity is often an integral component of counsellors' self-definition. The integration was to such an extent that one of the counsellors needed to respond to her own personal problem from her professional role. When Madhuri had a personal problem she asked herself, 'If I had a client with the same problem how would I deal with it?' Many of the other counsellors derived much of their self-identity, strength and fulfilment from their profession as accounted by some of the counsellors below:

> If I was a mechanic I would have remained a mechanic. Having made the decision to change my profession against my parents' and relatives' advice and having achieved so much, I feel proud to have chosen this profession; proud to have worked in an educational setting and I will learn till I die. It has definitely been a rewarding journey so far. (Vineeth)

For Latha, Rajesh and Renu it gave them a deep sense of satisfaction to make a difference to people but for Latha it was more than that. She said 'I now know why I was born. I found my niche; my purpose. I am satisfied'. Renu also expressed that psychiatrists and psychologists were considered to be in the field of failures and her confidence in the profession was seen when she said 'I try to succeed in this field of failures'.

For Suhasini, her life experiences have contributed to her success as a counsellor. She said

> I went through a lot in my life before I became a counsellor. All those experiences have helped, especially my age. My husband was ill for a long time before he passed away… I basically had a lot of empathy for human beings, and I was always good with interpersonal relationships. That helped me become a counsellor. (Suhasini)

It appeared that counselling others had a deep-rooted impact on the self, both personally and professionally. With experience and practice, counsellors have learnt to change those techniques and approaches which did not work and create new ones to tackle the newer issues they faced every day. This corresponds to the professional development and integration at the 'personal/environmental interactional level' that Ronnestand and Skovholt (2003) found in their study on practitioner's development. Previous successes and the diversity of clients and problems they have dealt with, have made them confident of their competence as a successful counsellor. For many counsellors, their professional development was more of a personal journey to fight against stigma, to create a niche for themselves in the helping field and to reach the status that they have achieved. These findings correlate to what Skovholt and Starkey (2010) said, 'To know and understand suffering on a personal level helps practitioners better understand client pain and suffering thereby increasing the practitioner's capacity for empathy'. p. 129

There appeared to be two main factors that were striking about counsellors from their narratives. One was the strong thirst for knowledge and learning endlessly and the other was an inclination or an interest to work with people.

4.5 The Road Ahead

Looking ahead, some counsellors have found their professions becoming monotonous. Although they are aware of the monotony, some wanted to continue and some did not. Vineeth gave both sides of the situation. He said

> It becomes monotonous to do the same thing every day - a routine to be in the same field. But at the same time, the longer you are in a setting, there is increase in trust and increase in clients following up as well. So I want to learn more, learn all that I can until I am 35. (Vineeth)

On the contrary, Madhuri left the school she was working in after 15 years because she wanted a change. Now after 10 years of her private practice she is looking for a change again. She wanted to use her experience and expertise for something more dynamic and challenging. She said

> But I need to see the sky and trees; I don't feel comfortable in a closed room, even in hotels during workshops. I would love to be a part of a think tank and I need to feel challenge and stimulation. I need a dynamic setting, may be in education but I get bored after sometime, may be for some years. I might not enjoy it endlessly. (Madhuri)

Other counsellors believed that awareness about the benefits of counselling needed to increase and that there needed to be more recognition and respect for counsellors. Prabhu would like to develop a 5-year integrated course in counselling, so that it was a more attractive and remunerative career choice for youngsters. He also emphasized on the need to have a national level body to accredit and monitor the practice of counsellors. It is Suhasini's dream to have a multi-facility mental health setup. She said

> One thing that I want to bring out in Chennai is to have one place for everything like a hospital; but a psychiatric hospital where there is a psychiatrist, a counsellor, a clinical psychologist, a remedial teacher and it is complete. It will be wonderful! (Suhasini)

4.6 Conclusions

The three primary areas of a counsellor's life that were influenced by the counselling process were the self, health and family. Most counsellors had experienced tremendous change and growth in their selves; they saw and lived life differently compared to when they were not in the profession (also found in Ortlepp and Friedman 2002). The finding that counsellors had a tendency to bridge the gap between their professional self as a counsellor and their personal self as an individual was also evidenced by Ronnestad and Skovholt (2003). For instance, they tried to be less perfectionist, worked on their own procrastination tendencies, and became more tolerant of others and valued others more. Half the counsellors consciously and unconsciously worked to 'be' a counsellor in all areas of their life rather than 'become' one only during a counselling session. In other words, 'being a counsellor' was considered as an ideal state, and many counsellors actualized their selves to reach that state. This corroborates with humanist theorists such as Rogers and Maslow who believe that humans have an innate tendency to self-actualize, evolve and strive towards achieving an ideal (McLeod 2003).

Apart from the inner willingness to change and to be consistent in all spheres of life, some counsellors went through a process of constant change and evolution because it was imposed by others such as their immediate family and friends. Such counsellors perceived the change as negative, where they became very analytical or aloof from the world. Thus, counsellors either integrated their personal and professional roles (which has been found to make therapy and counselling more effective (Ronnestad and Starkey 2003) as they continued working on themselves, or they chose to keep the two lives disconnected and expected significant others to accept them for who they were. In this study, it was found that those who were in the process of achieving such integration (a majority of the respondents) appeared to feel more positive about being in the profession compared to the one counsellor who did not achieve the same level of assimilation of the personal with the professional.

Second, there appeared to be a positive relation between the number of clients encountered in a day and the counsellor's physical and mental health. Although several studies warn mental health professionals and counsellors about adverse health effects (Oretlepp and Friedman 2002; Latha 2004), the findings in this study indicated that the counsellors who reported seeing six or more clients in a day had more severe health effects as compared to those who saw fewer clients. All counsellors saw the importance of taking care of themselves and engaged actively to either prevent ill health or proactively did something as soon as they saw symptoms of ill health (Hunter and Schofield 2006). Therefore, it is definitely a prerequisite for a counsellor to be aware and keep a look out for any signs of ill health (Etherington 2001; McLeod 2003; Dryden and Reeves 2008; Corey 2009).

Third, the effect of interpersonal experiences in the personal life on the professional development of the counsellor has been evidenced by Ronnestad and Starkey (2003). The finding from this study indicates that counsellors' self-growth (due to counselling process) usually had a positive impact on the counsellor's family members. Married women counsellors faced personal and professional role confusions as compared to married men counsellors.

Moving onto professional practice, it was found that counsellors learned on the job and hence develop mastery and expertise through experience (finding also supported by Skovholt and Starkey 2010). It was found that counsellors tried new techniques and approaches that they believe in, and had learnt through experience to contextualize various counselling approaches to work with their specific clients, which contributed to their professional development as counsellors. For instance, they had learnt not to depend solely on objective and physical tests and instruments but to make a more holistic assessment of the client and so on. Almost all counsellors were found to have a 'learning' tendency where they not only perceived their mistakes as opportunities to learn and grow in their practice but also to learn from their usual practice of what works and what does not (intense willingness and commitment to grow and learn was also reported in Ronnestad and Skovholt 2003). Over the years, counsellors were found to become more self-reflective, had improved their skills, had corrected their mistakes and established their own 'practice' of counselling by trial and error (Skovholt et al. 1997; Ronnestad and Skovholt 2003; Skovholt et al. 2004). This result strongly fits in with Kolb's experiential learning model and hence aligns itself with Fortin and Chevrier (2003) study on the process of counselling and experiential learning.

Finally, counsellors became more confident, earning credibility and recognition over time from their clients and other professionals. Their professional journey became so much a part of them that they began to define their own self in terms of their profession (Ronnestad and Skovholt 2003; Skovholt et al. 2004). Despite the many challenges that counsellors faced, unanimously all of them expressed a sense of purpose, a deep sense of satisfaction and fulfilment by being in this profession (Ronnestad and Skovholt 2003). Apart from their own progress and professional development, counsellors were found to be committed to the counselling profession growing at a macro level (for example, create awareness, initiate multi-speciality setups, etc.) and hence had many expectations from society and from themselves to accentuate its development.

Counsellors seemed to be in a constant dynamic from being attached and associated with the client (for providing a conducive environment where the client can be comfortable, being empathetic) to being detached and dissociated (to maintain objectivity, to deduce from the client's narrative and to take care of own self) and again to be associated with the self (to reflect and introspect on self and practice). This shift from association to dissociation to association again seemed to exemplify the entire counselling process.

It can be further added that the counselling process was not only a process with the client(s) in terms of sessions, but a process even with the self; it did not end when the client left the session, but continued thereafter. The counsellor's continuous review of self (consciously or unconsciously) extended the counselling process to mean more than a series of stages where a counsellor facilitates and empowers the client to resolve a problem, to a constant evolution of the self.

It is difficult for a counsellor to bifurcate their personal and professional lives. When change and growth is bound to happen, it is recommended that counsellors voluntarily accept the positive change and consciously work towards an 'integrated self' rather than struggle to keep the personal and professional selves separate. However, it is important for counsellors to be aware of themselves and what they are going through in order to quickly recognize ill health, changing attitudes and perceptions. This would reflect in 'physical and psychological vitality' of the counsellor and hence better efficiency in work (Corey 2009, p. 35). Although many of the participants spoke of reflecting on their practice and improving their skills and techniques, not all did. This indicates that reflection and introspection into one's own practice must be incorporated as a crucial module during the training of counsellors. Since supervision is not very common, or easily available for practitioners in India, this appears to be the only other way in which reflective and evolutionary counselling can take precedence in India.

A general willingness and openness to learn and a strong inclination to work with people could be possible prerequisites for anyone wanting to become a counsellor. Since burnout and physical illnesses were quite common amongst the sample of counsellors, it is recommended that counsellors keep track of their own mental and physical capacity and schedule sessions accordingly for the day. Sequencing sessions such that they are not back-to-back can take care of the counsellor's health.

Multi-speciality centres which incorporate counsellors, psychiatrists, clinical psychologists and remedial teachers need to come up so that clients can have a one-stop access to mental health professionals rather than go through the long process of going to other professionals. Finally, an authoritative body that issues a license of some kind, which has a check on practising counsellors and schedules regular reviews and license renewals, would enable the growth of counselling as a profession in India in the long run. A code of ethics that binds all practising counsellors to a common set of standards will also ensure equal and high-quality service to clients. The most efficient counselling practice that is culturally rooted needs to be identified, recorded, researched and tested. While counselling with its complex set of dynamics is an emerging and fast developing profession in India, it is still in its infancy and needs to be extensively explored.

References

Brown, C. (2002). Career counseling practitioners: Reflections on theory, research, and practice. *Journal of Career Development, 29*(2), 109–127.

Corey, G. (2009). *Theory and practice of counselling and psychotherapy* (8th ed.). USA: Brooks/Cole Cengage Learning.

Dryden, W., & Reeves, A. (2008). *Key issues for counselling in action* (2nd ed.). London: Sage Publications Ltd.

Egan, G. (1994). *The skilled helper: A problem-management approach to helping* (5th ed.). USA: Brooks/Cole Publishing Company.

Etherington, K. (2001). Training and Supervision issues for counsellors working in health settings. In Kim Etherington (Ed.), *Counsellors in health settings.* UK: Jessica Kingsley Publishers.

Fortin, G., & Chevrier, J. (2003). Process of counseling and experiential learning. *Canadian Journal of Counselling, 37*(2), 101–114.

Gibson, R. L., & Mitchell, M. (2003). *Introduction to counseling and guidance.* USA: Pearson/Merrill/Prentice Hall.

Hemalatha, P., & Suryanarayana, M. (1983). Working women: A study on their role interactions. *Indian Journal of Social Work, 44*(2), 153–156.

Hill, C. E., Sullivan, C., Knox, S., & Schlossern, L. Z. (2007). Becoming psychotherapists: Experiences of novice trainees in a beginning graduate class. *Psychotherapy Theory, Research, Practice, Training, 44*(4), 1–27.

Hunter, S. V., & Schofield, M. J. (2006). How counsellors cope with traumatized clients: Personal, professional and organizational strategies. *International Journal for the Advancement of Counselling, 28*(2), 121–138.

Jennings, L. G. M., Skovholt, T. M., Hanson, M., & Bannerjee-Stevens, D. (2003). Multiple factors in the development of the expert counselor and therapist. *Journal of Career Development, 30*(1), 2–15.

Jenson, P. (2007). On learning from experience: personal and private experiences as the context for psychotherapeutic practice. *Clinical Child Psychology and Psychiatry, 12*(3), 375–384.

Kolb, D. A. (1984). *Experiential learning: experience as the source of learning and development.* New Jersey: Prentice-Hall Inc.

Kottler, J. A. (2003). *The imperfect therapist* (3rd ed.). San Francisco: Jossey-Bass.

Latha, K. S. (2004). Work–Related stress among health professionals and coping mechanisms. *Indian Journal of Social Work, 65*(2), 190–212.

McLeod, J. (2003). *Introduction to counselling* (3rd ed.). Jaipur: Rawat Publications.

Orlinsky, D., Ronnestad, M. H., Ambuehl, H., Willutzki, U., Botersman, J., & Cierpka, M. (1999). Psychotherapists' assessments of their development at different career levels. *Psychotherapy, 36*(3), 203–215.

Ortlepp, K., & Friedman, M. (2002). Prevalence and correlates of secondary traumatic stress in workplace lay trauma counselors. *Journal of Traumatic Stress, 15*(3), 213–222.

Richards, K. A. M., & Marquez, J. (2005). Experiences of HIV/AIDS counselors in Zimbabwe and their perceptions on the state of HIV/AIDS counseling in Zimbabwe. *International Journal for the Advancement of Counselling, 27*(3), 413–429.

Ronnestad, M. H., & Skovholt, T. M. (2003). The journey of the counselor and therapist: Research findings and perspectives on professional development. *Journal of Career Development, 30*(1), 5–44.

Skovholt, T. M., & Starkey, M. T. (2010). The three legs of the practitioner's learning stool: Practice, research/theory, and personal life. *Journal of Contemporary Psychotherapy, 40*, 125–130.

Skovholt, T. M., Ronnestad, M. H., & Jenning, L. (1997). Searching for expertise in counseling, psychotherapy, and professional psychology. *Educational Psychology Review, 9*(4), 361–369.

Skovholt, T. M., Jennings, L., & Mullenbach, M. (2004). Portrait of the master therapist: The highly-functioning self. *Master therapists: Exploring expertise in therapy and counselling* (pp. 125–146). Boston, MA: Allyn & Bacon.

Smith, M. K. (2001). David A. Kolb on experiential learning. *The Encyclopaedia of Informal Education.* Retrieved from http://www.infed.org/b-explrn.html.

Theriault, A., & Gazzola, N. (2010). Therapist feelings of incompetence and suboptimal processes in psychotherapy. *Journal of Contemporary Psychotherapy, 40*, 233–243.

Williams, E. N. (2003). The relationship between momentary states of therapist self-awareness and perceptions of the counseling process. *Journal of Contemporary Psychotherapy, 33*(3), 177–186.

Chapter 5
Beginning the Journey: What Motivates Therapists to Join the Profession?

Chetna Duggal and Sujata Sriram

Abstract The choice of counselling and psychotherapy as a profession is determined by a range of factors. In India, psychotherapy as a profession is still in its early stages of development. There is limited research on what motivates individuals to take up psychotherapy as a career. A qualitative dominant mixed methods research study was conceptualized to explore factors contributing to therapists choosing psychotherapy as a profession. Sixteen practising psychotherapists, 10 women and 6 men, with 6–25 years of experience participated in the study. An interest in the human mind, in healing and reading and in working with children, led therapists to enter the helping profession. Personal qualities such as being a people's person and being a patient listener facilitated the choice. Experiencing life changing events and personal distress, receiving professional help or adopting certain roles within the family were mentioned as facilitating factors. Personal needs and the role of destiny and chance were also identified as contributing elements. Different therapists took different routes in their journey towards pursuing the profession of counselling and psychotherapy. Awareness of factors that contributed to entering the field through self-reflective practice in training and supervision is recommended.

Keywords Counselling · Psychotherapy · Motivation · Professional growth · Professional development

The reasons for therapists entering the profession of counselling and psychotherapy can be varied. Over the years, research has accumulated on what motivates therapists to join the healing profession and reasons that draw psychotherapy practitioners to the field of therapy; much of this research comes from the developed countries. This chapter examines some of the factors that motivate individuals to

Chetna Duggal (✉) · S. Sriram
School of Human Ecology, TISS, Mumbai, India
e-mail: chetnaduggal@gmail.com

S. Sriram (ed.), *Counselling in India*, DOI 10.1007/978-981-10-0584-8_5

take up the profession to become counsellors and therapists. Across the world, psychotherapy as a profession is not recognized as being a lucrative one; the benefits that accrue to a practising therapist are more often intrinsic, rather than extrinsic. In India, psychotherapy is still a growing discipline, yet to get the status that it deserves, from other mental health professionals and from the general public at large.

5.1 What Motivates Therapists to Join the Profession?

In a survey conducted with more than a thousand therapists, including psychiatrists, psychiatric social workers, psychoanalysts and clinical psychologists, Henry et al. (1973) found that more than 60 % of the therapists surveyed in Los Angeles, Chicago and New York, mentioned having few friends in high school, and feeling isolated. This study, with a focus on career determinants of psychotherapists was one of the earliest research studies in the area of therapist motivation for joining the profession. The authors concluded that although no single factor could be held accountable for settling on psychotherapy as a career, multiple factors such as being less authoritarian, more liberal, less religious, were important indicators for choosing the profession (Henry et al. 1973).

Recent research has found therapists' personal experiences, such as childhood experiences, family upbringing, life experiences, social circles, etc., to be strong motivators to pursuing therapy as a profession. In a study with eight practitioners, Farber et al. (2005) found that therapists joining the profession reported feelings of isolation, feeling alone and sadness, in their childhood, which spurred them to take up psychotherapy as a profession. According to the researchers, the therapists reported taking up roles of caretakers or parents early in their life, and experienced the warmth that came from caring for another individual. Additionally, Farber et al. (2005) mentioned that they found most therapists to be very observant as children and having a keen interest in understanding themselves and others, deeply.

A similar finding was obtained by Richardson et al. (2009), who found that the students in national training programmes for psychotherapy and counselling in Australia stated having undergone certain life experiences that instilled in them a need to be a therapist. Beatty (2012) conducted a survey-based study among trainee counsellors and psychotherapists in Ireland and found that an early experience of loss, a perceived lack of a confidant during childhood led the individual to undertake this prescribed role to others. Furthermore, 90 % of Beatty's participants mentioned the occurrence of at least one significant life event which influenced their decision. These experiences included childhood difficulties, addiction, mental health issues within the family of origin, personal encounters and loss.

Sussman (2007) indicated that unconscious motivations deeply rooted in the developmental past and the dynamics of the family of origin might have a role to play in those who choose to train and work as therapists. Sussman (2007) went on to say that 'an important determinant of the desire to practice psychotherapy involved the attempt to come to terms with one's own psychological conflicts' (p. 175). The cultural archetype of the 'Wounded Healer', coined by Carl Jung, refers to the therapist being eager to help clients as they themselves have been 'wounded' from life's experiences (Zarubavel and Wright 2012).

Therapist experiences of personal therapy have been identified as motivating factors for individuals to pursue therapy as a profession. Beatty (2012) reported that 60 % of the respondents mentioned their experiences of personal therapy to be a motivating factor for pursuing the profession. Additionally, personal values emerged as an important motivating factor leading individuals to become therapists. Hill et al. (2007) qualitatively analysed journals kept by five novice psychotherapists and found that values of giving back to the society in some way and also holding strong beliefs of empathy and sensitivity were central factors contributing to their desire to join the profession.

According to Norcross and Farber (2005), stating altruism as a motivation to be a therapist may be considered to be socially desirable, and the decision to help another being could be more complex and multifaceted; determined, by unconscious motives and chance encounters. They mentioned that these experiences may not be understood by the practitioner until late in their career.

In the Indian context, psychotherapy as a profession is still in its early stages of development as a career option. There is limited research in India that examines what motivates individuals to take up psychotherapy as a career choice.

5.2 Studying Therapist Motivations

This chapter on examining motivation to become psychotherapists is drawn from a larger research study. A qualitative dominant mixed methods research study was planned to explore the beliefs and values of therapists and understand how they impact their therapeutic practice. Psychotherapist's motivations to join the profession was one component of the larger study.

In the qualitative-dominant mixed methods research paradigm, 'one relies on a qualitative, constructivist-poststructuralist-critical view of the research process, while concurrently recognizing that the addition of quantitative data and approaches are likely to benefit most research projects' (Johnson et al. 2007, p. 124). In the present study, quantitative data were obtained from a self-designed questionnaire; yielding information on demographic details, information on the early training and supervision, therapeutic orientation and the nature of the practice of the respondents. This data informed the qualitative interviews.

The qualitative interviews helped understand therapist beliefs and values. Rich and detailed narratives of therapists and their meaning making of their own world views were obtained using the qualitative strand. The findings from the questionnaire and the interview were triangulated during data collection and analysis to obtain a comprehensive understanding of the research area.

The study was carried out on practising psychotherapists with a minimum qualification of a postgraduate degree in clinical psychology or counselling psychology, with at least 5 years of experience in the field. Therapists who participated in the study were obtained through personal contacts, through suggested referrals and through available information. The sample was collected purposefully, to include sixteen therapists. Ten women and six men finally participated in the study. The age of the therapists ranged from 30 to 68 years; while the years of experience ranged from 6 years and 2 months to 25 years. The therapists had different theoretical orientations, and practiced in a range of settings. Many of the respondents had their own private practice. While many of the therapists claimed to practice using an eclectic orientation, there was a distinct preference shown for a particular theoretical framework. There were two therapists who considered themselves as purists, and practiced using the psychoanalytic orientation only. Additionally, the nature of the clientele varied; while some of the therapists worked only with children and adolescents, the others worked with mainly adult populations. The sample was obtained from the cities of Mumbai and Pune.

Table 5.1 gives the details of the sample for the study.

The self-designed questionnaire was given to the participants, during the initial phase of rapport formation, wherein information about the study was conveyed to the participants and informed consent was obtained. In-depth interviews were conducted to collect data from the respondents over two sessions, in order to avoid fatigue for the researcher and for the participants. Data were collected till data sufficiency and saturation were obtained. Ethical considerations of anonymity, confidentiality and the right to withdraw were kept in mind while conducting

Table 5.1 Participant profile

Name[a]	Age in years	Gender	Place of practice	Years of experience
Arindam	46	M	Thane	19 years 8 months
Ameesh	45	M	Mumbai	13 years 4 months
Barbara	54	F	Mumbai	12 years 6 months
Ishrat	44	F	Mumbai	15 years
Dirghayu	36	M	Pune	8 years
Deepak	49	M	Mumbai	20 years
Joseph	68	M	Mumbai	25 years
Hina	37	F	Mumbai	11 years
Jiya	30	F	Mumbai	6 years 2 months
Keshav	38	M	Mumbai	15 years
Rita	52	F	Mumbai	25 years
Sheetal	44	F	Mumbai	18 years 11 months
Samira	49	F	Navi Mumbai	20 years 6 months
Sarah	36	F	Mumbai	13 years 6 months
Zeba	37	F	Mumbai	7 years

[a] All names have been changed to ensure anonymity of participants

the research. The interviews with the participants were electronically recorded and word-by-word transcription was done. The interview data were analysed using the grounded theory approach, while the data from the questionnaires were analysed using descriptive statistics.

5.3 Entering the Field of Psychology

All the therapists who participated in the study shared his or her personal journey into the realm of psychotherapy and shared what motivated them to join the helping profession. There were narratives of therapists for whom the decision to come into the profession was made early, and other stories of those who serendipitously stumbled into the profession. All the participants of the study self-identified as being psychotherapists and counsellors.

5.3.1 The Story of Ameesh

Ameesh had been practising as a therapist for the past 13 years, and was a trained psychoanalyst. He described himself as a very thoughtful person, who got interested in psychology as a child to know his own mind and fathom the depths of his distress. The story of his journey into the field of psychotherapy and counselling draws out the complex factors and motivations that contribute to the becoming of a therapist. This is how Ameesh outlined his beginnings:

> One was being thoughtful, and then … I always wanted to know people, I also wanted to know my own mind. I was depressed myself, my father was not a very kind person and nor was my mother. So there was loneliness, which I did not know, completely unaware. So it was also a struggle to know myself. And I loved language, I was thoughtful, I loved reading and I wanted to know people's mind, my mind. These were the things that were there. (Ameesh)

However, being a boy in India, pursuing psychology as a career was not an easy choice for him to make, given the gendered notions of appropriate professions among middle class families in India.

> Yeah, see I am a boy in India, I should not be doing anything but engineering. Indian boys should only be engineers and Indian girls should only be doctors. That is still there, even today my mother is very unhappy that I am a counsellor and not an engineer. (Ameesh)

Coming from a place of pain and loneliness and not being understood in childhood, Ameesh's thoughtfulness and interest in wanting to gain an in-depth understanding of the human mind led him to train in the psychoanalytic therapeutic framework, through the Tavistock course, despite the demands and gender expectations from home and outside. His was a story of vulnerability and courage waiting to be told and heard.

Ameesh's narrative about how he entered the field, and about some of the challenges he encountered along the way can be used to illustrate the story of the professional development of many of the counsellors who took part in the present study. The professional journey for most therapists began early, when they needed to choose the subjects they wanted to pursue in grades XI and XII in school. For a few, however, it was a life transition that prompted them to pursue psychology as a profession. Throughout the interviews, there were fond reminiscences about discoveries, joys and serendipitous events, and there were also moments of wistfulness and sorrow, some of which have been captured below through the voices of the participants.

5.3.2 Interest

When therapists spoke of the factors that influenced their decision to join the profession, a significant theme that emerged was interest; this has been illustrated in Ameesh's transcript above. Interest in the human mind, in healing, in reading and in working with children, have led therapists to pursue the helping profession.

Understanding the human mind

Interest in how the human mind worked, and being fascinated by human dynamics, was discussed by almost all participants as facilitating their decision to pursue the field and enter the profession. Ishrat, a practising psychoanalyst, like Ameesh, discussed her fascination with the human mind and how it worked. True to her analytic frame, she brought out how rich and varied the inner world of each individual was; and how the mind and the unconscious were something that intrigued her, drawing her to pursue the field of psychology.

Understanding human motivation, how people function and how they operate are the subject matter of psychology, and participants reported wanting to work in an area that would allow them to find answers to these questions. Sarah, amongst others, mentioned, 'I was always fascinated by the way people think, behave and figure things out … lots of times I would not be able to figure out why someone is doing this or not doing this, how is it working'.

Apart from wanting to understand what motivated people to behave and act in the ways they did, the participants spoke about how there were questions in their mind about what motivated people to change. Looking around them, they found that people were distressed and going through difficulties and were unable to cope with them, or were experiencing distress and unhappiness; leading them to wonder about questions of change and what motivated people to change. Sarah shared her confusion about growing up in her family, wondering why some people did what they did and over the years she began to look for those answers in psychology.

The findings obtained in the present study corroborate well with those made by Farber et al. (2005), who utilized two approaches, in an attempt to answer the question 'Why do people become psychotherapists?' (p. 1009). Apart from reviewing the literature on therapist motivations, they explored pathways to becoming a psychotherapist by considering the career trajectories of therapists. They found that therapists mentioned curiosity about the 'whys of behaviour—why individuals think, feel, and act as they do' (Farber et al. 2005, p. 1010). They linked this psychological mindedness—an endless curiosity and introspection on why people behave, act and feel the way they do—to psychological skills that helped these individuals around people and eventually motivated them to seek a career in psychotherapy and counselling.

Healing people

A couple of the participants mentioned that healing people and providing care and treatment to those who were suffering was what drew them to the field of psychology. Hina discussed how her need to understand people and wanting to heal them made her a therapist. Jiya shared a similar experience, and recalled how as a teenager, she saw people confused and not knowing what to do, and she thought to herself that this could be because people did not know whom to approach, and that led her to vision herself taking on a therapist role. For Samira it was a larger aim of helping people to come out of their misery. She also mentioned wondering to herself why people were so unhappy and distressed, when there was abundance and joy all around. She remembered these questions haunting her; 'Why are people so miserable, why do they want to be miserable, is there a choice they are making or accepting?'

Grappling with questions of human suffering and pain and alleviating human distress could be critical factors drawing individuals to the healing profession. Beatty (2012) found that one of the popular motivations mentioned in her sample of 30 psychotherapy students in Ireland, was altruism. Bager-Charlson (2010) also discussed that altruism could be an important factor for joining the profession, as being connected with and accepted by other people could be highly rewarding. Norcross and Farber (2005) shared that though the conscious motivation may be to help others, there could be other, not so conscious, motives that people might have that they might need to be aware of. The motive of altruism being socially desirable and acceptable is usually the reason that is most often stated.

The scepticism in Norcoss and Farber's discussion of the motive of altruism finds resonance in the study by Richardson et al. (2009). They asked professional counselling and psychotherapy trainers in Australia about what some of the possible reasons were for people not to become a therapist; or what people needed to reflect on before entering the field. The researchers found that 35.1 % trainers cautioned against the urge of 'wanting to rescue' others or to 'fix people's problems'.

Whether altruism or the need to heal others is the 'right' impetus to joining the profession or not cannot be said; at the minimum, an awareness of altruism as a motive would be critical, as therapist motivation and needs could deeply impact the therapeutic relationship and process.

Passion for reading

Most therapists discussed an early interest in reading, specifically in reading books on psychology, as a factor contributing to their entering the field of psychology. Availability of reading material, either through books at home or the fact that they were in a city where there was easy access to books and libraries, allowed them to read and discover the subject. Ameesh mentioned how his interest in reading and the availability of abnormal psychology books at home got him interested in the subject. Samira discussed her passion to read in great detail in her interview, discussing how she used to read everything, 'From religious books, and I was in a Jewish school so learning about the Jewish religion, to stories, to Nancy Drew, Enid Blyton'. She spoke of how she would scavenge the street bookseller collections to find cheap deals on psychology books and confessed to even having stolen money from home to buy the then popular Russian books. Rita shared that she kept reading all the books she could so she could find answers to how the human mind worked. It was through reading and books that Rita found out about therapy and it was this that drew her to take up psychotherapy as a profession. Farber et al. (2005) have illustrated and discussed the role intellectual curiosity and an early interest in reading played in a therapist's career choice.

Working with children

Jiya and Ishrat discussed how their interest in working with children had led to them entering the profession. During her second year in college Ishrat had to decide the subject that she would major in. The choice had to be made between literature and psychology; and she was inclined more towards psychology as she felt that it would help her work with children. Her interest in working with children was critical in her entering the field of psychology and then training in child psychotherapy.

While Ishrat shared her desire to work with children, Jiya discussed how being aware of the challenges experienced by less privileged children influenced her choice. Jiya wanted to work with underprivileged children, and children who had lost their parents. Her interest motivated her to interact with teachers and principals in schools where there were children from underprivileged backgrounds so she could be more certain about her choice.

Interestingly, both Ishrat and Jiya initially worked with children after they trained as therapists, though over a period of time they had also started working with adults. Jiya worked with children in schools; subsequently, she practiced with a not for profit organisation working with children who had experienced abuse. Ishrat had trained in psychoanalysis, and focused on observation studies of infants; additionally she conducted play therapy sessions for children and her outreach programmes also focused on child mental health.

5.3.3 Personal Qualities

Some of the therapists shared how their professional choice was determined by the personal qualities they felt they had. Choosing a profession that matched with their personal qualities was important. Understanding the personal qualities that they possessed, and aligning them with the qualities that were required for working in the field of mental health, were brought up in the discussion. Hina mentioned how her temperament and personality made her best suited for being in the helping profession. When she did the MBTI[1] programme, she discovered that her profile was of an INFJ,[2] characteristic of people who naturally gravitated towards the healing professions, towards counselling, writing and teaching, all of which she was doing. Her temperament, she believed, helped soothe and calm people down and that made her suited for the role of counsellor and therapist. The INFJ personality profile validated Hina's decision to take up counselling and psychotherapy as a profession.

A people's person

A couple of respondents described themselves as being a 'people's person' and gravitated naturally towards the profession. The fact that they were so comfortable working with people, and vice versa, led them to choose a profession that provided them the opportunity to work with people. Dirghayu changed his career from information technology and computers, and moved to psychology when he realized that what really motivated him was working with people and not machines. This was despite people trying to dissuade him from making this shift. In his own words,

> I was working in IT and computers don't talk back … and I have always been a people's person, I was always fascinated by the human dynamics, the shapes and things and that was one reason … that I was intrinsically motivated towards working with people. (Dirghayu)

The patient listener

Therapists shared that they were patient listeners and had an ear for the life stories of others. As Hina mentioned, 'I have the patience to deal with so many of them because it came naturally, it was second nature', and Samira went on to share her interest in the life stories that people shared with her. Ameesh too mentioned that he was a thoughtful and patient person and was interested in understanding others.

[1]MBTI—The Myers Briggs Type Indicator, a popular psychometric test used for assessing temperament and personality type.

[2]INFJ profile stands for Introverted iNtuitive Feeling and Judging; the counsellor type as identified by Keirsey (1998).

Therapist personal qualities have been constantly cited by the literature to be a crucial factor in the therapeutic relationship (Bowling and Hoffman 2000; Littauer and Sexton 2005; Luborsky et al. 2006), and significantly influencing the outcome of the therapy (Luborsky et al. 2006). Personal qualities such as a confidence-inspiring attitude, having a calm demeanour, being accepting and understanding and being an active listener were seen to be valued by clients in therapy (Littauer and Sexton 2005). Hill et al. (2007) found that personal strengths of listening, curiosity and willingness to help, along with external encouragement and positive social support from teachers, friends and family, emerged as factors motivating the therapist.

5.3.4 Personal experiences

During the interviews, the participants shared various personal experiences that influenced the decision to take up the helping profession. This sharing poured in after more factual data were related in the interview. As therapists eased into the interview situation and started going back in time, they began relating personal stories of relationships and experiences. These narratives included life changing events, personal experiences of psychological distress, receiving professional help and instances of family members undergoing psychological distress.

Life changing events and personal distress

Personal life crises or experiences were viewed by a couple of therapists as determining their trajectory of professional choice. Sheetal shared the story of her marriage break up and subsequent distress, as a life-changing event that led her to seeking the career path of a therapist. In contrast to Sheetal's relationship crisis in her thirties, Dirghayu's losing his eyesight, followed by a lung infection, at the age of about 18 years was a deeply personal crisis. His frank and open sharing of his pain as he saw his life slipping away before him stayed with the first author through the interview.

> …The turning point for me was around the age of 18–19, when I lost my sight; and for me that was a huge turning point … and the second turning point came for me around the same time, around '98 when I had a lung infection and I almost died. So, when you actually get so close to those experiences, then it kind of shapes you in a different way. I think these experiences were what made me…these experiences change the way you look at life, the way you look at how you spend a life and radically changed a lot of things for me. So partly it was somewhere inside me right from childhood but these events more acted like precipitating factors… and yeah that's what really made me get in this. (Dirghayu)

Though Sheetal and Dirghayu mentioned life events as crises that facilitated the movement to being a therapist, their stories drew out how these crises were fraught with personal distress and pain, and led to soul searching and looking for purpose in their lives. In the same way, Ameesh discussed his childhood experiences, the subsequent ensuing pain, loneliness and sadness and the searching for something meaningful that would lead him to a better place, making him seek the profession.

Ronnestad and Skovholt (2003), through their discussion of themes relating to psychotherapist development, suggest that personal lives of psychotherapists influence their development at all stages including the selection of work. In a survey of 238 psychotherapists in Ireland, Bager-Charleson (2010) identified 'own childhood' as the foremost reason for joining the profession, followed by 'later life crisis' and 'interest in people'. Early experiences of childhood loneliness, isolation and introversion (Barnett 2007) in the lives of professional therapists are drawn out by research as factors responsible for pursuing the therapeutic profession. Barnett (2007) pointed out that even though counselling was a solitary profession, it allowed the practitioner the possibility to obtain human contact, which may compensate for the loss of the same during childhood or adulthood. Bager-Charlson (2010) found that 75 % of the 238 participants, when asked about their motivations to train as a therapist, reported personal experiences, mostly crises.

Orlinsky and Rønnestad (2005) addressed the motivational aspect by asking therapists 'To what extent do you feel that your development as a therapist has been influenced by the motivation to explore and resolve your personal problems?' In response, 48 % of 3,577 respondents answered 'much' or 'very much', indicating that many therapists in their diverse sample were explicitly aware that their choice of career was at least somewhat a function of experiencing personal distress.

Receiving professional help

Both Dirghayu and Sheetal went through crises in their lives during which they sought professional help. The fact that they found therapy helpful in tiding over the crises motivated them to become a helper, and support those in need of psychological help.

As indicated by the literature, personal experiences in therapy provided a boost for the practitioners in the present study to enter the field of therapy. Beatty (2012) found that 60 % of trainee counsellors who had experienced personal therapy prior to their counsellor training reported it as being a factor in their career choice.

Roles adopted within the family

Hina discovered her motivation for joining the profession during her personal therapy. It was during her own sessions with her therapist that she discovered that she had taken on the role of counsellor very early in life, in response to family crises and stress. She shared how her maternal uncle was diagnosed with schizophrenia and there was a considerable amount of stress and disturbance in her family as she grew up. With marital conflict between her parents leading to a chaotic family environment, and with an anxious father, she found herself taking on the role of caring and nurturing almost unconsciously. During her personal therapy sessions she began making connections about how playing a supportive role in her family, as a child and adolescent, perhaps made her take up the helping profession, as an adult.

On similar lines, Sheetal discussed that her experiences as a first born child in her family required her to adjust and accommodate, and not make demands from others; this, she suggested, was a factor that contributed to her joining the profession. Sheetal recalled that seeing distress in close quarters, within her family, resulted in her becoming 'parentified', wherein she played the role of a parent, despite being a child. She mentioned that her being a parentified child had contributed to her coming into psychotherapy as a profession, as was often found amongst those in the helping professions.

Jurkovic (2014) in his book *Lost Childhoods: The Plight of the Parentified Child* details how therapists often shared stories of functioning in parentified roles within their families. He dedicated an entire chapter to document the narrative of a marriage and family therapist who shared how her parentification as a child impacted boundary issues in therapy with her clients in practice, and for which she constantly sought supervision. Jurkovic (2014) cautions that if this was not adequately addressed, it could create personal and ethical concerns for the therapist; however, at the same time he mentions that what cannot be discounted is that the dynamics in the family in some way prepared the therapist to be in the helping profession.

Murphy and Halgin (1995) compared the motivations of clinical and social psychologists and found that those in clinical practice were more influenced in their career choice by experiences of psychological distress in themselves and in their families of origin, and by their desires to resolve personal problems, than their social psychologist colleagues.

There has also been a discussion about the wounded healer hypothesis, i.e. whether therapists who had undergone psychological distress themselves were at an advantage or disadvantage to be a therapist. Burton and Topham (1997, as cited in Barnett 2007) propose that the processing and integration of the experiences was critical, if they had to be useful for the therapist in any way. For therapists who have had such experiences, personal therapy during training became important, as it then helped them to resolve personal conflicts and integrate and assimilate them in ways that would help them become better therapists.

Richardson et al. (2009) opine that though prospective students who want to pursue a career in psychology might think that personal life experiences that they have had would qualify them to enter into the profession, it is not necessarily so. Richardson et al.'s data from 92 psychotherapy and counselling training providers in Australia indicated that while personal life experience helped understand the complexity of life, and provided a foundation, it was not sufficient to allow one to be a good therapist. For the experience to be useful, it needed to be processed and integrated after self-reflection. Recognizing variations in personal experiences was important, as also was understanding the need to adapt, and change on the basis of the personal experience.

Zerubavel and Wright (2012) underscore a critical issue in terms of psychologists' perceptions of and responses to wounded healers. They mentioned how stigma from peers and seniors in the same profession and self-stigma could influence wounded healers' level of comfort in disclosing their wounds. While there is a trend to advocate reflective practice amongst practitioners, what would be required is to bear in mind the inhibitions or barriers in such self-disclosures. Zerubavel and Wright (2012) further propose that the relative absence of dialogue in the field regarding the experiences of those who may be wounded could be further encouraging secrecy and shame among the wounded. This atmosphere could be thereby preventing access to support and guidance. They recommend that the professional spaces promote greater openness and provide unconditional support to those who may be wounded, and in turn help to develop a safe space to promote individual resilience and post-traumatic growth.

5.3.5 Personal needs

The need for respect emerged as a motivating factor for Hina to join the helping profession. She shared during this interview how this was the first time that she was openly acknowledging her need to fulfil a void in her life and her need for respect, that got fulfilled through the therapist role. In fact, she was the only participant who approached the area of therapist personal needs that might consciously or unconsciously influence their therapeutic role.

Literature shows personal needs of the therapist were a boost in pursuing the profession. The need of the therapist to be valued and accepted by the client has been identified in the literature as a need that motivates therapists to join the profession (Beatty 2012; Guttman and Daniel 2001). Thus, early experiences in the family of origin, along with personal sensitivity to interpersonal stress and the desire to control interpersonal relations, could all contribute to the decision to be a therapist (Racusin et al. 1981).

5.3.6 Destiny and chance

Some of the therapists discussed how they were destined to be studying psychology and entering the profession of a therapist. Samira shared 'I was born to be a therapist', and Father Joseph discussed how he was destined by the Almighty to take up this role.

A few of the therapists began pursuing the subject of psychology by chance: for some it was a chance encounter with a mentor, while for others it was an admission into a particular course. 'Serendipity', as Deepak called it, was a factor that led him to join the profession. Zeba shared her story of how a chance admission into a psychology course set the ball rolling for her. Barbara, having studied and having taught psychology, stumbled on to her role as a counsellor by chance when she was recommended as a counsellor to the Eucharistic Congress. Beatty (2012) found that chance was the second most commonly cited motive for joining the profession among trainee counsellors.

The above discussion brings to light how the above mentioned factors may, alone or in combination, contribute to the decision to join the profession of psychotherapy and counselling. Different therapists took different routes in their journey towards pursuing the helping profession and many factors contributed to their decision to join the field.

5.3.7 Life stage

Through the interviews, the stage of life at which the therapists decided to enter the therapeutic profession was noted. The life stage or the age at which therapists entered the profession was variable. While some therapists discussed how the choices happened at critical decision points when they had to choose subjects in school, some others reported moving into it later on in life after having tried other things.

While few of the participants in the study entered psychology training in school, most of the others did so in college. Psychology as a subject is not a commonly offered subject at high school level in India. It is usually offered by few colleges and universities at the level of undergraduate studies. Ameesh was amongst the therapists who decided to enter the profession early in life, while in college. However, there were a few participants who decided to enter the field or train to be a psychotherapist later in life. Dirghayu was studying commerce in college, and worked in the IT sector for 6 years, before he joined college to complete his post-graduation in psychology at the age of 23–24 years.

Similarly, Father Joseph had trained to be a Jesuit priest and moved from mathematics to psychology after his training in the priesthood. He went on to join a college to teach psychology for 10 years, following which he started volunteering with the social service league. He then transitioned to the role of a counsellor in the college, where he had now been for over 30 years. Arindam had studied management and was pursuing his training in hypnosis out of personal interest, when he was invited to join an organisation and took on the therapist role. Barbara joined the profession very late in her career, again on invitation.

Just as there were no ideal motivations for joining the profession, there was no right time to decide to be a therapist. Even then, a majority of the therapists seemed to have been sure of their choice early on in their lives. This could in part be due to the nature of training for professional counselling and psychotherapy in India, which is through university and college education.

5.3.8 Gender issues

In the present study, out of the sixteen therapists who participated, only six of the participants were men; this was essentially because of the dearth of men in the profession. Gender stereotyping is still a challenge, especially in India, where professional roles of caring such as that of a therapist or a counsellor are viewed as being feminine. As Willyard (2011) highlights in her article, titled 'Men: A growing minority?' men also feel the effects of the gender imbalance in their profession.

Numbers suggest that women dominate the fields of psychology and counselling, usually for economic and cultural reasons (Blumenfield 2011). Similarly, as seen in Ameesh's narrative, there is a strong gender bias regarding career paths in India. There is a need to make the field of psychotherapy and counselling more available, accessible and lucrative to ensure that individuals interested in pursuing the profession are not hindered by such factors.

5.4 Conclusion

What is amply clear is that there is no single path, factor or motivation that is responsible for the therapist joining the profession, research does suggest that it is important for therapists to be aware of their motivations. This helps them take cognizance when these motivations manifest in their work with clients. The greater the therapist awareness of the personal needs and motivations that underlie their behaviour, the greater control they will have. This awareness of the motivations and needs will ensure the continuity in the field. Research into the motivation of therapists who discontinue practice may offer important insights into what make some therapists persist in the profession, while others do not, or cannot do so.

Sussman (2007) claimed that 'an important determinant of the desire to practice psychotherapy involves the attempt to come to terms with one's own psychological conflicts' (p. 175). Understanding what drives therapists to enter the profession is a crucial factor when reflecting on motivations to join and continue in the field (Richardson et al. 2009). Participants of the present study mentioned the lack of thought given to motivation for joining the helping profession, either before or during training, thereby indicating the need for increasing self-reflective practice in the field. Reflexivity, which involves the 'revisiting, re-examining and re-searching one's own motivations and strategies' encourages consideration of what we carry with us into our work 'in terms of our personal past, cultural values and belief' (Bager-Charleson 2010, p. 142).

Acknowledgments This chapter is based on the research conducted as part of the first author's Ph.D. dissertation titled 'Being a Psychotherapist: Exploration of Therapists Beliefs and Values' at the Tata Institute of Social Sciences, Mumbai under the supervision of the second author. The authors would like to acknowledge all the participant therapists for making time and sharing their experiences for the research.

References

Bager-Charleson, S. (2010). *Why therapists choose to become therapists: A practice-based enquiry*. London: Karnac Books.

Barnett, M. (2007). What brings you here? An exploration of the unconscious motivations of those who choose to train and work as psychotherapists and counsellors. *Psychodynamic Practice, 13*(3), 257–274. doi:10.1080/14753630701455796.

Beatty, E. (2012). *A study of motivations amongst contemporary trainee counsellors for pursuing a career in psychotherapy.* Dublin: Thesis, Dublin Business School. Retrieved from: http://esource.dbs.ie/handle/10788/830.

Blumenfield, M. (2011). Choosing a psychotherapist: Should gender matter? *Huffington Post.* Retrieved from: http://www.huffingtonpost.com/michael-blumenfield-md/choosing-a-psychotherapist_b_868475.html?ir=India&adsSiteOverride=in.

Bowling, D., & Hoffman, D. (2000). Bringing peace into the room: The personal qualities of the mediator and their impact on the mediation. *Negotiation Journal, 16*(1), 5–28. doi:10.1111/j.1571-9979.2000.tb00199.x.

Farber, B. A., Manevich, I., Metzger, J., & Saypol, E. (2005). Choosing psychotherapy as a career: Why did we cross that road? *Journal of Clinical Psychology, 61*(8), 1009–1031. doi:10.1002/jclp.20174.

Guttmann, J., & Daniels, S. (2001). What do school counsellors gain from their role as psychotherapists? *Educational psychology. 21*(2), 203–218.

Henry, W., Sims, J. H., & Spray, S. (1973). *Public and private lives of psychotherapists.* San Francisco: Jossey-Bass.

Hill, C. E., Sullivan, C., Knox, S., & Schossler, L. Z. (2007). Becoming psychotherapists: Experience of novice trainees in a beginning graduate class. *Psychotherapy Theory, Research, Practice, Training, 44*(4), 1–27. doi:10.1037/0033-3204.44.4.434.

Johnson, R. B., Onwuegbuzie, A. J., & Turner, L. A. (2007). Toward a definition of mixed methods research. *Journal of mixed methods research, 1*(2), 112–133.

Jurkovic, G. J. (2014). *Lost childhoods: The plight of the parentified child.* London: Routledge.

Keirsey, D. (1998). *Please understand me II.* CA: Prometheus Nemesis Book Company.

Littauer, H., & Sexton, H. (2005). Qualities clients wish for in their therapists. *Scandinavian Journal of Caring Sciences, 19*(1), 28–31. doi:10.1111/j.1471-6712.2005.00315.x.

Luborsky, L., McLellan, T., Diguer, L., Woody, G., & Seligman, D. (2006). The psychotherapist matters: Comparison of outcomes across twenty-two therapists and seven patient samples. *Clinical Psychology: Science and Practice, 4*(1). doi:10.1111/j.1468-2850.1997.tb.00099.x.

Murphy, R. A., & Halgin, R. P. (1995). Influences on the career choice of psychotherapists. *Professional Psychology: Research and Practice, 26*(4), 422–426. doi:10.1037/0735-7028.26.4.422.

Norcross, J. C., & Farber, B. A. (2005). Choosing psychotherapy as a career: beyond "I want to help people". *Journal of Clinical Psychology, 61*(8), 939–43. Retrieved from: http://www.ncbi.nlm.nih.gov/pubmed/15945069.

Orlinsky, D., & Ronnestad, M. (2005). *Therapists Look Into The Mirror. PsycCRITIQUES, 50*(29), 2. doi:10.1037/05177111.

Racusin, G., Winter, S., & Willam, D. (1981). Becoming a therapist: Family dynamics and career choice. *Professional Psychology, 12*(2), 271–279. doi:10.1037/0735=7028.12.2.271.

Richardson, J., Sheean, L., & Bambling, M. (2009). Becoming a psychotherapist or a counsellor: A survey of psychotherapy and counselling trainers. *Psychotherapy in Australia, 16*(1). Retrieved from: http://www.psychotherapy.com.au/fileadmin/site_files/pdfs/article.pdf.

Ronnestad, M., & Skovholt, T. (2003). The journey of the counsellor and therapist: Research findings and perspectives on professional development. *Journal of Career Development, 30*(1), 1025. doi:10.1023/A:173508081.

Sussman, M. B. (2007). *A curious calling* (2nd ed.). Lanham, Maryland: Jason Aronson.

Willyard, C. (2011, January). Men: A growing minority? *American Psychological Association*, p. 40. Retrieved from: http://www.apa.org/gradpsych/2011/01/cover-men.aspx.

Zerubavel, N., & Wright, M. O. (2012). The dilemma of the wounded healer. *Psychotherapy, 49*(4), 482–491. doi:10.1037/a0027824.

Chapter 6
Exploring Values of Therapists in India

Rashmi Rangarajan and Chetna Duggal

Abstract Psychotherapy research is replete with insights into therapy outcomes and the role it plays within the therapeutic alliance. However, much of the focus of research has been directed towards studying therapy, and not the psychotherapists. In order to fill this gap the current study intended to provide a comprehensive and in-depth understanding of therapist values in the Indian context. A concurrent triangulation mixed methods' study was developed to explore values of experienced therapists, to understand the interplay of their personal and professional values in their professional practice, and to study the various sources of their values. A self-designed questionnaire and the Portrait Value Questionnaire were used to obtain the quantitative data. The qualitative data was obtained through in-depth interviews with the participants. The findings of the study suggest an integration of personal and professional values. The four value priorities of the participants were benevolence (care and compassion), honesty, self-direction (growth and respect) and universalism (equality and justice). The main sources of their values were reported as family, training, clients and religion and spirituality. A model was developed to represent the interplay of therapists' personal and professional values and their influence on psychotherapeutic practice.

Keywords Therapist values · Experienced therapists · Benevolence · Self-direction · Universalism

Rashmi Rangarajan (✉)
Dehradun, India
e-mail: rashmir90@gmail.com

Chetna Duggal
School of Human Ecology, Tata Institute of Social Sciences,
Mumbai, India

S. Sriram (ed.), *Counselling in India*, DOI 10.1007/978-981-10-0584-8_6

6.1 Introduction

Most psychotherapeutic modalities acknowledge that a practitioner's fundamental tool is his or her self and that professional development involves resolving the struggle between the personal and the professional self through either splitting (or separating) or by integration (Hart 1985). Furthermore, Hart mentions that, as the therapist develops, psychotherapy moves from being seen as 'What I do' towards being perceived as 'Who I am'. Richardson et al. (2009) also claim that it is a generally held view that the therapist's most valuable tool is his or her 'self'.

Reviewing research on the contribution of therapist factors in psychotherapy outcome Miller et al. (2008), highlight that the individual who 'provides the treatment is a much more important determinant of success than what treatment is provided' (p. 15). In their study on therapist variables, Beutler et al. (2004) found that both therapist factors and the therapeutic alliance have a significant role to play in therapy outcomes:

> Despite the concerted effort to control, reduce or eliminate the effects of both therapist variability and extra diagnostic patient variables, research has not been able to escape the need to recognize either the roles of the clinician or the reciprocal influence of patient and therapist qualities on one another. (p. 227)

Regardless of this, several reviews of literature on therapist factors, such as the therapists' level of experience, training, expectations and intervention style, have been found to be inconclusively and unsatisfactorily related to therapy outcomes (Beutler et al. 2004). In recent years, however, therapist variables such as the therapist's personality and coping patterns, level of emotional well-being, values, beliefs and cultural attitudes have been receiving research attention. There is a dearth of research and understanding of the role of aspects of the therapist's self, such as personal values, irrespective of its influence on therapy outcomes, in the field of psychotherapy.

6.2 Understanding Values

Values have been defined as fairly stable, motivational characteristics (Bardi and Schwartz 2003) that direct individual behaviours, thoughts and feelings. Values influence interpersonal interactions and help regulate behaviour and thoughts. As Lindeman and Verkasalo (2005) ascertain, although linked with personality, motivation and behaviour, values are conceptually distinct. Further, values are more abstract and enduring, and are trans-situational rather than situation specific (Hitlin and Piliavin 2004).

One of the most influential conceptualization of values came from Schwartz (1994) who defined values as 'desirable trans-situational goals, varying in importance, that serve as guiding principles in the life of a person or other social entity' (p. 21). He proposed that individual differences in value priority are due to the unique interactions of biological qualities, social events and cultural influences that comprise each individual's life. Schwartz (1992) identified ten basic and motivationally distinct values: self-direction, stimulation, hedonism, achievement, power, security, conformity, tradition, benevolence and universalism.

6.3 Values in Psychotherapy

The role of values in the field of psychotherapy through the first half of the twentieth century was dominated by the premise that therapists functioned as blank screens upon which clients projected their beliefs and values, while the practitioner maintained a neutral stance (Patterson 1989; Vaughan 1963). As early as 1949, Hunt reported that, in theory, values were treated as lying outside the realm of science and should play no role in the therapeutic relationship. However, it was difficult to exclude values from the therapeutic relationship in practice. Around the same time, Ginsberg (1950) observed that practitioner hesitance to examine their own values could lead to a hindrance in the therapeutic processes. Research also confirms Ginsberg's observation that therapist values can significantly contribute to therapy outcomes, and the extent of congruence between the values of the therapist and the client influences therapeutic processes and outcomes in a way that clients often reflect the values of the therapist (Corey et al. 2007; Remley and Herlihy 2010).

Over the last six decades, there has been a growing understanding that values form an integral part of the therapy situation. It is widely acknowledged that therapeutic practice is an interaction between the value systems of therapists and clients (Tseng and Streltzer 2004). It has been recognized that the therapists cannot avoid communicating their values to the client, and therapist values are extremely crucial in the therapeutic process. As recent as 2010, Garza and Watts espoused the relevance of and the critical role social and cultural values play in filial therapy[1] as exchanges between the therapist and his or her clients. They bring to focus the dearth of knowledge and information in the area of therapy for culturally diverse populations, and how the understanding of specific cultural and social values can potentially influence how clients perceive, seek and receive psychotherapeutic services. They propose four Hispanic values (*familismo*, i.e. the family; *respeto,* i.e. respect; *personalismo,* i.e. personal relationships; and *confianza,* i.e. trust), which when interfaced with filial therapy leads to a more effective, culturally responsive treatment.

Values may also influence the selection of psychotherapy as a profession and therapists may endorse certain values that lead them to select the helping

[1]According to Garza and Watts (2010) filial therapy is both a therapeutic and a preventive approach. In filial therapy, unlike family therapy, the parent is placed in the therapeutic role, and the therapist utilizes the 'natural bond' between the parent and the child.

profession. In their work on why people choose to become psychotherapists, Norcross and Farber (2005) identified twelve themes as motivations to become a psychotherapists and found that values of self-growth, healing and altruism were among the twelve identified themes of motivation (Norcross and Farber 2005).

Practitioners often select a theoretical orientation on the basis of the congruence of the philosophy and values of the theory with their own values and philosophy. Research has shown that therapists usually choose a theoretical orientation which is compatible with their own values and beliefs, and how the theoretical orientations can in turn help shape and define the values and beliefs of the therapists (Myers 2013; Demir and Gazioglu 2012). Therapist values may seep in through the goals selected, the methods used in therapy, the way a practitioner relates to his or her clients and may determine the techniques used (Strupp 2001; Patterson 1989).

Tjeltveit (1986) has distinguished between the different kinds of values—political, moral, religious and mental health—among others, and that any and all of these may change in the course of therapy for clients. Clients may often express their values that are opposed to those of the practitioners', and may even display behaviour that can be in contrast to the practitioner's values, giving rise to value conflicts. It would seem that value conflicts are an inescapable process and a significant part of a therapist's practice.

While therapists are strongly discouraged from imposing their value system or philosophy on to their clients, it is recognized that the practitioner cannot avoid communicating his or her values to the client through the acceptance of an ultimate goal, the methods used in therapy, the way a practitioner relates to his or her clients and in the responses given (Patterson 1989; Strupp 1980). According to Farnsworth and Callahan (2013) it is imperative and critical for therapists to develop a larger understanding and awareness into their personal and professional values and recognize the impact it can have on their therapeutic practice.

6.4 The Experienced Therapist

In the professional journey of the therapist, the central developmental task of the experienced therapist according to Ronnestad and Skovholt (2003) is to create a therapy role which will be highly congruent with the individual's self-perceptions (including values, interests, attitudes and roles), which will in turn make it possible for the practitioner to apply his or her professional competence in an authentic way. Personal and professional values and their integration thus become a vital area of research and beckons for a greater understanding.

In their study, Ronnestad and Skovholt (2003) explored therapist professional development using a longitudinal interview approach in which they interviewed 100 American therapists at different experience levels in the year 1988 and later re-interviewed 60 of the 100 respondents after a gap of about 10 years. Based on the analysis of the data they obtained, they renamed their model as the phase model and collapsed their earlier eight-stage model into six continuous phases, consisting of the lay helper; the beginning student; the advanced student; the novice professional; the experienced professional; and finally the senior professional.

From the findings of research further exploring professional development, it has been observed that experienced therapists would have typically worked in different work settings, engaged in varied work-role modalities, and also worked with different types of clients over a number of years (Ronnestad and Skovholt 2003). Experienced therapists report positive skill change and have succeeded in overcoming their past limitations. They would have achieved the following developmental tasks:

1. Maintaining a sense of personal growth and avoid burnout and stagnation.
2. Integrating his or her personal self into a coherent professional self.
3. Envisaging a vision for one's future.

Experienced therapists and counsellors reported feeling more competent and effective as practitioners (Ronnestad and Skovholt 2003). The study on professional development of psychotherapy practitioners by Orlinsky et al. (1999) articulated the positive relation between the years of experience and levels of perceived mastery and growth among therapists and counsellors. Experienced therapists and counsellors reported being less defensive and inhibited in their work with their clients. They were involved in an individuation process whereby they developed unique and personalized ways of relating to their clients and reported a progression towards increased empathic engagement with their clients.

The central task at this stage of integrating one's personal self into a coherent professional self seems critical and requires attention. When therapists enter a value-based profession like psychotherapy, a considerable factor involved in the developmental task of integrating one's personal self into one's professional functioning could be to integrate personal and professional values in a manner that may be highly articulate and refined, so as to have an insight on how values may be entering psychotherapy practice.

Psychotherapy research is replete with insights into therapy outcomes and the role it plays within the therapeutic alliance. However, much of the focus of research has been directed towards studying psychotherapy and not the psychotherapists. According to Carlsson and Schubert (2009) psychotherapy has been examined mainly as a set of methods, techniques or procedures that are efficacious in themselves, regardless of the therapist who is using them.

In the recent years, there has been a consistent effort in trying to understand the trajectory of therapist professional development. However, the focus has rather been on novice and senior professional phases of professional development mainly examining their aspects of training and challenges, and its influence on therapy outcomes. There is an emerging need to explore the experienced professional phase, focusing on therapist experiences and the interaction between their professional and personal variables such as values.

6.5 Studying Therapist Values in India

While there has been a gradual impetus in psychotherapy research to study and understand the therapist's self, in India we continue to rely on western literature and thus, a greater need extends to generating an understanding of psychotherapy in the Indian context. Manikam (2010) mentioned the increasing demands for psychotherapeutic services and the need for trained therapists and counsellors in India. A handful of institutions in the country are offering courses in psychotherapy training, and a number of other avenues are steadily coming up pointing to the greater need of research and understanding of psychotherapy in India. All these aforementioned reasons indicate the need for developing an understanding of the therapist professional development in the Indian context, and build a knowledge base on the role values play within the therapeutic relationship in the Indian context. Indian culture is salient in the values and beliefs it propagates (Sen 2004), considering that the lens an individual adopts to view the world is heavily borrowed from the culture in which she or he is embedded, and research specific to the Indian context is needed.

The study aimed at exploring the personal and professional values of experienced therapists practising in India, and the sources of their values. To meet the objectives of the study the concurrent triangulation mixed methods' design was employed (Creswell et al. 2003). The qualitative and quantitative data was collected simultaneously, and the findings were triangulated to develop a comprehensive understanding of the research area.

A self-designed questionnaire was used to obtain basic therapist information about the respondents' demographic profile (i.e. age, sex, years of experience, practice settings and educational qualifications), and their practice characteristics (i.e. their theoretical orientation, professional identity, years of supervision received, ongoing supervision status and if they were currently supervising other therapists).

In order to obtain a personal value profile of the respondents, the Portrait Value Questionnaire (PVQ, as developed by Schwartz et al. 2001) was administered. The PVQ comprises 40 items, with each item consisting of a description of a person ('portrait') with two sentences. The PVQ asks about similarity to someone with particular goals and aspirations (values) rather than similarity to someone with particular traits (Schwartz 2003). The respondents are asked to assess how similar to the portrayed individual they were. The possible answers were as follows—*very similar, similar, rather similar, rather dissimilar, dissimilar and very dissimilar*. The responses were coded with scores ranging from 1 to 6, with 6 being *very similar* and 1 being *very dissimilar*. The forty items belonged to ten scales. The number of items in each scale was between two and six. The scales are briefly described as follows (Schwartz 2006):

1. Self-direction: The defining goal was independent thought and action: choosing, creating and exploring. It derived from organismic needs for control and mastery and interactional prerequisites of autonomy and independence. It included creativity, freedom, choosing goals for oneself, curiosity, self-respect, intelligence and privacy.

2. Stimulation: The defining goal was excitement, novelty and challenge in life. The value was a derivative of organismic need for variety and stimulation in order to maintain optimal, positive level of activation. It included aspects of a varied and a daring life.
3. Hedonism: The defining goal was pleasure or sensuous gratification for oneself. The value was derived from the organismic needs and the pleasure associated with satisfying them. It included enjoying life and being self-indulgent.
4. Achievement: The defining goal was personal success through demonstrating competence according to social standards. Performance that was competent and generated resources was vital for individuals to survive and for groups and institutions to reach their objectives. It included being ambitious, successful, capable and influential and having social recognition.
5. Power: The defining goal was social status and prestige, control or dominance over people and resources. It included aspects of authority, wealth, social power, preserving one's public image and social recognition.
6. Security: The defining goal was safety, harmony and stability of society, relationships and of the self. They were derived from basic individual and group requirements. It included the need for social order, family security, national security, cleanliness, reciprocation of favours, being healthy and sense of belonging.
7. Conformity: The defining goal was restraint of actions, inclinations and impulses likely to upset or harm others and violate social expectations or norms. It was a derivative of the prerequisite that individuals inhibited inclinations that might disrupt and undermine smooth interaction and group functioning. It involved exercising self-restraint in everyday interaction, being obedient, polite, honouring elders, being loyal and responsible.
8. Tradition: The defining goal was respect, commitment and acceptance of the customs and ideas that one's culture or religion provides. Tradition consisted of the subordination to abstract aspects like religious and cultural customs and ideas. As a value it demanded responsiveness to unassailable expectations from the past.
9. Benevolence: The defining goal was preserving and enhancing the welfare of those with whom one was in frequent personal contact. It was derived from the basic requirement for efficient group functioning and from the organismic need for affiliation. The value included being helpful, honest, forgiving, responsible, loyal, true friendship, expressing mature love, having meaning in life and leading a spiritual life.
10. Universalism: The defining goal was understanding, appreciation, tolerance and protection for the welfare of all people and for nature. It was derived from the survival needs of individuals and groups. The value included being broadminded, having sense of social justice, equality, world peace, beauty, unity with nature, wisdom, inner harmony and the presence of spiritual life.

An in-depth interview guide was developed to collect qualitative data for the study to explore therapist values and the source of the values. The domains of the interview guide were as follows: professional values, sources of professional values, personal values and sources of personal values.

The sample included currently practising therapists from New Delhi and Dehradun (both cities in north India), with an experience of ten to twenty years, with a minimum educational qualification of a Master's Degree in Psychology. Purposive and snowball sampling approach was used to select the participants for the study. Over forty therapists were contacted to participate in the study, out of which twenty-two therapists responded, and ten met the inclusion criteria. Of the ten, eight therapists finally took part in the study.

The data obtained from the questionnaire was analysed using descriptive statistics and represented in tables.

Based on the scoring key provided by Schwartz (2003), the forty items on the PVQ were scored under the ten value scales described earlier. The following steps for computing individual and group value scores were followed:

- Scores for the ten values were computed by taking the mean of the raw rating given to the items indexed/listed under the scales.
- Each individual's mean score was computed across all forty value items. Schwartz (2003) refers to this as the MRAT (mean rating).
- Next the scores of each of the ten values (as computed in step 1) were centred for the respondent around that respondent's MRAT (i.e. subtract MRAT from each of the ten value scales). This refers to the centred scores. The centred scores helped in identifying the relative importance of the ten values to a person, i.e. the individual value priorities. The top three value priorities of each respondent were chosen by selecting the values with the highest centred scores for that individual. These are referred to as the individual value priorities on PVQ.
- Subsequently, the mean of the individual centred scores on the values was used to derive the value priorities of the group of respondents. These have been referred to as the group value priorities on the PVQ.

The in-depth interviews were audio recorded and were transcribed word by word. The qualitative data obtained was analysed using Thematic Analysis. Thematic Analysis is a widely used approach for identifying, analysing and reporting patterns (or themes) within a data set. Thematic analysis is a flexible approach that facilitates rich and detailed, yet complex description of the data. It is also independent of theory and epistemology and can be applied across a range of theoretical and epistemological approaches. In Namey et al. (2007) words,

> Thematic moves beyond the counting explicit words or phrases and focuses on identifying and describing both implicit and explicit ideas. Codes developed for ideas or themes are then applied or linked to raw data as summary markers for later analysis, which may include comparing the relative frequencies of themes or topics within a data set, looking for code co-occurrence, or graphically displaying code relationships. (p. 138)

Thematic analysis allows the researcher to identify and determine in a precise manner the concepts and the relationships between these concepts and compare them to the data gathered from different situations at different times.

The findings from the qualitative and quantitative sections were triangulated to develop a comprehensive understanding of therapist values. The quantitative data (i.e. individual value priorities and group value priorities obtained from the PVQ), along with the values that emerged in the in-depth interviews were integrated to develop an understanding of therapist values in the Indian context.

The quantitative and qualitative data obtained from the study was an in-depth and rich account of therapist values and a first-hand description of the role values played in the participants' therapeutic practice.

6.6 Profile of the Participant Therapists

The profile of the participants of the study, related to demographic information such as age, sex, years of experience, workplace setting and their educational qualifications, theoretical orientation and their professional identity, is presented in Table 6.1.

The age range of the participants was between 33 years and 73 years, and as per the inclusion criteria of the study the years of psychotherapy practice experience ranged from 11 years to 20 years. Three of the participants reported having master's degrees (M.S./M.A.), while four reported having a doctoral degree (Ph.D./Psy.D.).

Table 6.1 Profile of participant therapists

Name[a]	Age (years)	Sex[b]	Years of experience	Setting	Theoretical orientation	Professional identity	Qualification
1. Shreya	52	F	20	Private practice	Existential, psychodynamic and humanistic	Psychotherapist and group facilitator	M.S. counselling
2. Meghna	37	F	13	Private practice	CBT and eclectic	Clinical psychologist	Psy.D. clinical psychology
3. Priya	48	F	20	Private practice and college	CBT and NLP	Psychotherapist and professor	Ph.D. developmental and educational psychology
4. Preesha	43	F	18.2	Private practice and school	CBT and eclectic	Clinical psychologist	Ph.D. clinical psychology
5. Vinita	40	F	16	Corporate hospital	CBT and eclectic	Clinical psychologist	Ph.D. clinical psychology
6. Sonali	35	F	14.4	Private practice	CBT and eclectic	Psychotherapist	M.S. family therapy
7. Padma	73	F	20	Private practice	CBT and eclectic	Counsellor	Ph.D. communication
8. Leena	33	F	11	NGO	CBT and biblical counselling	Developmental psychologist	M.A. applied psychology

Notes [a]Names of the participant therapists have been changed to maintain confidentiality
[b]F stands for Female

The work settings of the participants were varied; while most had their own private clinics and practice, participants also worked in colleges, schools, corporate hospitals and with voluntary, not-for-profit organizations. The therapists started their psychotherapy practice at different life stages. Leena, a 33-year-old therapist, had begun practising right after graduating from her master's degree programme in applied psychology, while Padma, a 73-year-old counsellor, had started practising counselling after taking voluntary retirement from teaching in a college.

In the study, majority of the experienced therapists reported cognitive behaviour therapy and eclecticism as their main theoretical orientations in their practice. Neuro-linguistic programming (NLP), biblical counselling and existential-psychodynamic-humanistic therapy were also reported (see Table 6.1). Another striking feature of the sample of respondents for the study was that all the participating therapists were women. To begin with there are few practising male therapists, and amongst those who were contacted for the study, there was, however, either no affirmative response, or they did not fit the requirements of the study. This may also indicate to a known fact that psychotherapeutic practice in India is a markedly female-dominated profession, and that there is a growing need for male therapists.

6.7 Personal and Professional Values

The personal and professional values of the experienced therapists based on the findings from the quantitative data which was obtained from the PVQ and the qualitative data which was obtained from the in-depth interviews are presented in this section.

The three individual value priorities, receiving the highest scores, for each of the participant therapists are presented in Table 6.2. Participant therapists gave priority to the values of benevolence, universalism and self-direction. Benevolence was an individual value priority for all the participant therapists, the value of universalism was important for seven of the participants, and finally the value of self-direction received a high score for six participants.

Self-direction was prioritized for six of the participant therapists indicating the significance for independent thought and action, creativity, freedom, growth and privacy in their lives. Seven therapists ascribed significance to tolerance, social justice and welfare of all people and nature (i.e. the value of universalism). All eight participants assigned significance to being helpful, empathic, responsible, loyal and loving, with the value of benevolence emerging among the three most important values for all the participants.

The top three group value priorities which were derived from the top three individual priorities of the participants were benevolence with the highest mean score of 0.97, self-direction with the mean score of 0.88 and universalism with the mean score of 0.85 (see Table 6.3).

Table 6.2 Individual value priority of experienced therapists on the Portrait Value Questionnaire (PVQ)

Names	Top three values	Value scores
1. Shreya	1. Universalism	0.54
	2. Self-direction	1.38
	3. Security	0.48
2. Meghna	1. Benevolence	1.73
	2. Universalism	1.31
	3. Conformity	0.98
3. Priya	1. Universalism	1.14
	2. Self-direction	0.98
	3. Benevolence	0.73
4. Preesha	1. Benevolence	1.43
	2. Universalism	0.68
	3. Self-direction	0.18
5. Vinita	1. Benevolence	1.18
	2. Self-direction	0.93
	3. Universalism	0.59
6. Sonali	1. Self-direction	1.63
	2. Universalism	1.13
	3. Benevolence	0.63
7. Padma	1. Universalism	1.21
	2. Stimulation	1.21
	3. Benevolence	1.05
8. Leena	1. Benevolence	0.93
	2. Self-direction	0.68
	3. Stimulation	0.43

Table 6.3 Group value priority and their mean scores on the Portrait Value Questionnaire (PVQ)

Top three values of the group	Mean scores
1. Benevolence	0.97
2. Self-direction	0.88
3. Universalism	0.85

The in-depth interviews with the participants explored the personal and professional values endorsed by the therapists. Participants reported that the values they considered as most important to them personally were also values they considered equally important professionally, indicating an integration of values in both their personal and professional lives. Based on the description of the values given by the participants, the values reported in the in-depth interviews were triangulated with the top three group values prioritized on the PVQ to extrapolate an understanding of the values that therapists rated as important, both personally or professionally. Four important value domains of benevolence, honesty, self-direction and universalism emerged as important for therapists, which are discussed below.

6.7.1 Benevolence

This value scale had the highest mean score of 0.97 among the top three individual value priorities, indicating that the participants considered benevolence as their most important value as per the PVQ. Benevolence was also found to be the most important value for the participants through the interviews conducted, and included extending help to people, being empathetic and considerate.

On being asked to describe and talk about the values they believed were most important to them, all the participant therapists discussed that the value of being caring, empathic and understanding to be their most important characteristic. They also said that while this was a value they practiced within the ambit of their personal lives, it was also something they conscientiously practiced in their professional lives. Shreya articulated that being caring and compassionate was important to her both as a professional and as an individual, and that she also expected compassion towards her from people she knew.

> Caring and compassion is a very important value for me… in my supervisors, I look for someone who is caring and compassionate… even for my clients… I care a lot about them and that's very important because it's the same I expect from other people. So yes, caring and compassion has been a constant value both personally and professionally. (Shreya, 52 years)

Benevolence also seemed to be close to the participants' role of being a therapist, and being in a helping profession. It is often seen that therapists take on a nurturing role with their clients apart from other roles such as a trainer, mentor and supervisor. Hovrath's (2001) meta-analytic review of therapist variables also found that empathy among other factors had an impact on effective therapeutic alliance, especially in the early treatment phases.

6.7.2 Honesty

As another salient value that influenced their behaviour, especially in their professional practice, all the participant therapists reported honesty as a priority. When asked to describe how honesty played a role in their interactions, the respondents shared myriad experiences with their clients, family members, friends and workplace colleagues. In her narrative, Sonali described how the value of honesty played a significant role in both her personal and professional experiences.

> A very personal value is honesty, it sounds very clichéd, but it is very important… it's a real and hard core thing that also comes out in my sessions a lot and I don't mean clients being honest with me, that doesn't translate to that, it translates to when a couple is dishonest and the issue is to work on their honesty and not anything else… I don't expect clients to be absolutely honest with me, I accept clients hiding things from me and in time share things, but honesty becomes a very important issue to deal with in my therapy sessions. (Sonali, 35 years)

Although Sonali talked about how honesty was one of the priority issues she worked with in the therapy sessions with her clients, other participant therapists reported that they made sure they were honest with their clients, and the significant people in their lives. Thus, the narratives of the participant therapists reflected the crucial role the value of honesty played in their lives both as individuals and practitioners.

6.7.3 Self-direction

The value of self-direction (which includes independent thought and action, choosing, creating and exploring, self-respect and growth) was mentioned by six of the participant therapists as a value priority on the PVQ. Specifically, the values of growth and respect (also aligning with the value of self-direction) were perceived as highly significant both in their personal and professional practice by all the participant therapists in their narratives.

The value of growth was reflected in their effort towards professional development, wherein all the participants reported that they actively sought additional training, attended workshops and consulted relevant articles, and engaging in dialogues with other professionals. Padma described how growth as a value motivated her to read, in order to update herself. The value of growth also became relevant in her relationship with both her clients and interns.

> Growth is very important for me because of which I read a lot, and not just journals; I read novels and biographies too in order to expand my knowledge and understanding… growth is important because it's the foundation of all humans… the need to grow. Even in my counselling relationship with my clients I make it a point that I give them the space and freedom to grow in the relationship. With my interns also, I give them the freedom and the space to grow and explore. It's very important for me and for them. (Padma, 73 years)

Growth and respect was a significant value which was especially displayed in their professional pursuits, whether it was through seeking additional training, or engaging in regular dialogues with other professionals.

The value of respect under self-direction was described in terms of behaviour towards people, such as greeting in a positive manner, refraining from using verbal or physical abuse and desisting oneself from rebuking or being sarcastic to another person. Vinita described how, in her interactions with not just her clients but also with the people outside of her professional setting, she continually practiced showing genuine respect.

> Respect is probably one of the most important values, both personally and professionally… for me it is about respecting people and that they respect me back. It's always important to respect everybody and respect oneself. In my relationships with my clients, I always make it a point that I greet them, I show them respect and never make them feel small. (Vinita, 40 years)

It was found that respect and growth were two important values that also fell under the value domain of self-direction. These values also influenced the participants' current and past professional training and their therapeutic practice.

6.7.4 Universalism

The final important value domain that emerged was universalism that included having a sense of social justice, equality, wisdom, inner harmony and the presence of spiritual life. It primarily constituted the goal of understanding, appreciating, tolerating and protecting the welfare of people and nature. In the current study, it was found that, in the narratives of the participant therapists, the values of equality and justice were significantly relevant to their practice and interactions.

Leena reported that she valued every human being, whether the individual was an adult or a child. She described in an eloquent manner that children and adults were equal and that they were created for a purpose, and her job as a therapist was to try and help them see that they were valued.

> What I believe is that every person, every child is undoubtedly created with a purpose.... so their lives have a message... my belief is that every child has value...whether they are with or without an obvious disability... The purpose for which we work is, [because] each of those children deserves a life of dignity. They deserve the life where they are celebrated and it's my job to be able to provide that for them in my own way. (Leena, 33 years)

Other respondents such as Meghna, Vinita, Padma, Priya and Preesha also reported that they highly regarded the value of equality in terms of every individual having the right to make his or her own choices, be treated with dignity, given equal opportunities and not discriminated against on the basis of their race, religion, caste or economic status. As therapists, the participants of the study reported that they strove to bring this value in their practice by continually empowering their clients.

Shreya expressed that the value of justice was quintessential for her, both personally and professionally. She reported that she would find it very hard to work with clients who were not being fair to people in their lives. She also said that she often used confrontation as a method to address it in the therapy sessions with her clients.

> Justice is very important. If a client is being unjust or unfair in their life they're going to have trouble because, I'm not going to understand their weak points, and still be there if the person is being unfair to another person or being extremely superior. So justice and a strong sense of fair play are there in both my personal and professional life. (Shreya, 52 years)

Participant therapists also reported that they continuously strove to uphold equality in their therapeutic practice by not discriminating among their clients, i.e. the therapists did not refuse or decline to offer their services to a client based on his or her caste, religion, gender, sexual orientation and nationality. The respondents also reported that they often gave their clients the right to exercise their choice and empowered them by sharing accurate information to the best of their knowledge The value of justice was appreciated as being important, and it involved being fair in their interpersonal interactions both in their personal life and their professional practice.

Apart from the above-mentioned value domains, some of the participants such as Sonali, Meghna, Priya and Preesha also mentioned fidelity and commitment as important values. They reported that the value of fidelity and loyalty was one of the significant values that they upheld both professionally and personally, including the value of commitment.

6.8 A Summary of Therapist Personal and Professional Values

Findings revealed that benevolence (under which respondents reported the values of care and compassion), honesty, self-direction (under which they reported the values of growth and respect) and universalism (under which they reported the values of equality and justice) were important values for therapists. It was also found that these values continually played a role in their therapeutic practice and contributed to their professional development. The value of growth was particularly linked to professional growth and development in which participants reported going for additional trainings and workshops, and consulting relevant articles and books.

Pirzadeh et al. (2007) conducted a survey of genetic counsellors' personal values on 292 genetic counsellors in the United States of America using the Schwartz Universal Values Questionnaire (SUVQ; Schwartz 1992). The results of their study also indicated that the respondents highly valued benevolence, self-direction, achievement and universalism, indicating a strong pattern of concern for the welfare of others.

Patterson (1989) suggested that therapists should not impose their value system on their clients; however, therapists cannot avoid communicating these values to their clients through acceptance of a therapeutic goal, their behaviour towards their clients and through the methods and techniques they use in executing their therapeutic practice (Strupp 1980). Thus researchers urge therapists to continually analyse and reflect on their value system to keep the values from causing hindrance in their professional practice (Ronnestad and Skovholt 2003; Odell and Stewart 1993; Patterson 1989; Vaughan 1963).

An area which continues to be relatively unexplored is the source of therapist values. While a considerable chunk of literature focuses on training and theoretical orientations as having a significant role to play in contributing to a therapist's professional values (Richardson et al. 2009), a case in point being the Humanistic approach, which lends support to the values of empathy and positive regard, there is still a need to further explore the other possible sources of therapist values. In 1959, Glad had noted that values were essentially inherent in the theories of psychotherapy, and that psychotherapy and values could not be examined as two separate entities. Schwartz (1992) suggested that individual differences seen in value priorities arise from the unique interaction of an individual's innate qualities, social events and cultural pressures. Consequently, the next section will examine more closely the different sources of values that the participant therapists reported in their narratives.

6.9 Sources of Values

The participants of the study identified and described the different sources of their values—family, training, clients and religion and spirituality.

6.9.1 Family

All the participant therapists reported that they acquired values from different people they considered as their family. Family for the respondents included parents, siblings, spouse or partner, friends and children. The respondents also described how their family members had contributed to their value system, considering them as one of the most important sources of their value system. Care and compassion, commitment, equality and unconditional acceptance were some of the values participants reported as having acquired from their intimate relationships. Participants reported that value influences from their intimate relationships also translated into their therapeutic practice in ways that they were now aware of after years of practice.

Participants described the influence of their family members on their value system in a very expressive manner, sharing their personal narratives and accounts of interactions that happened to leave a lasting impression on both their personal and professional self.

Meghna described how, as a child, she saw the value in care by watching her father and grandfather interact with their patients in their clinic.

> My upbringing has contributed to who I am… my family is a family of medical doctors so I've grown up seeing them work with people. Their interactions and their humanity with their patients … my grandfather and my father would spend time with their patients for hours and hours and they would talk to them… it wasn't [just] discussing about their cold, cough and fever, it was like they were their confidante, discussing about life … so I grew up watching that, respecting it and seeing the value in that sort of care. (Meghna, 37 years)

Priya described how her friends, spouse and children had contributed to her value system in a significant manner.

> My friends have contributed to my values of endurance or being able to unconditionally give and accept… my spouse and my children have contributed tremendously by not only admiring my values, and acknowledging them, but also valuing them… And that probably has cemented it further… (Priya, 48 years)

6.9.2 Training

Almost all the respondents of the study reported that their training was another important source of their values. Through training, participants reported that they were oriented to the ethics of practising therapy (i.e. confidentiality, honesty, focus on the clients' needs and welfare, and equality, etc.). Meghna reported on how she was instilled with the value of growth through her training in psychotherapy, which continued to motivate her to develop herself as a therapist.

> I think I got the value of growth from my training … it was not something that was ingrained in me but my training contributed to it … my training was so thorough in its ethical teachings and about how to conduct yourself as a therapist… [That] I got instilled with the value of growth, to keep myself moving ahead and not becoming stagnant. (Meghna, 37 years)

Some of the respondents such as Shreya, Sonali and Vinita also reported that apart from training, their supervisors and trainers also contributed to their value of growth as therapists. Consequently, training was reported as an extremely important source of their value of growth as individuals and practitioners.

6.9.3 Clients

Out of the eight respondents, six described that their clients were one of the most important contributors to their values of care, compassion and commitment. Therapists shared close and strong relationships with their clients within the purview of their therapeutic practice. As noted, majority of the participant therapists reported having learned many positive aspects from their clients including the values of care, compassion and commitment.

Shreya described the level of connection she shared with her clients and how important they were in helping her understand the value of commitment in her life.

> Some of my clients have been so accepting of me… with couples the kind of complete candidness and honesty with which they have shared their inner reactions to each other, like the level of suspiciousness, the level of jealousy, the level of hurt, the level of being caring and, commitment to the relationship regardless of how bad it was in that moment, the commitment to hang in there, I think has had a huge influence in the way I saw intimacy in my own life and valued commitment. (Shreya, 52 years)

Ronnestad and Skovholt (2003) had found in their study on professional development of therapists that clients continued to be a very important source of influence on the experienced therapists. Schwartz (1992) has suggested that one of the main sources of values for people is the interpersonal interactions and relationships they shared with other people.

Leena described a moving experience with her clients where she was influenced by the kind of contexts they came from and how she learned to value the quality of her life, and the value of empathy in practice. As a result, empathy also became an important tool to practice the value of care and compassion.

> When I was in Delhi or Chennai, people we met had issues to do with things like...having an affair or being dumped by a boyfriend... and then when I came here, you suddenly met people for whom you have absolutely no idea what they would say because... They were struggling with issues like, there is no food to eat, they live in a house where there is severe water seepage during the rains and therefore they have not slept since the last one week... they are sitting in front of you and weeping away saying I can't take all of this anymore. I had never seen anything like that before... My life is quite protected and... here they were just facing issues of survival and you have no idea what to say. And that's when I learned the value of compassion, of empathy, of being able to be there for somebody in greater need. There is no way I'm going to walk away complaining about the food I get in the mess when I know I met somebody who didn't have two square meals to eat the same day. (Leena, 33 years)

6.9.4 Religion and Spirituality

Some of the participants expressed the role and influence of religion and spirituality on their value systems. Leena reported how the spiritual relationship she shared with God contributed to her value system by helping her value each and every life. She also reported that she practiced biblical counselling with her clients, indicating to the extent of influence religion and spirituality had on her professional practice. Post and Wade (2009) acknowledged that often religious and/or spiritual interventions for some clients may be more effective in addition to traditional therapy interventions.

Shreya described how she learned the values of equality and justice from mythological and religious stories she heard and read about as a child.

> The fables or folklore about Krishna and some incidents in his friendship with Sudama, being humble and caring, valuing Sudama's poverty and simple gifts. Stories about Guru Nanak and his calm demeanour, wisdom and clarity about faith ... about the Mullas trying to move his feet as he lay under a tree so that they would not face Mecca, in the face of his assertion that God and thus Mecca is everywhere and appearing in every direction, they moved his feet back to how they were... some Zen fables and the Panchatantra tales that talked about fairness and justice. (Shreya, 52 years)

It was found that religion, religious fables and stories, and spirituality contributed to some of the respondents' value systems to a significant extent. Values of care and compassion, humility, wisdom, clarity about one's faith, fairness and justice were derived from religious stories and spirituality.

6.10 The Model

The findings obtained from the analysis of the quantitative and qualitative data on personal and professional values of the experienced therapists were further developed into a model that presented the interaction and integration of personal and professional values. Through the triangulation of the data analysed from the PVQ and the transcribed interviews, it was found that the participants identified the following as core values—benevolence, under which they identified the value of care and compassion; honesty; self-direction, under which they identified with growth and respect; and universalism, under which they identified with equality and justice. Interestingly, all the participants described how these values were influential both in their therapeutic practice and their personal interactions, thus, indicating the integration of their personal and professional values. Further, participants also described the various sources of their values—family, training, clients and religion and/or spirituality.

The model depicted in Fig. 6.1 illustrates the complex interaction and integration of personal and professional values, wherein the sources of the values contribute to the development and strengthening of the core values, which in turn influence the therapist's personal and professional lives, and subsequently the different experiences in their personal and professional lives further feed into the sources of their values.

While an influential body of literature offers us some insight into the role theoretical orientation and training plays in contributing to a therapist's values, there is almost none that explores some other sources of values, such as the ones found in the current study: family members, clients and religion and/or spirituality.

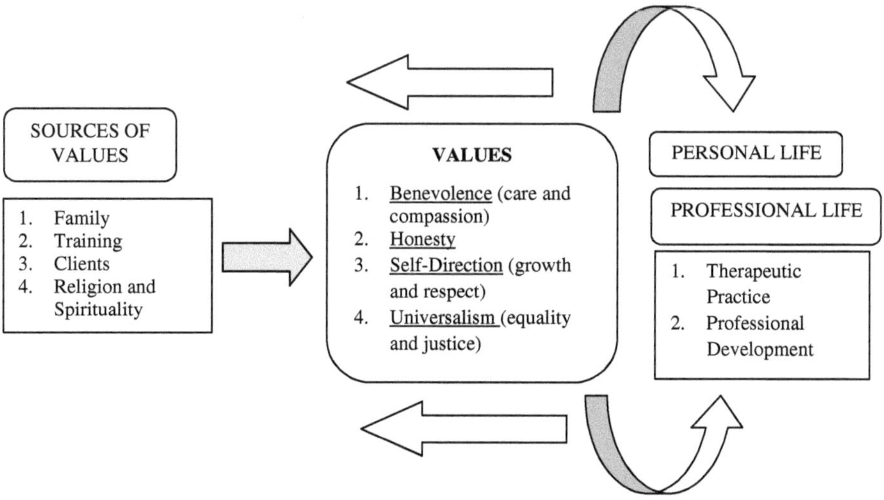

Fig. 6.1 Schematic representation of the model of personal and professional values and their integration in the experienced professional phase

Although the mainstream scientific community may regard values in psychotherapy with caution, despite the availability of substantial research to prove it otherwise, there is no denying that therapist values play a significant role in not just professional practice, but also in personal interactions. As established in the current study, values such as benevolence (care and compassion), honesty, self-direction (growth and respect) and universalism (equality and justice) influence not just the choice of therapeutic methods, but also style of interaction and the quality of the therapeutic relationship.

6.11 Implications for Psychotherapy Practice

Participants of the study were able to identify their core values and how they played out in their personal and professional lives. There were times during the interview when it was suggested by the participants that it was the first time they were thinking of these issues. Large caseloads and no formal spaces for self-reflection made it very hard for practitioners to pursue regular self-reflective practices. Considering that self-reflection is so critical to professional growth and development, both supervision and training might need to create more space and formats for such practices.

While research in psychotherapy is steadily increasing in India, there is hardly any data and research available to understand the complex experiences of therapists in the Indian context. The present study attempts to develop an understanding of the interaction and integration of personal and professional values of experienced therapists; however, further research to examine and explore the role of values in therapeutic practice is needed with a larger sample and with therapists across different stages of professional development. The current study also did not include the voices of male therapists in India. It would make the available literature more inclusive and complete if future research could also incorporate the narratives of male therapists.

An in-depth study of the sources of therapist values, including a more detailed understanding of the role of religion and spirituality in the lives of therapists, could also be explored. A study on the clients' perspective of the role of values in their therapeutic experiences within the Indian context would also be a line of enquiry worth exploring and developing an understanding of.

Acknowledgments The authors would like to acknowledge all the participant counsellors for making time and sharing their experiences for the study.

References

Bardi, A. & Schwartz, S. H. (2003). Values and behaviour: Strength and structure of relations. *Personality and Social Psychology Bulletin, 29.*

Beutler, L., Malik, M. L., Alimohamed, S., Harwood, T. M., Talebi, H., Noble, S., & Wong, E. (2004). Therapist variables. In M. J. Lambert (Ed.), *Bergin and Garfield's Handbook of Psychotherapy and Behaviour Change* (5th ed., pp. 227–306). New York: Wiley.

Carlsson, J., & Schubert, J. (2009). Professional values and their development among trainees in psychodynamic psychotherapy. *European Journal of Psychotherapy & Counselling, 11*, 267–286.
Corey, G., Corey, M., & Callanan, P. (2007). *Issues and ethics in the helping professions* (7th ed.). Belmont, CA: Thomson Brooks/Cole.
Creswell, J. W., Clark, V. L. P., Gutmann, M., & Hanson, W. (2003). Advanced mixed methods research designs. In A. Tashakkori & C. Teddlie (Eds.), *Handbook of mixed methods in the behavioral and social sciences* (pp. 209–240). Thousand Oaks, CA: Sage.
Demir, I., & Gazioglu, I. E. (2012). Theoretical orientations of Turkish counselor trainees: The role of thinking styles, epistemology and curiosity. *Psychology, 3*, 527–533.
Farnsworth, K. J., & Callahan, L. J. (2013). A model for addressing client-clinician value conflict. *Training and Education in Professional Psychology, 7*(3), 205–214.
Garza, Y., & Watts, E. R. (2010). Filial therapy and hispanic values: Common ground for culturally sensitive helping. *Journal of Counseling & Development, 88*, 108–113.
Ginsberg, S. W. (1950). Values and the psychiatrist. *American Journal of Ortho-psychiatry, 20*, 466–478.
Glad, D. D. (1959). *Operational values in psychotherapy*. New York: Oxford University Press.
Hart, H. A. (1985). *Becoming and psychotherapist: Issues of identity transformation.* Paper presented at the Annual Meeting of the Eastern Psychological Association, Boston, MA, March 21–24, 1985.
Hitlin, S., & Piliavin, J. A. (2004). Values: reviving a dormant concept. *Annual Review of Sociology, 30*, 359–393.
Hovrath, A. O. (2001). The alliance. *Psychotherapy, 38*(4), 365–372.
Hunt, J., & Mc, V. (1949). The problem of measuring the results of psychotherapy. In O. H. Mowrer (Ed.), *Psychotherapy: theory and research.* New York: Ronald Press.
Lindeman, M., & Verkasalo, M. (2005). Measuring values with the short Schwartz's values survey. *Journal of Personality Assessment, 85*, 170–178.
Manikam, L. S. (2010). Psychotherapy in India. *American Journal of Psychiatry*, 366–370.
Miller, S. D., Hubble, M., & Duncan, B. (2008). Supershrinks: What is the secret of their success? *Psychotherapy in Australia, 14*(4), 14–22.
Myers, K. J. (2013, November 13). *Counseling theories converge: Person, client, therapist.* Retrieved from Counseling Today: A Publication of the American Counseling Association: http://ct.counseling.org/2013/11/counseling-theories-converge-person-client-therapist/.
Namey, E., Guest, G., Thairu, L., & Johnson, L. (2007). Data reduction techniques for large qualitative data sets. In G. Guest & K. M. McQueen (Eds.), *Handbook of team based qualitative research* (pp. 137–162). Lanham: Altamira Press.
Norcross, J. C. & Farber, B. A. (2005). Choosing psychotherapy as a career: Beyond "I want to help people". *JCLP\In Session, 61*(8), 939–943.
Odell, M., & Stewart, P. S. (1993). Ethical issues associated with client values conversion and therapist value agendas in family therapy. *Family Relations, 42*(2), 128–133.
Orlinsky, D. E., Ronnestad, M. H., Ambuehl, H., Willutzki, W., Botermans, J.-F., Cierpka, M., et al. (1999). Psychotherapists' assessments of their development at different career levels. *Psychotherapy, 36*(3), 203–215.
Patterson, H. C. (1989). Values in counselling and psychotherapy. *Counselling and Values, 33*, 164–176.
Pirzadeh, M. S., Veach, M. P., Bartels, M. D., Kao, J., & LeRoy, S. B. (2007). A national survey of genetic counselors' personal values. *Journal of Genetic Counselling, 16*, 763–773.
Post, B.C., & Wade, N.G. (2009). Religion and spirituality in psychotherapy: A practice-friendly review of research. *Journal of Clinical Psychology*, 65(2),(pp. 131–146). DOI: 10.1002/jclp.20563.
Richardson, J., Sheean, L., & Bambling, M. (2009). Becoming a psychotherapist or a counsellor: A survey of psychotherapy and counselling trainers. *Psychotherapy in Australia, 16*(1). Retrieved from: http://www.psychotherapy.com.au/fileadmin/site_files/pdfs/article.pdf.

Remley, T. P., Jr., & Herlihy, B. (2010). *Ethical, legal, and professional issues in Counseling* (3rd ed.). Upper Saddle River, NJ: Merrill/Pearson Education.

Ronnestad, H. M. & Skovholt, M. T. (2003). The journey of the counsellor and therapist: Research findings and perspectives on professional development. *Journal of Career Development* 5–44.

Sen, A. (2004). How does culture matter? In V. Rao & M. Walton (Eds.), *Culture and Public Action* (pp. 37–57). California: Stanford University Press.

Schwartz, S. H. (1992). Universals in the content and structure of values: Theoretical advances and empirical tests in 20 countries. In M. Zanna (Ed.), *Advances in experimental social psychology* (pp. 1–65). Boston, MA: Academic.

Schwartz, S. H. (1994). Are there universal aspects in the structure and content of human values? *Journal of Social Issues, 50*, 19–45.

Schwartz, S. H., Melech, G., Lehmann, A., Burgess, S., Harris, M., & Owens, V. (2001). Extending the cross-cultural validity of the theory of basic human values with a different method of measurement. *Journal of Cross-Cultural Psychology, 32*, 519–542.

Schwartz, S. H. (2003). Basic human values: Their content and structure across countries. In A. Tamayo & J. Porto (Eds.), *Valores e Trabalho [Values and Work]*. Brasilia: Editora Universidade de Brasilia.

Schwartz, S. H. (2006). A theory of cultural values orientations: Explication and applications. *Comparative Sociology, 5*(2–3), 137–182.

Strupp, H. H. (2001). Implications of the empirically supported treatment movement for psychoanalysis. *Psychoanalytic Dialogues, 11*, 605–619.

Strupp, H. H. (1980). Humanism and psychotherapy: A personal statement of the therapist's essential values. *Psychotherapy: Theory Research and Practice, 17*, 396–400.

Tjeltveit, A. (1986). The ethics of value conversion in psychotherapy: Appropriate and inappropriate therapist influence on client values. *Clinical Psychology Review, 6*, 515–537.

Tseng, S. W. & Streltzer, J. (2004). Introduction: Culture and psychiatry. In W. S. Tseng & J. Streltzer (Eds.), *Cultural Competence in Clinical Psychiatry,* American Psychiatric Publishing, ISBN 1585621250, Washington D.C., pp. 1–20.

Vaughan, P. R. (1963). Religious belief, values, and psychotherapy. *Journal of Religion and Health, 2*(3), 198–209.

Chapter 7
Training in Counselling: Trainers' Perspectives

Sujata Sriram and Sneha Anant Nikam

Abstract This paper examines educator's perspectives on training for counselling in Mumbai. Thematic analysis, with a pre-coded questionnaire was done with ten institutes running counselling programmes of varying duration—short-term, diploma and degree programmes. Counselling training imbued counsellors with theory and practice. An absence of a standardized curriculum for counselling training produced inconsistency in graduates across programmes. Over the years, there was an increase in the number of students being admitted into counselling programmes, these students were from across social class. A gender divide was clearly seen, with more women taking admission in counselling programmes. Curriculum revision was easier in short-term programmes. Trainers believed that there was insufficient attention on practical learning. Intensive fieldwork was required, with supervision and internship. Regulation of the field was important for entry of trained professionals. Participants expressed a need for training counsellors to use vernacular languages for counselling.

Keywords Counselling as a profession · Fieldwork · Curriculum development · Licensing

Counselling is a relatively new field in India, slowly gaining visibility. In the age of competition and stress, the need for counselling is apparent. While there is a growing awareness about counselling, people are often not comfortable with the use of services and may be sceptical about the effectiveness. At present, only some urban educated groups from the elite and middle class populations avail of these services. Economic factors also operate in the use of psychological services, as available services are scarce and are often expensive.

S. Sriram (✉)
School of Human Ecology, Tata Institute of Social Sciences, Mumbai, India
e-mail: sujatasriram@gmail.com

S.A. Nikam
CanKids, KidsCan, Mumbai, India

S. Sriram (ed.), *Counselling in India*, DOI 10.1007/978-981-10-0584-8_7

7.1 Counselling Training in India and Issues Thereof

In India the need for counselling services have been acute, and these needs have manifested themselves within a specifically dynamic social, cultural, and economic ethos. A survey conducted by Arulmani and Nag (2006) (as cited in Arulmani 2007) indicated that the Indian counselling fraternity was not prepared for the increased demand for services. The survey, carried out in 12 different Indian regions reaching a sample of over 7000 young people revealed that less than 10 % of the sample had access to any form of counselling. In their communication with 26 colleges located in different parts of the country, it was found that only six lecturers in charge of career counselling had a background in behavioural science, and only three were trained in counselling. These findings corroborate the belief that though there is a felt need for counselling, services offered by trained counsellors were not available, even in higher education institutions (Arulmani and Nag-Arulmani 2004, as cited by Arulmani 2007).

The parameters for counsellor qualifications have not been defined in India. As a result, 'counselling' as a term is loosely used; counselling services could be offered by anyone at all. Those who are 'interested in helping others' like well-intentioned individuals and social service clubs quite often assume the role of counsellors. The teacher or lecturer who is deputed to be the student welfare officer often carries out this responsibility in school and college contexts (Arulmani 2007). The nature and scope of counselling are poorly understood. Everything falls under the rubric of 'counselling', including courses such as rehabilitation, career guidance, marital problems, HIV/AIDS, school mental health, and life skills.

The number of professionally qualified counsellors, psychotherapists, psychiatrists and clinical psychologists in India, are far fewer than would sufficiently meet the requirements of the population (Manickam 2010). The human resources review on mental health revealed that, there were three psychologists per ten million population, in contrast to the global figure of 60 (cited in the speech of the Vice-President of India, on the 16th convocation at National Institute of Mental Health and Neurosciences (NIMHANS), India News: Mental Health 2012). The current training infrastructure in India produces about 300 psychiatrists, 50 clinical psychologists, 25 psychiatric social workers, 185 psychiatric nurses every year; figures that are not adequate given the need and the size of the country (Kakuma et al. 2011).

Despite the shortage of trained counsellors, and simultaneous awareness of counselling gaining recognition among the populace, the profession remains underpaid. The absence of a central accrediting body or policy of licensure to regulate counselling as a profession has complicated matters even more. There is neither a governing body to regulate ethical standards and practices nor is there a check on private practitioners and/or their qualifications.

Little exists in the way of regulation and accreditation of counsellors and training for counsellors in India, as seen in countries like USA, UK, etc. Counselling training in India is offered by a number of training and educational institutions and universities. The duration of the programmes vary from short-term programmes of a few months' duration to longer programmes extending from 1 to 2 years.

While the short-term programmes offer a Certificate on completion, the longer programmes provide for Diploma and Degree options. There are no regulations existing at present in India for the nature and content of the training programmes.

Much of the training done for counsellors in India draws from Western models and therapies. There are few attempts to consider how to contextualize these Western models to Indian contemporary reality. The need to develop indigenous models of therapy has been expressed often; the development of such contextual models has been slow (Arulmani 2007; Kapur et al. 1996; Varma 1982).

7.2 Ground-Level Issues Related to Counselling Training

Ten institutes offering training in counselling in Mumbai were approached for a qualitative dominant embedded mixed methods approach study. Quantitative data was embedded within the larger qualitative phenomenological design. Both qualitative and quantitative data was collected simultaneously from the participants.

The sample consisted of universities, colleges affiliated to universities and private institutes offering training and education in counselling in the city of Mumbai. Counselling programmes of differing durations were identified, such as short-term Certificate courses, 1-year Diploma and 2-year Degree programmes. Purposive sampling was carried out to cover training programmes for counselling of differing durations available. Perspectives from a range of training programmes were sought for the study. Thirteen institutes were approached for the study of which ten individuals who were teaching and coordinating the counselling programmes agreed to take part in the study and responded to the questionnaire.

A self-designed questionnaire with closed-ended multiple-choice questions, and open-ended questions was prepared. The questionnaire consisted of questions under the following broad categories:

1. Programme Details: Pertaining to the name of the programme, its objectives, duration, number of seats for the programme, number of teaching faculty, number of guest and visiting faculty, faculty–student ratio, etc.
2. History: When the programme started, nature of preliminary discussions held before starting the programme, reasons for initiating the programme, target group for the programme and rationale for choosing the same, etc.
3. Admission: Admission procedures, advertising of the programme, eligibility criteria for applying to the programme, procedure for selection of candidates, number of people applying every year, etc.
4. Content, Structure and Revision: Courses included in the syllabus, courses taught, elective courses offered, credit hours for each course, views on the course content and the way the course was structured, duration of the programme, role in the development and transaction of the course, if there had been any revisions in the course, whose inputs were considered during the revision process, and so forth.

5. Teaching: Methods of teaching used, developing practice-based learning, number of hours of teaching in a week, kind of reading and reference material available for the programme, etc.
6. Fieldwork: This part covered items related to fieldwork and practice in the programme, nature of the fieldwork, number of hours of fieldwork students are expected to do, planning fieldwork for students, records maintained by students of their fieldwork, number of hours of supervision per week, views on need for supervision and format for the same, etc.
7. Personal Development: This section included items on personal development of the student, if it was part of the programme, means of carrying out personal development, etc.
8. Evaluation: This consisted of questions on method used for evaluating performance, views of the most effective way for evaluating performance, etc.
9. Placement Opportunities: This section dealt with placement opportunities, various settings in which students get placed, percentage of students continues to work in the field of Counselling, how the institute kept track of where the alumni were working, etc.
10. Experience: This portion focused on whether practising as Counsellor or Therapist helped trainers to be more effective, if it helped in teaching, number of faculty members from the institute who are practitioners, nature and frequency of training programmes organized for trainers for their development, challenges experienced as a trainer and how they were dealt with, etc.
11. Future of Counselling as a Profession: This section had questions related to the demands of the counselling profession from the point of view as a trainer and practitioner in the field, gaps perceived between available training and the demands from the field, measures needed to overcome the gap, the need for a licensing body in India, views on future of the field of counselling in terms of its prospect for growth in development of the field in Mumbai and in India, views about possible obstacles in development of the field.

Thematic Analysis was carried out from the eleven broad themes, wherein common and similar themes and sub-themes were picked up for analysis.

7.3 Programme Details

There were three distinct types of programmes that varied according to the programme duration, objectives and the course content. Four colleges offered 2-year postgraduate degree programmes, for students who had completed a basic graduation degree, usually in psychology. Additionally, there were three diploma programmes, which offered postgraduate Diplomas in Counselling (as stated in the title of the programme). There were also two short-term programmes, which gave aspirants a Certificate. The colleges offering degrees were affiliated to two universities; two of the diploma programmes were also affiliated with universities, while the other two were run by private institutes. Both the short-term programmes were run by private institutes. Table 7.1 gives the details of the programmes.

When the course curricula and details were examined, the objectives of the programmes varied depending on the ideology of the institute and the duration of the programme. The objectives of all the programmes were geared towards developing skilled professionals, who were familiar with different models of counselling, with sufficient skills and knowledge to deal with different problems and situations in their counselling practice. The emphasis was on the continued development and enhancement of skills, enabling the trainee counsellor to work in various settings and enrich the quality of the services already rendered.

Private counselling institutes ran short-term and part-time programmes of duration of 6–8 weeks to 6 months. One of the private institutes offered two short programmes; one on the Carkhuff model of therapy, and the other on Rational Emotive Behaviour Therapy (REBT). The other short-term programme was a Certificate on general counselling skills and processes, which could be used in a range of situations. The short-term programmes claimed to be skill-based programmes, which helped fill the skill gaps that were evident in students who had completed the longer, full-time degree programmes. One of the participants involved with running a short-term programme bemoaned the lack of practice skills in graduate students in psychology, which made it necessary for students to seek skill-based training programmes.

The programme duration for diploma programmes extended from 9 to 10 months to 1 year. The scope of the curriculum for the diploma programmes was larger than that of short-term programmes but less than that of the 2-year degree programme. The diploma programmes straddled the middle ground of trying to integrate theory and practice components.

There was little commonality between various programmes. All of them were unique, designed independently by their respective directors and the team based on their personal or the institute's ideology, and preconceived rationales about the requirement of counselling training. Even when the same programme was offered by colleges under the same university, there was no common curriculum which specified the number of hours and the content.

Table 7.1 Programme Details

	Degree programme		Diploma programme			Short-term programme
Number	4		4			2
Programme offered by	Universities and colleges affiliated with universities		Universities and colleges affiliated with universities and private institutes			Private institutes
	Univ A	Univ B	Univ B	Univ C	Pvt. Institute	
	3	1	1	1	2	
Duration of the programme	2 years		1 year		9 months	2–6 months

The total number of seats provided for students ranged from 10 to 40. One degree programme admitted only ten students on a yearly basis and this number was strictly adhered to. The other programmes had varying numbers of seats, with two colleges affiliated to the same University having 40 seats for the 2-year degree programme. The total seats for all the programmes was about 250, which provided an indicative number of individuals wanting to be trained in counselling in different programmes.

Across the different types of programmes, the number of faculty members teaching ranged from 1 to 12. It was seen that, some programmes had only one full-time faculty member, while others had at least four full-time faculty members. Except for one short-term programme, all institutes had guest and visiting faculty teaching their programme. There were guest/visiting faculty who taught specialized areas or were specifically nominated to cover certain portions of the syllabus according to the arrangement between them and the institute. The number of guest or visiting faculty varied from 2 to 20. It was seen that these visiting faculty came from other universities, colleges, voluntary organizations, hospitals or were practitioners in the field. For selection of guest faculty, experience in teaching and field practice was given importance, followed by knowledge and expertise. The educational background and the number of hours of their teaching were not specific and primarily depended on the course requirements, so it varied from one programme to another.

Faculty–student ratio ranged from 1:2 to 1:30. While some trainers preferred low faculty–student ratios, others did not feel that the ratios needed to be as low as 1:3, but could be as high as 1:35. The higher ratios were indicated by trainers from some of the degree programmes. Specifically there was demand for trainers in some of the programmes, as expressed by the participants. During the study, turnover in faculty was seen in one of the colleges, where two trainers left in quick succession for personal reasons, leaving it to the Head of Department to try to appoint fresh faculty in order to complete the programme with no disruption for students.

According to Thorne and Dryden (1991, p. 13) counselling courses must have a high ratio of staff to students. Training counsellors was seen as a demanding role, requiring inputs in skills and in theory, equally. They recommended that the core staff should probably be in the ratio of at least one to every 8–10 trainees and no course should be run by one solitary individual. A range of supervision opportunities required the involvement of more teaching and supervisory workforce; a small core staff could not adequately cover the curriculum.

7.4 History

The oldest programme was a diploma programme run by a private institute, started in 1992. The most recent programmes were a diploma programme and a short-term certificate programme set up in 2010. The other programmes had been initiated after 2000. It was interesting to look at the reasons behind initiating the programme, which matched with the current demand for counsellors in a variety of areas. The need for counsellors and the demand for intensive training programmes appeared as one of the strongest reasons for starting a programme; given the nature of problems in the country, there was a need for trained counsellors. Additionally, while the people involved in a particular programme had some previous expertise in running short-term programmes in allied areas, a need for trained professionals was recognized and therefore a programme was initiated. As a trainer from one of the diploma programmes said:

> We have been running a short-term programme on Interpersonal skills for 12 years; and every year at least half the class would demand for more intensive counselling programmes. There were many short, market-oriented programmes of poor quality and very high fees so we felt that with the kind of expertise we have, we should start a quality programme with reasonable fees for professionals who deal with human services.

For a trainer from a college running a 2-year degree programme, the reasons for starting the counselling programme was more practical. In her words,

> Basically we wanted to start a programme; I'll be very honest, because some people felt that it would be good for the future of the college for NAAC[1] purposes. But I look at it as a challenge because after having taught for so many years I always wanted that we should have a PG programme; but I am looking at it as a challenge. But mainly it was for the accreditation purposes and now I realize that there is a very strong need for counsellors and 'maybe' we'll able to fill that lacuna, that's it.

There was one college which offered a 2-year degree programme in Counselling in Marathi medium; and the purpose here, was to increase access for training and provide for gradual increase in counsellors who were able to work in the vernacular medium. There was a need expressed for developing proficient counsellors in languages other than English. This participant said, 'This programme is specifically meant for BA (Psychology) Marathi medium students, as it was found most MA programmes are in English, which these students found difficult'.

The target group for the programmes varied according to the nature of the programme. Whereas 2-year degree programmes preferred students with psychology and human development backgrounds, the diploma programmes cast their net much wider and preferred candidates with a background in the helping professions. The short-term programmes admitted students who were interested in working as counsellors, with no specific background required.

There was a perceptible relaxation in the criteria required for student admissions as the shift occurred from the degree programmes to the short-term programmes. The emphasis on psychology for the degree programmes was because concepts in counselling were based on concepts from psychology. The compulsions of degree awarding institutions that required correspondence between the basic degree and the higher postgraduation degree could be seen in both the universities offering postgraduate programmes in psychology. Hence, a basic degree in psychology was considered necessary. Such restrictions were not felt by the

[1]NAAC—National Assessment and Accreditation Council, an autonomous body that assesses and accredits institutions of higher education in India, to promote quality in education and research.

diploma and short-term programmes. In one of the diploma programmes, while admission was open for people from a range of specializations, there was an unwritten preference given to students with a background in psychology.

The age of the students ranged from 20 to 45 years. Across all programmes, majority of the students were women, reinforcing the reality that counselling was a woman-dominated profession. One of the diploma programmes had 2–4 male students in each batch of 20 students, a short-term programme estimated women–men ratio as 80:20 which was sometimes 60:40. While most students were from the middle and upper middle classes, there were some students from the lower income groups as well.

7.5 Admissions

Advertising the programme played a crucial part in spreading information about the programme and increasing the number of applicants. It was found that some institutes had advertised before initiating the programme by distributing pamphlets in colleges with undergraduate programmes in psychology, while few advertised in the newspaper. Whatever the type of programme, it was observed that public advertisements appeared before admissions, at various times in the calendar year.

Admission procedures for the programmes varied. For the degree programmes and one of the diploma programmes, marks obtained during graduation were taken into consideration. In one of the diploma programmes, a pre-admission test was taken. All programmes included an interview as part of the admissions process. A group discussion was used by one diploma and short-term programme, and one diploma programme used an essay as a means for selection. These interviews and group discussions were intended to help identify the right candidate, who could benefit from the training offered.

The number of people applying for these programmes ranged from 20 to 150. The difference in application rate was high, but it was not dependent on the duration of the programme. The highest number of applicants was observed in a short-term programme and a 2-year degree programme. In most of the cases it was observed that there was an increase in number of applications in the last few years. The reasons for the same were related to greater awareness in students about the counselling profession and in particular about the course and the programme. In some cases, specific details of the programme such as the teaching methods and structure of the programme had increased by word of mouth.

7.6 Content, Structure and Revision

The course content of all the programmes overlapped, considering the ultimate aim of the programmes was training for counselling. Main topics or themes like techniques, theories and therapies were offered by all the programmes. Within this paradigm, courses offered sub-topics that were both common and varying. It appeared that there was a similarity in the course content, but the titles of the courses were different.

Participants reported that to ensure that students are able to clarify philosophical and theoretical concepts and apply them to their practical counselling work there needed to be sufficient emphasis on reading and written work. Thorne and Dryden (1991) emphasize that while training for counselling, it is important to consider the cultural background and context that the students came from. Additionally, participants revealed that the training should include concepts from other social sciences, in order to develop perspective. Elements of human development and theory had to be integrated into the programme in order to make it meaningful for the students.

All the diploma programmes introduced aspects of the counselling process and skills, accompanied by theoretical perspectives on therapy and intervention. There was an introduction to development over the lifespan and psychopathology. Vocational and educational guidance was the core component of one of the diploma programmes. For the 2-year degree programmes, there was some parity in courses across the two universities to which the four colleges were affiliated. Inputs on psychological assessment, therapeutic interventions and practicum components were provided in the degree programmes, which were not there in the diploma and short-term programmes.

There was a defined and definite structure in the programmes with reference to the courses offered. Courses were offered according to a specific calendar, which the students were expected to follow. When the programmes followed a semester system, the students took a minimum of 3–4 courses in a semester. One of the diploma programmes and three of the degree programmes followed this pattern. In the case of a year-long programme, the student was also expected to take a similar number of 3–4 courses. Two of the diploma programmes offered six and eight courses per year.

Views about the course content and the way in which they were structured along with the duration of the programme were interesting. The director or coordinator of the diploma and short-term programmes were satisfied with the structure and duration of the programmes offered by them, though issues such as longer training period and supervised internships were mentioned. A participant from a diploma programme opined about course content, 'The programme is good but more emphasis should be put on practicum. We cover much more practicum than mentioned in prospectus'.

In the case of the 2-year degree courses, it was seen that course revision took time, because of the formal structure in place for such revision. All revisions and changes had to be put forward and approved by a Board of Studies before they could be implemented. This often meant that individual faculty members and course coordinators did not have actual control over updating course content. If faculty members were senior enough to serve on the Board of Studies, they could steer the changes needed in the curriculum, as they desired. The revisions in the 2-year degree programme generally happened every 5 years. This was unlike the short-term programmes and the diploma programmes run by private institutes, where there was flexibility and possibility to revise the courses according to the needs of the participants and other faculty.

Six out of ten participants had made revisions in their programme over time. The revisions pertained to adding components that were felt to be missing in the existing curriculum; aspects such as disability were included. Revisions and modifications were based on feedback and the need of the students. Inputs from boards of studies, panel experts, faculty members, professionals, and students were taken during the revision process. Three institutes spoke of revisions in the programme content, with emphasis on internships which were supervised and more rigorous practice components.

7.7 Teaching

Participants in the study were asked about the teaching methods used for transacting the course. The didactic mode of lectures were the instructional mode most commonly used across programmes. Four programmes mentioned using panel discussions. Only one programme, a short-term course, mentioned using video and audio recording as a teaching method. Case presentations were mentioned, as also were role-plays and discussions on films and books. The degree courses mentioned peer mentoring for student learning. Only two programmes, a short-term programme and a diploma programme, made variations in their use of methods of teaching as per requirement, while rest of the programmes used a specified method of teaching for the entire programme. It was observed that one short-term programme had live counselling sessions with case presentations which were practice-based learning for their students. One of the diploma programmes asserted that the entire course was practice based which included training in skills, work with clients and self-work. Fieldwork and visits, mock sessions, enhanced training programme, community outreach programme visits and experts' discussion, practicum, internship, and case study were the other methods through which practice-based learning happened in the 2-year degree programmes.

Diploma programmes and 2-year degree programmes had books, journals, handouts, faculty resources, journal articles, and psychological tests available in their library and department. Two of the diploma programmes mentioned not having relevant books and journals in their library for the courses. Readings in Marathi were available for students doing the programme in that medium; however, the instructor said, 'Though we have readings in medium of instruction, i.e. Marathi, but we encourage students to read English books as well, so as to improve communication'. Another participant from a 2-year degree programme said, 'We do not want to make student dependent on us by spoon feeding, they are at PG level so our preference is to encourage them to search for books and do referencing on their own'.

7.8 Fieldwork

In this study, seven institutes had fieldwork or a practice element, as an integral component in their programme (one short-term programme, two diploma programmes and all the 2-year degree programmes). The nature of the fieldwork varied as follows:

- Short-Term Programme: Field visits to institutions, observations and writing of personal experience, practical work internships.
- Diploma Programme: Two programmes had the concept of working with clients identified by the student, followed by supervision. Another diploma programme expected fieldwork of at least 10 h of work per week in any setting offering counselling services, such as in voluntary organizations, private clinics, schools, vocational guidance centres, etc. Another programme had organizational visits, a counselling assessment workshop and field placement in a variety of settings as a form of fieldwork.
- 2-Year Degree Programme: One of the 2-year degree programmes required students learn administration, scoring and interpretation of psychological tests for individuals and for groups. Case studies, field visits to different institutions, conducting workshops and exhibitions on specific topics at schools and colleges all formed part of the fieldwork. For the three other degree programmes, the internship format as prescribed by the university was placement in settings such as schools, remand homes, old age homes, etc. Each student was expected to do individual case studies with two children and one adolescent in the first semester and five adult case studies with tests administered and counselling sessions, and one case study of a senior citizen in the second semester.

The number of hours of actual fieldwork varied across the programmes. It was reported that students had 8–20 h of fieldwork per week. One of the diploma programmes which did not have fieldwork expected 20–25 h of counselling done by the student; another diploma programme had 1 month block placement so there was approximately 36 h per week; three of the 2-year degree programmes had fieldwork three times a week which resulted in 18 h fieldwork per week in a semester.

Fieldwork for students was planned and structured through coordination with agencies for chalking out the programme, and the role of the student in the field setting. Choice of fieldwork settings was determined partly by interest and work areas of the students, and geographical proximity. Records of fieldwork were variously maintained across the programmes; most of the programmes required students to maintain journals or a diary as a record of their fieldwork. One of the diploma institutes made their students submit summary reports to the agency and faculty.

Supervision was offered both for individuals, and for groups of students. Modes of supervision included listening to taped recordings of sessions, use of transcripts, case discussions and journals. The frequency of students meeting their supervisor varied from twice a week in some programmes to once a month in others.

Participants were asked whether there was adequate field exposure for students. It was found that three institutes (one short-term programme, one diploma programme, one 2-year degree programme) felt it was adequate and four felt it was not (two diploma programmes, two 2-year degree programmes) because there was scope for improvement. They opined that the number of hours and number of case studies should be increased. Trainers from the degree programme in Marathi said that when there was inadequate fieldwork exposure they asked the student to change the setting..

Most participants reported that it was important to provide supervision in order to help students stay motivated and to get direction. Opinions about the format for supervision however, varied. A trainer from a 2-year degree programme said, 'Students should work under experienced counsellor once in a week; maintain the record of the day. Thereafter should discuss about those cases with the supervisor. This is like 'on the job training''. Yet another diploma programme trainer shared about the significance of supervision:

> Without supervision, fieldwork is like a shot in the dark. You'll just be functioning with the common sense. Idea is to remove it (common sense), and to replace it with professional understanding. It's only supervision which can bring a professional behaviour, understanding, attitudes.

A trainer at a 2-year degree programme said, 'We maintain records and cross-check things. As there are many girls we do not do regular supervision but if required and once in a month we visit for supervision in fieldwork setting'. From the remark, it appeared that they did not have sufficient trainers or staff, which may have resulted in inadequate supervision. The number of students admitted in this institute was 20–30. Considering about 25 students per year, a minimum of 5 teachers would be required. An interesting fact was the same institute referred the ideal faculty–student ratio as '1:10' which meant the current staff of three should have been able to handle 30 students, yet they were facing challenges with 25 students.

Fieldwork was a part of a student's evaluation and this evaluation happened through processes such as maintaining record forms (feedback form) by supervisors in the field and at the institute, and personal discussions with students. Grading of fieldwork; case study discussion and presentation; examination of test reports and interpretation; therapy with clients; presentation of block fieldwork at the end of the course; evaluation form for fieldwork being filled by teachers, students, and the organization, followed by discussion; the students' ability to take forward their learning to actual practice and plans for the same, i.e. ability to link theory with practice, were some of the methods used. The different modalities of fieldwork, the structuring, supervision and grading, and record keeping used in the various settings is depicted in Fig. 7.1.

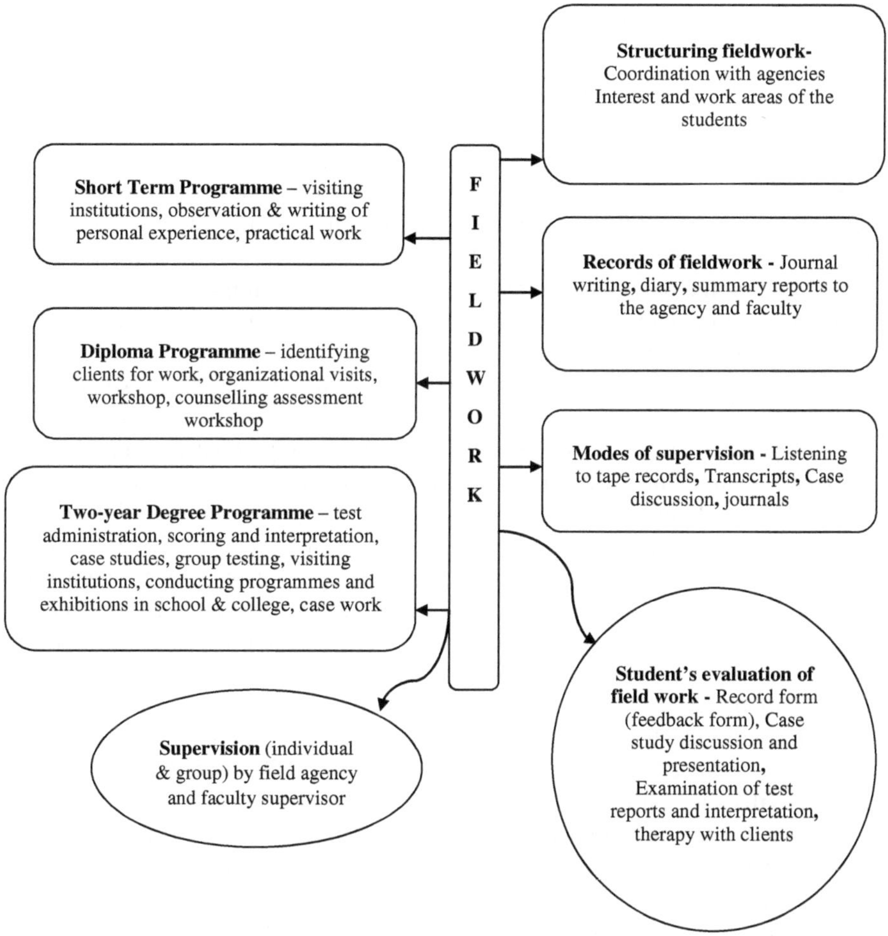

Fig. 7.1 Fieldwork

For the short-term programme which did not have fieldwork, the assumption was that the lack of fieldwork did not adversely affect the quality of the programme. The explanation given was,

> On the contrary, have I wondered in the name of fieldwork, very often people waste time. Here, we are teaching the techniques which has to be taught only in the presence of the trainer. Students do practice within their own group or with people in home [*sic*]. We encourage them to practice the skills in all the informal relationships because counselling skills are very highly refined communication. If one has to practice it, why can't they practice it otherwise, why do they need someone in counselling session? We encourage them to use counselling skills from day 1 in all their informal interactions.

7.9 Personal Development

According to Thorne and Dryden (1991, p. 15), trainees should be provided with learning opportunities through the means of self-exploration, supervised work with clients, the acquisition of counselling skills and counselling theory and relevant academic material. Personal therapy is a crucial factor of counselling training. It is recommended that counsellors or psychotherapeutic practitioners undergo therapy to resolve personal issues and to experience being a client to feel what it is like to sit on the other side of table. Resolving ones own issues becomes important before commencing with practice. There are more chances of transference and counter transference if the practitioner's self-healing has not happened. In order to build self-confidence and ability to think rationally one of the aids is personal therapy.

In the present study, all the institutes stated positively about the importance of personal development of the student being part of the programme at their institute. This was definitely an encouraging sign, every institute mentioned items such as: *self-exploration*, *group activity*, *individual activity*, *personal therapy* and *reflection through journal writing*, as being a part of the programme. In one short-term programme, they had workshops for self-development for the students. Another short-term programme used the first week of the programme for sensitivity training, 'In sensitivity training they go through series of exercises where they work on themselves. They share their own inner issues with the class in a particular format thus sharpening their skills'. One of the diploma programmes had sessions on self-esteem, self-exploration, leadership skills, assertiveness, communication skills, etc., built into the curriculum. These exercises appeared to be similar to what Thorne and Dryden (1991, p. 18) referred to as personal development groups, where trainees were given a chance to explore their relationships with one another and to benefit from the curative factors that groups provide (e.g. universality, cohesion and interpersonal feedback). They provided a platform for the airing and resolving of interpersonal conflicts among trainees which may otherwise spill over to other parts of the course and thereby inhibit learning.

None of the degree programmes mentioned a separate component on personal development of the counsellor in the curriculum, indicating that such processes did not necessarily find space in a structured degree programme.

7.10 Evaluation

Written evaluation in the form of end of term examinations and class assignments were used by most of the programmes. Other forms of written evaluation included journal writing. Some programmes included evaluation formats of practical exam such as role-plays, and viva voce as well. A research project was a compulsory part of the curriculum in one of the 2-year degree programmes and one of the one-year diploma programmes. In contrast, the three other degree programmes had a research project as an optional element.

Class assignments could be case discussions, which were monitored, along with practice sessions. Efforts were made to ensure that confidentiality was strictly maintained in the classroom. Case presentations were used by the degree programmes, along with workshops and book reviews. One of the short-term programme trainers said, ‘In the advanced training in counselling based on cognitive behaviour, we tell the students to record the case and write the transcription of the entire recording as it is and submit to us, and then it is evaluated’.

While methods of evaluating performance differed across the programmes, it was observed that emphasis was given on practical application of theory and students’ effectiveness in handling theory and learning from it. An appealing response from an instructor in a diploma programme was, ‘Evaluation has to match the objectives. So there is no one best way, it depends on the objectives’.

7.11 Placement Opportunities

It was found that eight institutes provided students with placement opportunities. Both short-term programmes, two diploma programmes and all the 2-year degree programmes had the facility of offering placement opportunities. This placement was regulated by bodies within the institute, with participation from the students completing the programme.

As an instructor from one of the 2-year degree programmes said,

> There is a placement cell but mostly the head of department and lecturers guide students. They are aware about vacancies through ex-students who approach them to say, ‘Our supervisors are very happy about the training our college gives, so they want to know if you could recommend someone else for our place’. Also, MA-2 students performance impresses most agencies where students are placed and most get absorbed there itself. Every student is helped during the course to find out her area of passion through counsellor series, guest lectures, field visits and then the selection of field of work becomes easy for them. The Counsellor of India site provides useful information about vacancies and these mails would be put up on notice boards earlier. Now the mails are forwarded by a lecturer to the Yahoo groups formed by each batch.

Data showed that 50–80 % of students continued to work in the field of counselling. Students completing the programmes were placed in varied settings, such as: voluntary organizations, helplines and employee assistance programmes, private clinics, day care and rehabilitation centres, hospitals, educational institutions, vocational guidance agencies, schools (normal and special needs), corporate and research organizations.

Participants said that graduating students kept in touch with the institute and the faculty members. In most cases, the institute kept track of where the alumni were working through student forum, internet (email), mobile contacts, invitation for talks and seminars. In most cases, records of alumni were maintained, along with their biodata. The alumni group served as a possible route for placement of students, both for fieldwork and for jobs. One of the instructors in a 2-year degree programme said,

> If we get information about any vacancy we forward those details. After completion of programme if student feel they require revision of some tests or if anything is not clear then we do allow them to sit for classes with ongoing batch.

7.12 Experience as Practitioners

All participants affirmed the importance of practising as a counsellor even if they were not currently practising. It was found that eight participants practised as counsellors or psychotherapists in the field. When asked about how practice helped, one of the trainers said, 'It helps give practical, hands on job approach and also helps to give enough case studies'.

Yet another trainer said,

> Yes of course, the trainer has to be a practising counsellor otherwise the trainer should not be trainer. Yes, we are very insistent about it. How can a trainer not be practising: then what are you teaching? Only a practising counsellor or psychotherapist should be a trainer.

Thorne and Dryden (1991) also raised similar issues, where they said,

> Core members should themselves be practising counsellors and this goes without saying for there can be few occupations where the continuing interaction between practice and theory is of such primary value in the training process. The trainer who is no longer practicing as a counsellor will quickly lose the immediacy of experience which provides the major stimulus for creativity and is the principal source of his or her credibility in the eyes of trainees. (p. 13)

Along with keeping abreast of personal area of counselling training, it is necessary for trainers to keep track of developments in the counselling field. The 'self' of the trainer and supervisor needs to be ensured through continuing professional enhancement; accompanied by availability for supervision, good quality of life, relationships and leisure. This can help in preventing burnout and the growing counselling field will be supported. There is a need for organizing refresher courses for supervisors to give new orientations.

For the trainers' own development, it was seen that participants attended workshops and tried to keep abreast with the new developments in the field. Efforts were made to find out about the ongoing research in order to keep abreast with the developments in the field. This was specially the case when the institute they were working in did not offer specific opportunities for the development of the trainer.

When participants were asked about the challenges and problems that they faced in running the training programmes, some of the issues raised related to matters of submission of assignments and journals by students. In time bound programmes, it was sometimes difficult to ensure that all students completed the required assignments on time. Other issues related to ‘finding means to teach a heterogeneous group’ and, ‘getting students in touch with themselves’ were expressed. A similar concern was also raised by one of the trainers in a 2-year degree programme where she said,

> Students come from different backgrounds and getting all of them to look in the same direction as our goals is challenging. Concepts of ‘right’ and ‘wrong’ are already formed, so instilling values in some of them becomes challenging. Many of the current batches have only short-term gains in mind and many throw a lot of attitude.

Limitation of time was seen as an issue by some trainers. This was the case in some of the practicum training. If attitude change had to be brought about, it need not happen in the limited time duration of the programme; it was hoped that some of the seeds of change would be sown during the programme. Providing good role models during training, and providing opportunities for development were mechanisms that could result in attitude change. Some issues such as dealing with alcoholism and marriage conflicts were difficult to convey in a classroom setting. Another challenge faced by trainers was related to the need to keep oneself updated and informed about the recent changes and innovations in the field. It was necessary for the trainers to keep themselves abreast with the ongoing developments through books and journals available.

For a participant who coordinated the 2-year degree programme in vernacular medium the issue was related to criticism received from outside about the course content. She said:

> We are criticized as our course is new, so we don’t have teachers with good work experience. People have doubts about the course but we are confident of what we are providing for our students. The challenge is to maintain the effort and try for the best. We make an effort for our students’ improvement in English communication as English is a language in demand in the market; we refer to English books and also ask them to translate text from Marathi to English.

7.13 Future of Counselling as a Profession

When the participants were asked about the future of the counselling profession, all the respondents said that in the present situation, there was a tremendous need for trained counsellors. The unfortunate part of it was that there were not enough institutions to provide training. As one of the trainers who ran a short-term programme said,

> There should be more available counsellors who will listen to people and counsel people. Thus, there should be more training programmes where more training will be provided; we are unable to meet the demands of the society. The amount of pain that exists in families, couples … the number of counsellors actually available is disproportionately low. People are suffering, so there is definitely an increasing need of more people to be counsellors or [those who] can function as counsellors.

They mentioned that apart from training more counsellors, it is also important to recognize that the training should be practical and relevant, with an emphasis on skills, so that they can deal with the problems that they confront. The challenge was to be able to function according to ethical and moral principles when confronted with difficulties in the field. This challenge could only be met through adequate training.

One of the factors stressed by a trainer was related to more people willing to come for counselling. This was considered as one of the significant changes over time, with people willing to spend money to see a professional counsellor. However, many clients wanted quick solutions, and were resistant to come for a number of sessions, even if necessary. This was accompanied by an increase in awareness about the need for counselling in schools, hospitals, and other private institutions, which were employing counsellors, and were referring patients and clients for counselling if needed. It sometimes became the responsibility of the trainers and the training institutes to inform about the job opportunities and put people in touch, especially if the contacts had not been built.

While the profession was growing, it was beset by the problem of low salary. The poor income that came in the beginning was one of the factors that made fresh trainees reluctant to enter the field. The low salary may be responsible for counsellors losing heart and eventually leaving the field. The training did not help the counsellor reconcile with such issues; this was expressed by a number of trainers.

A lecturer from one of the 2-year degree programmes brought up the issue of specialized degree courses in counselling, with graduates with Counselling Psychology having skills above and beyond those available for social workers and diploma holders. She lamented, 'Today anyone comes in with a diploma or certificate course and declares oneself as a counsellor. This should not happen. Counselling psychologists and counsellors are different. Students with only a diploma are allowed to practice'.

In her opinion, this should not be so, and there should be notice and recognition given to students who have studied for 2 years, learned theories and therapies and done fieldwork in supervised settings. This view was echoed by others teaching in degree programmes. Participants felt that large gaps existed between the available training and the demands of counselling field. These gaps were primarily because of the nature of the training which was not practice based. One of the trainers in a diploma programme felt that the need for the short-term courses came up because many of the existing courses were not practical in orientation. In the words of a trainer from a short-term programme,

> At present whatever training programmes are available, most of them are theory based and I am very unhappy with that because students who have done these programmes have come here, and they don't know the practicality. We wonder … so and so has done such and such programme at such place … we wonder how can one still be raw, why haven't they learnt earlier?

The gap between theory and practice was reiterated by more than one trainer. There was often a lack of confidence in trainers to demonstrate actual procedures, which would be of great help in practical learning. In such situations, the availability of practitioners for teaching was clearly advantageous; practitioners brought their case experiences and knowledge into the classroom, using the case material to substantiate the theory components.

Many trainers were of the opinion that the duration of most training programmes was insufficient, irrespective of the length. In a diploma programme, one academic year was felt to be insufficient to provide the kind of supervised learning that was essential for the development of the field. It would also be beneficial to the students if exposure in more than one field setting could be provided. An increase in the time in the field would be of great use for the potential counsellor. One of the faculty teaching in a 2-year degree course said that she noticed the gaps in training once she entered the field. She felt that she had not had sufficient exposure as practicum. She said, 'When I graduated I realized there are gaps in training provided to us. We didn't have such proper practicum, etc. So I tried to fill the gap by providing appropriate things for my students, which I didn't receive'.

An issue raised by one of the participants related to the fact that specialized settings often required specialized techniques and methods. It may not be possible to provide all such inputs in a training programme. In such cases, it may be necessary for additional training to acquire competencies once the basic training was over. Retraining and updating of skills was felt to be essential, given that new methods of counselling were always being developed.

Another gap that was expressed was related to the inadequate research being done in the field of counselling. One of the diploma programme participants expressed that there was need for research to fill gaps in knowledge about what the demands were from the field, and how to meet those demands. Such research was not being emphasized on. It is pertinent to note here that only one of the 2-year degree programmes and one diploma programme had research as an essential component of the programme. In case of the other colleges offering degree programmes, research was optional, and not many students did the research project, instead preferring to do additional practicum hours.

All participants expressed the opinion that licensing was needed in the field of counselling. A commonly expressed view was that the absence of a licensing body resulted in untrained people entering the field, claiming to be counsellors. As one of the trainers who taught in a 2-year degree course said,

> There are pseudo-counsellors as there is no licensing body in India. They are not trained counsellors. They can't help resolve the problems of people. They don't counsel but just give advice to their clients. The problem remains as it is. As a result of this people think that counsellors are unable to help them.

This opinion was variously expressed by all the participants. It was felt that some forms of counselling, such as career counselling was seen as being very lucrative. This meant that it could be seen as a means to make money, without providing the essentials of counselling. The view that the term 'counsellor' was loosely and inappropriately used was expressed by one of the participants. It was felt that licensing would result in some restrictions about what counselling was, and what counsellors did. Licensing would be a means of ensuring the job description of counsellors. As a trainer from a short-term programme said, 'Seriousness and standardization are the main requirement of growth which is missing in the field today' Hence licensing was a means of ensuring quality of services being provided. Licensing would also ensure that unethical practices in the field would not be allowed.

Yet another trainer who ran a short-term course expressed the opinion that the Government, whose duty and role it was to ensure standards, was doing very little to ensure that some standards were being maintained. He was of the opinion that introducing licensing would only result in corruption. In his words,

> Now, of course, the government does things in a shoddy manner; it will recruit a group of people who are themselves corrupt. They will take money and will give a licence wrongly. That's why sometimes I feel, let things be as they are.

At the same time, he also felt that licensing should be introduced, and the licensing body should have the right to examine candidates, issue licences to successful candidates for fixed periods. After the lapse of that period, the licence would have to be renewed.

One participant felt that licensing could be detrimental for growth in the field. This participant said that licensing had a pro and a con. In terms of the negative aspects of licensing, this participant felt that it would limit the number of people entering the field. At present, in the absence of a licensing body, there is growth in the number of counsellors. Additionally, given that the field was still growing in India, she opined that licensing be introduced only after a certain level of professionalism was reached. In her words,

> There is freedom now that people with counselling skills in spite of not having a licensing body are getting into it. People are already getting trained; see, if there were a licensing body they would not be practising. So the field is already growing, but once the field has grown, what we need to do is now make it more refined.

When asked about who should do the licensing, the commonly held view was that it should be a body made up of counsellors in the field, trained psychologists and psychiatrists. As one of the participants from a short-term programme said, 'A uniform group headed by prominent psychiatrists and psychologists who would screen every professional, visit the place of work, regularly conduct workshops and conduct upgrading programmes'. It was felt that this body could have elected representatives who could function under government control. It was shared that it may be necessary to set up such up bodies at both the State and the Central level. The need for a government initiative was clearly articulated, which helped bring together the voices of the various psychology associations that are presently functioning in the country.

One trainer who taught in a diploma course was more cynical about the process and the outcome of licensing, while holding on to the belief that licensing was the right thing for the growth of the profession in the country. He said, 'All the licensing bodies in India are more like a 'damage control mechanism' to protect misuse of services'. He gave the example of the Medical Council of India which had been under controversy. He went on to say, 'However, for me it must be a proactive measure to provide more quality service to those who are in need'.

With reference to the counselling profession's prospect for growth in Mumbai and in India, participants responded that there was extremely bright scope for the profession of counselling in the light of rising necessity of it in the increasingly competitive twenty-first century. The need for counselling was felt in a variety of settings and not just limited to 'conventional form of counselling'. As one of the participants from the 2-year degree programme said,

> The 20th century was the era of anxiety but 21st century is full of stress. Right from the school age we face different problems. Lots of adjustment problems in individual and social life are being faced by the people. They need trained experts to help them resolve their problems. Counsellors are required in schools, colleges, in social settings, in industries and other organizations.

The need for counselling was reiterated by the other participants as well. It was necessary to try to create awareness in people. Even professionals such as doctors were not aware of the benefits of counselling. A participant said, 'Growth is slow but it is happening for sure. People did not have any idea, as in, there are doctors who did not know what and how counselling is actually. I have to give lectures to them on what is counselling'.

Participants shared that there was still lack of clarity between counselling and advice—counselling has often been considered as a kind of advice giving. It was necessary to write more about counselling to prepare publicity materials that could be distributed to the public. Writing about counselling in newspapers helped in spreading awareness about the nature and scope of the field. It was felt that there was awareness about the field of counselling in metropolitan cities such as Mumbai. However, in smaller places, the appreciation was low, and the spread of the profession was slow. This did not mean that there was no need for counselling in smaller towns; it was just that the penetration was poor. The fact was that the number of counsellors in the field was much lower than the required numbers. This disparity between supply and demand was also responsible for inadequately and poorly trained people entering the field. There needed to be more colleges that offered quality training in the country. In the words of a trainer from one of the 2-year degree programmes,

> Preparing as many as possible good psychologists with proper knowledge is essential for people to solve their problems. Colleges offering PG programmes are also very few; so, there is a lot of scope and demand for the counselling profession; it is the need of the hour.

7.14 The Road Ahead

The field of counselling in Mumbai is still in the early stages of development. It is a new professional field for both the supply and demand sides. It is still to develop as a strong independent entity. There is a growing demand for more training programmes, trainers, and trained counsellors, with the requisite skills. The demand has arisen as an indicator of a greater need for counselling services by people. The need has always been there, but has been suppressed by cultural beliefs in India.

Indian cultural norms do not allow or encourage sharing of emotions; and when it comes to a 'counsellor' who is a third person, it becomes 'taboo'. We have been 'socialized' to believe that it is not good to share emotions or personal/family matters with a stranger. Alongside, there is the stigma associated with mental illness and seeking help for the same. Seeking counselling is seen as the 'last resort' in resolving a 'problem' due to the common tendency to procrastinate over the problem, and the added resistance to avail of outside help.

Despite several cultural beliefs and resistance towards seeking help and counselling, the scene is improving in urban middle and higher middle class populations who are the seeking counselling support. In this section of the society, there is an increasing awareness about counselling, and why professional help should be sought, when necessary.

The present study indicated that the content, nature and kind of practical counselling experience varied across programmes, with varying expectations from students. There is no grounding in the design of the fieldwork modules across institutes and universities. This is compounded by differences in the number of hours that students are required to spend in the field; all institutes have different requirements about how many hours students spend in the fieldwork setting. There is clear absence of uniformity about fieldwork, and the absence of uniformity does not mean that institutes are not providing thorough training.

However, there need to be guidelines for 'training in counselling' through which some common parameters should emerge, to become the compulsory part of that training and which represents the counselling training curriculum. This is particularly important for the professionalization of the field. To realize this, it is important to standardize the curriculum across all the institutes followed by the need to form a regulatory body which can look at these affairs more systematically. Currently there are no defined guidelines in India to decide programme duration and to scrutinize and supervise the curriculum. Short-term and diploma programmes can be started by institutes and individuals according to their own preference and convenience. Overall standardization of the programme will take care of variations in the programme design. The programme duration needs to be regulated according to the demands from the field and the needs of the students.

It is important to recognize that the aims of the three types of programmes are substantially different. Short-term programmes offered by practitioners are useful for professionals in the field to update themselves on new models and practices in counselling. This service is essential. However, the practice of trainees completing a short-term programme of a few weeks' duration in counselling and then setting up practice as a counsellor is more problematic. Institutes that offer short-term programmes offer their training for people from diverse arenas of life, often without even having an understanding about the issues that confront individuals over the lifespan. The short-term programmes may be excellent as means of increasing awareness about the need for counselling and the nature of issues that may be amenable to counselling. The risks of applying this learning without supervision and exposure to fieldwork in diverse settings have to be considered and examined.

Diverse fieldwork settings are necessary to broaden students' exposure and experience. This necessitates widening the network and collaboration with a variety of field settings, making them understand what counselling is and what students should be provided in order to aid in their theoretical understanding, and building the linkages between theory and practice. It is necessary to increase the awareness about counselling across a variety of settings and professions.

Providing counselling services in a culturally diverse country like India, requires culturally competent counsellors, who can work with people from different caste, ethnic, sociocultural, economic, regional and linguistic backgrounds. The study demonstrated that there was a lacuna of ethical training or ethics component as part of teaching. This is an aspect of training that requires attention.

The trainer's job in the counselling training is a herculean task, and is an emotionally taxing experience where they deal with responsibilities not only of teaching, but also of mentoring students for the 'real' practice. It goes beyond mere teaching, in that there is the need to integrate theory with practice. The fact that many trainers are themselves practitioners increases the pressures on them. While being practitioners allows the ready integration of cases into theory lessons as illustrations, there is the added responsibility of training potential counsellors, and translating the lessons learned through practice into the classroom, and building theory.

There is a paucity of indigenous theoretical perspectives on psychotherapy and counselling. Most of the therapeutic interventions referred to by the trainers in the study were drawn from the Western models of theory and practice. There is a need for the development of indigenous models of therapy that may build on Western models, but have more cultural relevance (Arulmani 2007; Kapur 2001). The integration of local level understanding about mental health and means of dealing with mental health with the western discourse communicated in the classrooms has to be brought about (Arulmani 2007; Kapur et al. 1996).

Membership to professional associations such as Counsellors' Association of India, Association of Indian School Counsellors and Allied Professionals, and the Indian Association of Clinical Psychologists provides an additional opportunity to meet once a year or on a six monthly basis, where trainers across programmes can meet, present papers on relevant issues and upcoming innovations and advances in the area of counselling and psychotherapy, followed by discussions. There should be more openness and exchange of thoughts among the practitioners across all the institutions. Additional research pertaining to the field of counselling training with new goals and objectives should be discussed adding to the knowledge base of counsellors. The contextual researches should be focussed upon to provide the counsellors with research based data in handling several different clients' issues.

There is a pressing need of having a 'licensing body'. All the participants in the study have supported the idea of a regulatory and licensing body. The modalities for the functioning of such a regulatory body need to be worked out. A licensing body can act as a body of scrutiny where a person with requisite qualifications will be examined, to determine the eligibility to practice as a counsellor or psychotherapist. This will help in providing counsellors with intensive quality training to enter the field, thereby enabling growth of skilled practitioners. The practice of referring and using the term 'counsellor' in the manner it currently is, will be managed and controlled.

Acknowledgments The authors would like to acknowledge the role of all the participants who took part in the study for their time and inputs.

References

Arulmani, G. (2007). Counselling psychology in India: at the confluence of two traditions. *Applied Psychology: An International Issue, 56*(1), 69–82.

India News: Mental Health. (2012). *Tracking mental health media coverage in India—by remindindianews*. The Vice President of India speaks on mental health from http://remindindianews.posterous.com/the-vice-president-of-india-speaks-on-mental/.

Kakuma, R., Minas, H., van Gineken, N., Desiraju, K., Morris, J. E., Saxena, S., & Scheffler, R. E. (2011). Human resources for mental health care: current situation and strategies for action. *Lancet*, pp. 1654–1663. doi:10.1016/S0140-6736(11)61093-3.

Kapur, M. (2001). Training objectives in psychotherapy from the perspective of clinical psychology. In: Kapur, Shamasundar, Bhatti (Eds.) *Psychotherapy training in India*. (2nd Edition). NIMHANS, Bangalore: Anju Graphics.

Kapur, M., Shamasundar, C., & Bhatti, R. S. (1996). *Introduction. Reprinted in Psychotherapy training in India. 2001* (2nd ed.). NIMHANS, Bangalore: Anju Graphics.

Manickam, L. S. S. (2010). Psychotherapy in India. *Indian Journal of Psychiatry, 52*(Supplement), 366–370.

Thorne, B., & Dryden, W. (1991). Approaches to the training of counsellors. In W. Dryden (Ed.), *Training and supervision for counselling in action* (pp. 15–32). London: SAGE Publications.

Varma, V. K. (1982). Present state of psychotherapy in India. *Indian Journal of Psychiatry, 24*(3), 209–226.

Chapter 8
Exploring Expressions: Therapists' Use of the Creative Arts in Therapy

Afshan Mariam and Aparna Joshi

Abstract Arts such as painting, dance, drama or music have been part of Indian culture since ancient times. The use of creative arts in therapy (CAT) is a modern profession, still in a fledgling stage in India, with few trained individuals. A qualitative study to explore experiences of ten therapists using CAT (art, dance, drama, music and intermodal) for mental health in Mumbai, Chennai and Bengaluru, was carried out. The healing aspects of CAT included alternate expression, body mind connect and creativity. Therapists highlighted the unique features of the therapeutic processes such as use of physical space and arts materials, use of metaphors and symbols, use of art work for expression, assessment and intervention and use of rituals.

Keywords Creative arts therapy · Dance therapy · Music therapy · Art therapy · Metaphor · Symbols

While talk is still the traditional method of exchange in therapy, practitioners using creative arts in therapy know that people also have different styles of expressing—one may be more visual, another more tactile and so forth. The creative arts therapies (CAT) include art therapy, dance/movement therapy, drama therapy, music therapy, poetry therapy and psychodrama. These therapies use arts modalities and creative processes during intentional intervention in therapeutic, rehabilitative, community or educational settings to foster health, communication and expression; they promote the integration of physical, emotional, cognitive and social functioning, enhance self-awareness, and facilitate change (National Coalition of Creative Arts Therapies Association 2011).

Afshan Mariam (✉)
Chennai, India
e-mail: afshanmariam15@gmail.com

Aparna Joshi
School of Human Ecology, TISS, Mumbai, India

S. Sriram (ed.), *Counselling in India*, DOI 10.1007/978-981-10-0584-8_8

Art, dance and music therapy, as they are now practised, were formally organized in the twentieth century. Before that time, art, dance and music played an informal, although continuous role in Eastern and Western medicine. Through the centuries, the healing nature of these creative therapies has been primarily reported in anecdotes that describe a way of restoring wholeness to a person struggling with either mind or body illness (Pratt 2004). Music, dance, drama, etc., have been a part of rituals and healing practices since ancient times. There have been documented reports of the use of the arts, highlighting their effectiveness as an aid in healing practices of physical and mental illnesses. As a result, an art therapist or music therapist is now recognized as complementary healthcare professionals in countries such as the United States, Britain and other developed countries.

8.1 History of Creative Arts Therapies

The use of arts as a method of healing can be traced back to ancient times across cultures. In the Greek civilization, the God of medicine, Apollo was also the God of music. Greek philosophers Plato and Aristotle promoted the use of music as they felt that music had mood altering effects. The cathartic effects of drama were also advocated in the Greek culture. In the east, the Samaveda chant is said to bring about harmony, well-being and balance to the body, mind and soul. Ayurveda still advocates the use of music, mantra and sounds for healing at a deep level (Ranade and Ranade 2004).

If we look at history in the West of how the arts entered the realm of healing in the twentieth century, we can see that several influential figures advocated them. The work of Freud and Jung introduced the therapeutic benefits of using arts in therapy. Freud (1923) understood creative expression as a defence mechanism that allows the transfer of sexual impulses and anxieties towards a more socially acceptable form. This he felt could lead to catharsis. Jung's work was related to his examination and use of universal archetypes in artistic expression. Jung himself continued to explore his inner psyche by drawing and sculpting. He felt that art allowed him to examine his inner world and create a bridge between the demands of his inner needs and the outer world (Gladding 2011). Apart from the few mentioned above, under each modality there have been crusaders who have taken up the cause and gained support from the community around him or her.

Another reason for the growth of CAT that has been cited in literature was the need for novel ways of dealing with the World War II veterans. Apart from the talk therapies, inclusion of other non-intrusive forms of healing such as arts, dance, drama, music and literature was considered important. The interest of health care practitioners was piqued and the arts as an adjunct to traditional healing practices was further explored. Professional associations were formed, universities started to provide degrees in arts therapies and journals publishing the effectiveness of these therapies were circulated in the academic milieu.

At the beginning of the twenty-first century, the creative arts therapies are firmly established as an important part of complementary medicine for psychological and physiological illnesses. The arts therapies are being used in every facet of medical practice such as hospitals, hospices, other health care institutions and private practice (Pratt 2004).

8.2 Creative Arts Therapies and Their Effectiveness

Several studies highlight benefits of the use of the creative arts as effective therapeutic tools. Research on the effectiveness of art therapy as mentioned in the review article by Slayton et al. (2010), which identifies studies from 1999–2007 that measured effectiveness of art therapy, across age, with clinical and nonclinical populations. The authors identified a small body of research that reported art therapy was statistically significant in improving a variety of issues such as cancer, sexual abuse, physical illness and behavioural issues for a broad range of people and ages.

Music therapy has been used across age groups to deal with a diverse range of issues. Among children and adolescents, music therapy interventions have been effective in dealing with behavioural and developmental issues (Voracek et al. 2004); reducing depression and increasing self-concept (Hendricks 2001); and facilitating self-expression (Montello and Coons 1998). Among adults, music therapy has been seen to reduce emotional distress (Chang and Chung 2008; Benenzon 1981); to achieve clinically relevant goals among individuals with psychosis (Silverman 2003; Pavlicevic et al. 1994; Tang et al. 1994). Music therapy has been used to deal with emotional and interpersonal difficulties among individuals with chemical dependence (Dingle et al. 2007; Cevasco et al. 2005).

Drama therapy has been used widely among children along the autistic spectrum to help them develop socioemotional functioning skills (Corbett et al. 2011). The arts have been perceived as serving a ‘unique voice’ for this group with limited communication and verbal skills (Schonmann 2011). Drama therapy has also been used extensively among individuals who have experienced trauma such as sexual abuse or war (Grayer 2005; Mulky 2004; James and Johnson 1996; Mackay 1989) and with individuals who have experienced symptoms of psychosis (Casson 2004).

Dance and movement therapy has broad applicability as well—among adolescents to address body image issues (Emunah 1990); among women who have been sexually abused (Meekums 2000); among older adults to improve memory, alertness, judgment and personal insight (Ashley and Crenan 1993).

The integrated arts approach or the intermodal approach (also known as multimodal) therapy involves two or more creative arts therapies to foster awareness, encourage emotional growth and enhance relationships with others. This approach is also referred to as expressive therapy. Intermodal therapy distinguishes itself from its closely allied disciplines of art therapy, music therapy, dance/movement therapy and drama therapy by being grounded in the interrelatedness of the arts. It is based on a variety of orientations, including arts as therapy, arts as psychotherapy and the use of arts for traditional healing (Knill et al. 1995). Use of intermodal approach is effective in enhancing communication and social skills, improving emotional expression, bettering motor movement, stimulus perception and memory and reducing impulsive behaviours among individuals at a rehabilitation home for mentally challenged adults and a de-addiction centre (The World Centre for Creative Learning Foundation 2010).

8.3 Creative Arts Therapies in India

A web search of *arts therapy in India* provides a number of links which directs one towards newspaper articles, web pages and blogs, with a sporadic mention of the use of art, music or drama for specific populations. There are also various groups and social networks started by individuals sharing their common interest for using creative arts therapies. Books are available on the use of music therapy, which are written and published by Indians (Menen 1998, 2002).

The arts as therapy have been practised in India since ancient times. Music and dance have been associated with reaching transcendental states and relieving psychological distress. Every historical era has its collection of art work, dance, music and poetry. Communicating using artistic symbols has thus been an inherent part of the Indian mind—starting the day by creating *kolams*[1] on the entryway, initiation of religious ceremonies through dance and music, are few examples of how the arts have been a central way of communicating and expressing in Indian culture.

However, psychotherapy by itself has been a new field in India (Laungani 2004). The use of arts in a structured profession is still at its nascent stage (Kiran 2011). It is heralded by a select group of professionals who have either been self-trained or trained in courses abroad. Some of these individuals have started new initiatives in using creative arts therapies for addressing needs of specific groups such as children in special needs (RASA Centre for Theatre Arts and Special Needs 2007). Some on the other hand have undertaken pioneering efforts to initiate training courses for creating trained arts-based therapists (World Centre for Creative Learning Foundation 2010). There has been an increase in the use of CAT since the twenty-first century in India. This can be seen in the number of trusts and voluntary organizations that have adopted and promoted these therapies.

[1]*Kolam* refers to decorative patterns drawn with rice flour or white chalk powder drawn at the threshold of the house, by women. They are intended to bring prosperity to the household. There can be many motifs and designs in the *kolam*, representing creativity.

8.4 Researching Creative Arts Therapies in India

One of the needs that have been felt in the area of CAT across the globe is the generation of research (Gladding 2011). The need arises because the practice must be credible and accountable to the people involved in receiving the services as well as those who promote them. Such credibility can also promote the use of CAT and increase its recognition in the field of mental health (Malchiodi 2007). Given the nascent status of Creative Arts Therapies in India, there has been sparse research regarding the same. Some effectiveness studies have been carried out by Indian NGOs who use creative arts therapies in their intervention programmes and by those who offer training (Machado et al. 2005) but the results have limited circulation and have not entered academic circles.

This certainly points to a dire need to carry out research in the Indian context—to explore practitioner's perspectives of processes involved in therapeutic practices and interventions that use the creative arts, theory of change behind the same and the nature of the therapist client relationship. The present study was an attempt to answer some of these questions, related to understanding the processes involved in using the creative arts such as art, dance, drama and music in the therapeutic context. The study was exploratory in nature and adopted qualitative methods to obtain the subjective experiences of therapists using creative art(s). The methods allowed an openness to study the knowledge and practices of the respondents and take into account the diverse viewpoints and perspectives in the field influenced by their social reality (Flick 2010).

Ten participants were interviewed for the study. There were two therapists under each modality—visual art, dance, drama, music, expressive/intermodal approach. The respondents worked with mental health issues and self-identified as therapists using CAT. They were trained in the use of creative arts therapies through formal and informal means. Since there is no regularized body of certification in India to validate counselling practices, the criteria to select the sample was drawn based on whether or not they met the general criteria for a 'good informant' (Cresswell 2009). To ensure that the informant had the necessary knowledge and experience on the issue, a criterion of a minimum of 2 years of experience in the field, using creative art(s) in therapy was set. The informants of the study were located in Mumbai, Bengaluru and Chennai. The settings they worked from included schools, hospitals, corporate settings and privately owned spaces.

Data was collected using an interview guide. Verbal consent was obtained prior to data collection. Appointments were scheduled with the respondents. All the interviews were audio recorded after consent, except for one where notes were taken. The audio recordings were transcribed for analysis. Publicity material as well as information on websites and press coverage was collected. Field notes on each interview were maintained in a research diary.

Thematic analysis was used to code the data. Both concept-driven and data-driven coding were used to build themes from the transcribed interviews. The themes were the primary domains that guided the interview. However, it has been recognized that the data can also throw up new ideas and codes which the researcher must be able to adopt into a pre-existing framework (Gibbs and Gibbs 2008).

8.5 Theory of Change

Counselling is seen as a dynamic process. It consists of certain features which structure natural human interaction into a purposive and directed effort towards achieving a desired outcome. The respondents who took part in the study had different ideas of *why* the art(s) could be used as a tool for promoting the mental health of an individual or individuals; and what about the art form(s) they believed could be therapeutic for the individual(s) they were working with. The following section details therapists' theories of change.

8.5.1 Body Mind Connect

The use of arts in therapy is said to be experiential in nature (Malchiodi 2007), engaging all the senses. This stimulation of the senses is said to have an effect on the mind of the individual. The connection between the physical self and mental self is referred to as *body mind connect*. The therapists believe this to be one of the processes which benefits the individual.

Aahna, an art therapist, through her training in Reiki, was aware of the body–mind connect that the art processes have on a person. Reiki, as a healing practice, is based on the assumption that there are subtle energy fields that surround a person. Illnesses in the person can be due to these energy fields. Reorganization of the subtle energy fields can lead to relief from the illness (Wilson 2011). She wanted to bring in energy or consciousness, which was there and channelize that into her work.

The primary tool for intervention among dance therapists was the body. The philosophy of the dance therapists was based on the mind–body connection. The dance therapists encouraged expression of mental states through the body and attempted reorganization of the mental states through bodily movements.

Tripura, a dance therapist and a trainer said that a person was able to *speak* more authentically through the body because the 'movement' was more 'primal and instinctive'. Through this expression, emotions and feelings formerly suppressed were brought to the awareness of the individual, which could be therapeutic. This expression can also be interpreted by the dance therapist, allowing her to understand the client and assess ways in which the body can be reorganized to 'cultivate more wholesome personalities' (Kashyap 2005).

Shazneen, a dance therapist, worked on a similar philosophy of the body–mind connect. She suggested changes in body movements to her clients, if she found them stuck in certain aspects of their body. This was helpful in changing their perception of their bodies and mind. It helped clients express, connect and restructure one's inner state.

The music therapists utilized traditional Indian music to promote a healthier mental state. Their art form involved sound vibrations and frequencies. The quality of the sound had an impact on the physiological constitution of the individual, which in turn had an impact on the mental composition. Stimulation of the brain through sound vibrations regulated the brain in a balanced manner, proving to be therapeutic. Anjali, a music therapist, believed that musical expression helped the individual experience pleasure, as it was universally and inherently enjoyable. Anjali elaborated on this:

> Take the neurological element. … Even before the thoughts and feelings, music is directly experienced as a mechanical sound which is then transformed into an electrical signal. Music is a refined sound which naturally provides enjoyment. When we listen to music, the left brain dominates. The logical arrangement is processed by the left hemisphere. However, the aesthetic quality of the music is perceived by the right hemisphere. There is a transfer of information, as well as simultaneous activation of both sides of the brain. (Anjali, music therapist)

Vijay, a music therapist, drew his learning from his theoretical understanding of traditional music. The curative knowledge of particular ragas was an ancient tradition which remains relevant today. Ragas are related to the time of the day as they can regulate different mood levels and emotions (Menen 2002). Talking about his idea of why music is therapeutic, Vijay said, 'These chords… they trigger the brain chords… there are morning raga, night, midnight, post-midnight. As mood changes the ragas change…'.

8.5.2 Alternate form of Communication and Catharsis

The arts have the inherent ability to tap into the subconscious; as a result, more authentic and organic forms of expressions emerge. These lead to deeper insight which promotes problem resolution. The notion of the arts being an *alternate* expression that can lead to the achievement of therapeutic goals is one of the primary reasons cited by the therapists in the study.

Claire, an art therapist, defined art as allowing open expression. She saw artistic expression as a 'language' that could be seen as an alternative to words. She said,

> Once there is expression of the soul, the contents of the soul are purged; catharsis. This catharsis leaves an 'empty space' which needs to 'reorganized' into a healthier way of being. This reorganization is done through artistic expression- facilitated by the use of colours and exercises structured by the therapist. (Claire, art therapist)

The drama therapists working with children felt that drama processes replicated real life and contributed to 'holistic development'. Drama helped create a non-threatening environment whereby children were able to express themselves more openly, truthfully and innocently, allowing healing. Research on effectiveness of drama therapy has shown that it is capable of providing cognitive organization in autistic children (Chasen 2011).

Use of creative therapies is cathartic not only for young children, but also for their parents and adults in general. Bhavya, a therapist using the intermodal approach, found creative arts therapies helpful especially with adult clients, who had extreme difficulties in expressing their own feelings. Art became an easier way of communication and realization. The inherent ability of the art to tap into the subconscious allowed for a quicker bridging of the inner self and outer world leading to deeper insights and quicker problem resolution.

The expressive therapists, Theresa and Bhavya, emphasized the benefits that expression through dance, drama, music or imagery could have in comparison to verbal forms. Theresa felt that expression through arts not only led to a quicker resolution, but also provided a more enriching experience for the client. She illustrated this point through her personal experience with a client:

> I tell them to draw a barren tree and talk about a relationship that is troubling them now. They draw a barren tree and tell me that this is my marriage. Thus a symbol or a colour can take you very far. (Theresa, expressive therapist)

8.6 Nature of Therapeutic Relationship in Creative Art(S) Therapies

The relationship between a client and a therapist is compared to a social relationship where it is based on trust, safety, openness and sharing where both the individuals put in their effort and commitment to nurture it. However, the relationship is nurtured to meet the needs of one person—the client (Cormier and Hackney 1987). The relationship between the client and the therapist is based upon what the therapist thinks are the necessary conditions to meet the goals or desires of the client. Therapists used various descriptions to explain the nature of the therapeutic relationships. Some therapists talked about the facilitative nature of the therapeutic relationship, while others highlighted the importance of adopting a more directive stance.

Aahna, an art therapist, defined her relationship with the clients as being 'facilitative'. The only 'suggestion' given to the clients was to draw what they felt. Aahna said that the client's inner potential to heal, eventually allowed them to express themselves accordingly. She talked about having a tentative plan and theme for her work with her clients. But she also talked about changing the same to suit the clients' mood and needs. She opposed the idea of imposing the therapist's agenda on clients, and favoured the idea of giving them their space and being in synchrony with their needs. The expressive therapists emphasized the role of 'core qualities' such as empathy, genuineness and positive regard as necessary components for establishing a warm therapeutic relationship.

Tripura and Shazneen, the dance therapists, used their movements to communicate to their clients that they were on the same page. Tripura said that she liked to take a more 'participatory approach', wherein she joined the clients in their exercises and moved along with them. Shazneen emphasized the role of 'empathy' (also at a physical level), as she felt that it was only through moving authentically with the client, that the client could get in touch with his or her inner feelings and thoughts.

Both the drama therapists worked with children. Hence, their interaction was primarily that of facilitation, with emphasis on limit setting. They believed that the theatre arts helped develop children's abilities, creating a safe space. One of the drama therapists brought attention to the distinction between the more 'rigid teacher student relationship' and more 'fluid counsellor child relationship' that allowed for positive outcomes from the therapy session.

A group of therapists talked about the importance of adopting a directive stance in therapeutic relationship. One of the art therapists, Claire, believed that the role of the therapist was to be the higher voice who directs clients to paint in a style that can heal them. She talked about being similar to the master or conductor of the orchestra—telling people when to start and stop. This she said was particularly necessary during the later phases of therapy. She talked about an implicit hierarchy in the therapeutic relationship whereby the therapist eventually guided the clients so that the painting became therapeutic and the nature of the colours began to have a healing effect on them.

Talking about the hierarchy of another kind, Anjali, a music therapist, identified herself as a doctor, as it gave her the authority to direct the clients in a manner she deemed appropriate for the situation. This included directions regarding the number of sessions required and the kind of music they needed to listen to. Vijay, also a music therapist, talked about an interesting distinction between the role of a musician and that of a music therapist; he said that a musician could afford to keep his/her eyes closed or be lost in his/her music during the performance. A music therapist, on the other hand, was expected to maintain a relationship with his audience, to be present, to maintain eye contact and to talk about the music.

8.7 The Counselling Process

Therapy can be seen as a process—one where there is an initial contact with a purpose and moving towards achieving that purpose or goal. This progressive movement is guided by the theoretical orientation of the therapist. Cormier and Hackney (1987) have conceptualized the counselling process as a series of stages through which the counsellor and client move—Rapport or relationship building, Assessment or definition of the problem, Goal setting, Initiating interventions, and Termination and follow-up. The following section discusses themes that emerged through data analysis and organizes them into the stages mentioned. This is not to say that the therapy moved through these discrete phases in a linear fashion, but points to a tentative flow of sessions in creative art(s) therapies.

8.7.1 Publicity and Referral Mechanisms

Given the fact that the use of creative arts therapies is in a nascent stage in India and is therefore not widely available and accessible, the researcher asked therapists to talk about ways in which they publicized their services and ways in which clients got to know about them. Their answers showed that it clearly depended upon the nature of settings in which the therapists worked. For those who were in private practice, the clients learned about their services through 'word of mouth'. Some therapists had their own websites which gave an account about their programmes, the nature of the services, the methods used, the prognosis, along with some client statements about efficacy. For therapists working with schools or other organizational settings, the clients were referred through the organization. Some therapists approached organizations to offer their services. The therapists who were in private practice provided services other than therapeutic services in their spaces, such as dance lessons, Reiki healing or talk therapy, which in turn brought in new clients.

8.7.2 Preparation for the Therapeutic Session

Before the therapist and the client met for the therapy session, there was a stage of preparation which facilitated the therapeutic session. Preparation involved the therapist readying themselves, and readying the space to be used, before meeting the client in a therapeutic encounter.

Readying the Self

Preparatory self-work referred to work that the therapists engaged in, in order to orient themselves to the session. It involved work with one's *personal self.* Many therapists talked about creating the right energy or bringing in positive energy in order to perform better as a therapist. Some spoke about themselves as 'carriers of energy'. It was through this preparatory work that they could understand deeper issues of the client rather than the superficial ones. Aahna, an art therapist, who was influenced by the theory of subtle energy, emphasized the need to meditate and bring in a certain mental state which she felt helped in the therapy session. She also talked about doing spiritual practices, using mantras, Reiki, crystals and aroma oils. Some of the other therapists spoke about breathing or meditative practices. Many of these therapists had a theoretical orientation based on the 'theory of subtle energy'.

This idea of 'centring' oneself is recommended to help the therapist focus and be more sensitive to the therapeutic session. It helps a therapist remain in the here and now and become more aware of what one is feeling in relation to the client

(Moursund 1985). Atkins and Williams (2007) talked about the therapeutic relationship as a 'container' for the artistic exploration to take place and emphasized the need for the therapist to be fully present in the session.

Space

The space referred to the physical environment created by the therapists; which included not only the room but also the materials that the therapist used in the session. While preparing for a session where more than speech was required, the space and the materials to support the techniques became a part of the therapeutic process (Wadeson 2010). The process was not limited to only the verbal transaction between the therapist and the client but was equally facilitated by the environment and the products the client utilized. As a story was expressed differently when one used dance, drama, music or art, one took into consideration the fact that even the 'materials themselves have lessons to teach us' (Atkins and Williams 2007, p. 22).

One of the art therapists, Aahna, conducted her therapy sessions in the living room of her apartment where her artwork was displayed on the walls. Before beginning a session, she created a space that was conducive to the needs of the client. This required her to have an array of materials ready in her space—different aromas and music. These had to be matched with the client's energy levels. The products she used to create the space depended on what she felt could create the right 'energy' for the person. This was in tune with the sensory experience of the arts—visual, tactile, auditory, etc. She drew upon her knowledge of colour and aroma therapy and integrated it into the physical space to create a therapeutic environment for the client.

The preparatory work done by Claire, also an art therapist, before an art therapy session was elaborate and specific to the techniques she used. This required each individual to have several materials in front of him or her, such as a flat board, wide blank white sheets of paper, bowls of specific colours, glasses of water, brushes, tissue paper, etc. In her studio space, she arranged the tables and chairs to facilitate a particular style of group interaction. This was based on the theory of human nature conceptualized by Anthroposophy.[2] Based on this understanding, she had spaces where the lighting was milder, where chairs were close to the door; while in other spaces the chairs were in the centre of the room. This helped clients sit in spaces that appealed to their temperament. While, a choleric person might prefer the centre of the room with more lighting, an individual with a melancholic temperament might prefer a corner. Before the clients entered the session, the art materials were laid out for individual use. For clients who had already been to a session, their files with previous artwork were placed in front of them. Their place

[2]Anthroposophy is a spiritual philosophy that addresses the spiritual questions of humanity, the artistic needs, the need to relate to the world, and develop a relationship with it. It is based on the philosophy of freedom.

was predetermined by the therapist. The space that was created by the therapist was as much a part of the therapeutic process as the interactions that transpired in the later part of the session.

In dance or movement therapy, 'physical space' was required to explore oneself. The dance therapists talked about other preparations such as music—recorded or live (with the help of musical instruments)—that needed to be ready as they were seen as important components of the therapeutic process.

Props, music, costumes and space were part of the stage. Hence, these elements are included in drama therapy as well. Chesner (1995) mentioned that physical environment in drama therapy should be conducive to risk taking and experimentation. To facilitate this a few factors that needed to be kept in mind while preparing for a session were privacy of the studio, flexibility in structuring the space and atmosphere, and ethos of the work space.

Kimiya, a drama therapist, mentioned how privacy was an important aspect. She worked in a school setting. She had to see that the manner in which activities were conducted did not interfere with other activities occurring in spaces around her. Size of the space was important to encourage physical movement—a crucial aspect in drama therapy. Flexibility in terms of creating a space where imagination and creative processes could be stimulated was also considered. Kimiya stressed several aspects of the physical environment which were required when using drama processes in therapy; she says

> An open set up … an open space which is not cramped by other things. I set up things such as when children come in they can say '*aaj hum jungle mein jayengey*' (today we will go to the jungle) so I will put up props and things. A lot of artistic creativity and those kinds of things such as instruments…. I have to ensure that we are not near other classes… Even room temperature shouldn't be too hot and sweaty. (Kimiya, drama therapist)

The music therapists worked primarily in hospital settings. Anjali had a room of her own, which was provided by the hospital. When asked if she engaged in any kind of preparatory work, she said that she did not have the time to do so as the '*patient*' just came in and she had to '*prescribe*' the type of music that could help them.[3] Vijay performed concerts for particular groups in hospitals and corporate settings. He needed to get equipment to support his performance. These were provided by the hospital and the organizations.

Expressive therapists used multiple modalities and hence their space had to be flexible enough to shift from one modality to the other along with the materials needed to do so. Theresa said, 'I have organized my room such that everything I want is there; including water, if I want to paint in that room. It just takes me a matter of 5 min to understand what medium we should use'. The therapeutic space created should communicate a sense of support—both physically and psychologically (Atkins and Williams 2007). The space created should be such that there are certain expectations that the therapist creates for the client (Beier and Young 1998).

[3]The words 'patient' and 'prescribe' were words used by the respondent.

This encourages emotional experience and exploration. Theresa said that the presence of art work and art material, mentally prepared clients for what was going to happen next. This reduced their fear and resistance for the therapist's later suggestions to use arts during the therapeutic process.

8.8 Therapeutic Assessment

Assessment served a variety of purposes in the therapeutic setting—it allowed one to establish rapport, enabled an understanding of the client's strengths and weaknesses, clarified the cause for the problem, decided on the most appropriate intervention and provided data for research or audit, to name a few (McLeod 2003). Assessment could be with standardized tools, or frameworks constructed by an organization based on their needs. However, the nature of assessment depended on the theoretical model used by counsellors (Mace 1995). Assessment used by the therapists included practices that helped them determine the issues of the client, and appropriate interventions for the same. It helped the therapist direct the therapeutic process. The assessment tools used by the therapists using CAT could be standardized tools or self-designed by the therapist.

The art therapists used the art making process and the art work produced as the primary grounds to assess the state of the individual. Informed by their study of lines, colours, brush strokes and other nuances of the art making process, the therapists made their observations and inferences about the client. An example cited was asking the client to draw a line and observing how they drew the line—hard or light, upward, downward or horizontal, which part of the page, colours used, etc. All of this said something about the person. Some creative arts therapists used drawing and colouring body maps[4] as assessment and interventive tools.

One of the art therapists, Claire, used the knowledge of anthroposophy to provide a framework for her observations. She said she was influenced by the Jungian orientation. She also used ideas of psychogenealogy—by sketching the genealogy tree and by understanding the projections from clients' ancestors through generations, she got an idea of their life transitions.

The dance therapists, Shazneen and Tripura, used the assessment tools designed for dance therapists. They learnt about these specific assessment tools (covering emotional, intellectual and spatial domains) from their training in dance therapy. The assessment tools included sensitivity to certain cues such as facial expressions, body attitudes, social interactions and the like. It required them to be sensitive to the movements the client made, so as to answer questions such as 'what

[4]Body mapping is a creative arts technique that allows a client to explore and creatively communicate the stories lived in the body. It involves drawing a life-size representation of the body, and using symbols, images, and words to indicate parts of the body that hold pain, pleasure, hope, etc. The process helps draw links between the parts of the body represented and the personal power to heal oneself (Schwalbe 2014).

movement qualities were practised?', 'why did a particular movement unfold the way it did', and 'where did the movement happen?'

The expressive therapists talked about having designed their own techniques to assess individuals through art forms. One of the therapists (Theresa) talked about using storytelling as an art form for this purpose. She asked her clients to tell her a story from their childhood. It might be some fairy tale or whatever they had heard and then asked them what in this story was appealing to them and what was the 'core value' of the person involved in the story. This gave her an idea of what was important for the clients.

Therapists also spoke about use of standardized assessment tools in their practice. Since Kimiya, a drama therapist, was a clinical psychologist who worked in a school, she used standardized tools to measure IQ, social intelligence or other emotional issues, if necessary. She also talked about using 'plain observation notes' on what works and what does not. Amala, also a drama therapist, assessed the children to structure their lesson plans and build a 'baseline' to get an understanding of where they need to start from. The children were assessed along physical, emotional, social and intellectual domains. Standardized assessment tools were also used to measure the progress of the clients.

The process of assessment for most therapists also became an intervention strategy. It gave them qualitative information about the clients which in turn allowed them to understand the position of the client as well as core issues and design interventions that might prove advantageous to the client. As Payne (1993) noted, the basic assumption behind creative arts therapies is that the person used the art medium to express themselves. This required the therapist to be sensitive to the non-verbal communication that emerged within the session. The special language that was communicated served as the base upon which the therapist could assess the needs of the client and set appropriate goals.

8.9 Creative Art(s) Therapies and Goal Setting

The therapeutic process moves towards an ultimate goal—the purpose for therapy. Once the problem was assessed and clarified, a positive psychological atmosphere created, goal setting took place (Manthei 1997). Setting goals was considered an important determinant in the process as it gave a base to see whether the therapy had worked and when the process could be terminated. Goal setting allowed therapists and clients to make a commitment (Cormier and Hackney 1987). It gave the therapist and the client an idea of what the outcome of the session would be and what they could do to achieve this end. Dryden and Reeves (2008) have divided goals in counselling into two kinds—explicit and implicit. Explicit goals were goals that were external to the client such as getting better grades or making friends. Implicit goals on the other hand were goals that were internal or 'experiential' such as internal thoughts, beliefs and perceptions.

All the therapists established goals that centred on issue resolution—depending on the population, these could include behavioural, physical, emotional or spiritual goals. However, the therapists talked about the resolution of these goals as a means to establish complete balance within the person.

8.10 Creative Art(s) Therapies and Intervention Strategies

The techniques used by the therapists were unique to the art(s) modality they used. Though the goal or the purpose of therapy was similar across the therapists, the techniques used to achieve these goals varied based on the art(s) modality used. The style of using the techniques depended on the population and the setting. The progress of the session developed in three phases—warm up, theme building and closure.

8.10.1 Warm Up

Cormier and Hackney (1987, p. 19) have described rapport as 'the psychological climate that emerged from the interpersonal contact between the counsellor and client. Consequently, good rapport set the stage for positive psychological growth, while poor or bad rapport lead to undesirable or even counterproductive outcomes'. The ways in which the psychological climate was created, and the nature of the psychological climate varied, based on the therapist's personal preferences and the nature of relationship that would facilitate the process.

Warm up referred to those activities where the therapist invited the client into the therapeutic journey. It prepared the client to start the session and warm up to it. This could occur in several ways based on the personal style of the therapist and the art modality they used.

Both the art therapists began the session with a verbal interaction with the client. This verbal interaction served to not only introduce the role of the therapist but also get an idea of the client and their issues. As Aahna said, this social interaction of general 'small talk' helped her 'break the ice', make the client comfortable and slowly lead them into the session. This interaction was important to know if the client had received any diagnosis in the past and if the client was on any medication. Along with these, assessment of the individual and problem definition also started to take shape through this verbal interaction.

The dance therapists oriented their clients to what they would be doing in the session. This was a general orientation to dance/movement therapy—how the body influenced the mind and vice versa. This occurred not only through a short verbal exchange but through body movement exercises (Kashyap 2005, p. 98). As Tripura said,

> Warm ups include moving, bending and stretching body parts in isolation as well as moving the whole body in unit … they enhance awareness of the body and its movements, increase range of motion and flexibility in various joints and heighten energy levels in individuals. (Tripura, dance therapist)

These short warm-up exercises lasting for about 15 min, prepared the mind and the body to enter the therapeutic session. Assessment of the client in terms of 'The energy level and what they're going through and a sense of why they have come there and their expectations' also took place through these movement based exercises. Since the drama therapists mostly worked with children, they usually used free play or interacted with children using an art modality of the child's interest so that he or she familiarized oneself with the space and the materials in the room.

In case of a group session, the warm up was usually a *ritual.* The ritual attempted to separate the individual from the world he or she had come from and helped move towards the world that he or she was going to be a part of. This ritual was established at the beginning of the session and was repeated in every session, marking the beginning of the session. Put simply,

> The classic example of where they say 'Good morning miss'. They know that the teacher has come in and they have to begin. So it's a daily repetitive ritual…. It's just something we always do when we come together to create some sort of semblance and say that, ok now we are in our little circle and we are going to have a session today and we have started. (Kimiya, drama therapist)

Similarly, Amala also started her session with a 'warm up' where a song might be sung or a prayer might be recited. With the music therapists, the warm up session primarily involved verbal interaction. As Vijay went as a performer, he started the session by introducing basic information about his instrument and the theory behind music. Bhavya, an expressive therapist, worked in a setting where the families functioned as a community for the time that they were there. When they entered the community space they were given the responsibility to clear the space and arrange the materials for the session. This initiated a sense of togetherness and prepared them for collecting in the space to perform an activity. Once this was done, she began the session with a ritual such as breathing exercises, physical exercise or body movement. Theresa, also an expressive therapist, identified herself as a counsellor and started a therapy session by structuring the session—timing of the session, frequency, payment and the like. This gave the client a boundary to work within and inducted him or her into the structural process of therapy.

8.11 Theme-Based Techniques

Theme-based techniques were those that centred on addressing the core issues of the client. These included art specific techniques and were largely influenced by the therapist's style, preference of art form(s), and nature of the client population they were working with. Aahna, the art therapist, after clarifying the problem of the client and deciding whether to use Reiki or art therapy, selected strategies to address the needs of the client. This involved selection of an activity which revolved around using art materials—colours, newspaper clippings, pencils and the like. After the initial problem clarification, she did not discuss the problem at all. She and the client just got into the art work. Her belief that change can occur through transformation of energy and removal of negative energies within, guided her session structure and strategies used to address the issues of the client. The process of art making is the therapy in itself. Slayton et al. (2010) identify the healing and life enhancing ability of art therapy with children, adolescents and adults, with varying challenges. Aahna talked about using mandalas in the therapy session. She saw these figures as a symbol of completeness and had read extensively about them. Apart from drawing mandalas, she also encouraged clients to express what they were feeling or thinking through drawing and then interpreting the colours or themes that emerged from their art work. Another art technique used was collages.

Claire used her specific technique of wet painting where the colours were applied to the wet paper and allowed to take their own form. This art work was then left for interpretation by the client, complemented by the therapist's perspective. Though the art making process was itself considered therapeutic, the art work produced was used as a tool to make interpretations and give insight to the client. The structure to Claire's session was consistent across clients. The first eight sessions required the client to work with specific colours with a theme in mind, provided by the therapist. These eight sessions were diagnostic sessions which helped her diagnose the personality of the client and the issues that needed to be addressed. The theme of the session would be using the colour to complete the exercise described by the therapist. In between the painting, the therapists and the client had minimal verbal interaction.

In anthroposophical art therapy, the session consisted of painting and reflecting. This reflecting helped the client to balance out his actions with thoughts, thereby creating harmony and not overwhelming oneself with a single act. Anthroposophical art therapy is based on the holistic understanding of health that incorporates body, soul and spirit. 'Illness has its' roots in the soul; and artistic work is an expression of the soul… The therapy aims to strengthen and bring balance to the person to resolve and prevent illness and guide towards a happier life. It allows clients to become more aware of natural processes in and around themselves and of the healing potential of colour, line and form' (Arts Therapy London 2015). The communication became a 'three way process', between the therapist, the client, and the image or artefact created (The British Association of Art Therapists 2011).

Dance movement therapists spoke of specialized techniques such as mirroring, Chasian technique, Kerstenberg technique and the like. They also spoke about body movement exercises based on yoga techniques and folk dances (Kashyap 2005). In theme building, dance therapists used 'therapeutics of dance' fully in the session. Exercises designed to encourage exploration and resolution of client problems were utilized by the therapists. Shazneen described this part of the session as the 'thematic movement experience'. It is in this part of the session, where a symbol is selected to build upon the theme or the issue that needed to be addressed. The symbol determined the exercises that were chosen and the manner in which expression might take place. To illustrate this further, Shazneen used the symbol of water and described how this was developed into the theme of the session:

> Imagine that you are water. How do you imagine water to be? You could think of ice. You could think of fluidity you could think of it as vapour.... When the person is moving their body they are taking the shape of an emotional story that they are unravelling through movement, on the dance floor.... Unravelling the story and telling it when they can't necessarily talk about it. It's happening in the imaginative process, calming them down. Inevitably they will associate what was in the past and the present and how they can work with it in the future. (Shazneen, dance therapist)

Tripura considers this theme development to be the 'central core in which the therapeutics of dance unfolded through a combination of movement experiences…' (Kashyap 2005). It is through the activities designed for this part of the session that the goals of the session are achieved.

The drama therapists used song, dance, movement and role plays with special children to develop social, emotional and behavioural skills. Depending on the skill level of the child, the activity was designed by the therapists to address his or her needs. As Amala said, 'If it's mobility we use dance, if it's social skills, we use drama.... We can use dialogue and music too. If it's hand function issue, we use arts and craft'.

The music therapists either played live music or recorded music. Vijay performed his sarod recitals at the hospitals; playing songs which he felt would have certain affective changes in the patients. The expressive therapists used multiple art modalities. These included two or more modalities in a single session. As Theresa mentioned, 'We have bottles, masks, dolls. So we use anything. Some people… we make them do papier-mâché stuff and that's also therapeutic. We use drama. We get people to roll. We use props. So, we use pretty much whatever we can'. Theme building of the session in music therapy involved direct administration of the music to the client. As Anjali said, 'They come in; they listen to the music for 22 min. They have received one dosage here…'

Expressive therapists, Theresa and Bhavya, used a number of modalities to address the theme of the session such as guided imagery and music along with some body movement. Following which, they could express what they are feeling through painting. The theme development happened through various modalities and a single theme was addressed using various techniques.

8.11.1 Relaxation Techniques

The relaxation techniques could consist of meditation or breathing exercises. Since arts therapies are action oriented therapies, techniques to relax the body and mind after a session of intense 'doing' were required.

8.11.2 Reflecting Techniques

The reflecting techniques helped the client to elaborate on the experience he or she has had. These techniques primarily involved words—verbal or written. Clients were encouraged to maintain a journal or have a discussion with the therapists and the group about how they felt and about what they thought about the session. These techniques sometimes took the shape of homework activities, where the clients were expected to go back and think further about the session. This was recommended especially by the dance therapists and the expressive therapists. The expressive therapists encouraged reflection through other means as well—such as a song or poetry or art work. The drama therapists, due to the profile of clients they dealt with (children with special needs) did not use reflecting techniques. One of the art therapists discouraged the use of reflective techniques, since she wanted her clients to leave behind what was done in the session and not take it home. This was based on her theory of energy, where once the energy is transformed, that needs to be carried forward.

8.11.3 Use of Metaphors

The use of metaphors was a technique mentioned by many therapists. Metaphor is anything that can represent something else. It could take the form of a visual image, object or a word. This metaphor was then used as the glue that tied the session together. Kimiya (drama therapist), illustrated the use of river as a metaphor to give an idea of 'the transformative power of a metaphor in therapy' (Loue 2008). She narrated an incident that occurred while she was working with a group of children. She mentioned that everyone except one boy was participating in a story building exercise. The boy kept looking at her and would not respond. There were *dupatta*s (stoles) and things lying around; she asked him to pick up whatever he wanted and become that object. Both she and the boy took blue *dupatta*s and became the river:

> … And then we said a big wave is coming and we moved like that. First he was like this (bodily closed and shy) and then as he physically opened up, you could see his energy levels also changing and how he was moving around the room because we were supposed to be in floods or something. And I had to move with him … and soon we were all over the room. (Kimiya, drama therapist)

Geldard and Geldard (2009) have explored the significance of using metaphor with adolescents in therapy which can be seen through this snippet of a session—The boy had an increase in interest levels when the metaphor was used, as he went from being closed to being energized. He was not being pushed to move, but through using an external symbol such as a river, the boy was encouraged to move around the room. This had a therapeutic impact on him—emotionally and behaviourally.

Moon (2007), elaborated on the significance of using metaphors in art therapy. Metaphors play a powerful role in therapy as they help stimulate the creative processes and encourage insight. They are discreet in nature and do not threaten the individual. This allowed a person to explore threatening experiences and emotions in a safe manner. They contain layered meanings, and could have a powerful impact on the individual at the conscious and subconscious level. Metaphors provide the link between the art work, the client and the therapist which allowed the session to be held together and not dissipate into abstractions. Metaphors in this way helped build rapport and engaged the client in a positive direction.

8.12 Closure of the Session

Closure primarily consisted of relaxing and reflecting on what had happened in the session. Since the arts therapies are considered 'action therapies' (Malchiodi 2007), seven of the ten therapists included 'relaxation techniques' in their closure session. These relaxation techniques included breathing exercises or meditation. These closure exercises were a ritual where the client was prepared to leave the safer therapeutic space and move into their everyday lives.

> The closure is also very important. A closure can also be a very ritualistic thing where you go by giving a handshake to everyone or you sing a song or you say goodbye or you hold hands. We chant 'om' or do breathing exercises. So you tell yourselves you've had a lovely session, you calm down and then you go back to your homes. Communion and closure are both important. (Kimiya, drama therapist)

Anjali (music therapist), handed over music CD's that clients had to listen to throughout the week and planned a follow-up session. Vijay, who acted as a therapist and a performer to hospitals, the closure consisted of a question and answer session where he interacted with the audience.

In fact, the therapists who used closure rituals in the latter part of the session mentioned how it was necessary for the clients to leave behind the experiences of the therapeutic session and resume their normal activities. Art making experiences can result in an altered state of mind which can leave one feeling relaxed. Closure helped one focus and centred the self so that they could enter their normal lives (Atkins and Williams 2007).

8.13 Termination and Follow-Up

Termination is the last phase of the therapeutic encounter where the therapist and the client decide to end therapy. Depending on their experience, theoretical orientation and setting, the therapists worked with the clients to establish a period of termination and follow-up. All the therapists had a certain number of sessions which they felt was necessary for the clients to experience change. They ranged from 'at least six sessions' to a 'minimum of ten to twelve sessions'. In group work, the group was already aware of the duration. Nearing the end of the session, a discussion was facilitated to summarize. Drama therapists, working in the school did not have a specific time framework within which they worked. Children met them almost regularly.

For the music therapists, the duration of the therapy depended on the client's resources and availability. Anjali (music therapist) said

> I am above all that. I am a doctor. The patient comes in, I give them the treatment. If I tell them that it is a six month package, they pay and come. If I say it will take four months then they come for that time. I just give them the treatment and they leave.

For some others, the duration of the therapy was determined by the hospital or company who availed their services. In case of group work, the therapists had an idea of how many sessions would be required and the module was developed accordingly. The group was informed about this at the beginning. The last session was seen as a celebratory event: 'The whole atmosphere is created by preparing for it way in advance. So a story is created, a painting with a story might be created that will show that everyone is together and that this is a party with everyone' (Bhavya, expressive therapist).

The creative arts were used as a means to bring about closure and tie together the sessions for the group. Moursund (1985) felt that termination must occur when the goals of therapy have been met or when the client was no longer moving towards the goals. Among all the therapists, regardless of whether the sessions were predetermined or determined through the process of therapy, the notion that termination occurred when a desirable outcome was achieved underpinned their therapeutic interactions.

8.14 The Scope of Creative Art(s) in Therapy

Through their experience with the art form and its use in therapy, the therapists had developed a theoretical framework which gave the rationale about why they used this approach, but also guided their interactions with the individual in therapy. The arts have the inherent ability to tap into the subconscious because of which more authentic and organic forms of expressions emerged. These lead to deeper insight which promoted problem resolution.

The understanding of the therapy influenced the nature of the therapeutic relationship with clients. The therapeutic relationship was influenced by the theoretical orientation of the therapist, and the experience they gained as practitioners in the field. Therapists used either a facilitative approach or a more directive approach. In the former, the client was given the baton to guide the session, and the therapist played the role of the shaping and guiding the session to move it towards achieving the goals. In the directive approach, the therapist adopted the role of expert.

In order to achieve therapeutic goals, the therapists assessed the need of the client. Standardized tools as well as self-designed forms of assessment were used. Therapists trained in clinical psychology adopted and adapted standardized tools in the therapy process. However, most others relied on the art form they used as the basis for assessment. The tool helped the client in responding and expressing himself or herself, which was then observed and analysed by the therapist, within the framework provided by theory they followed.

Based on the assessment of the individual(s), the goals were formulated by the therapist and the client. These goals were both explicit and implicit (Dryden and Reeves 2008). The goals were inclined towards the client's needs, and included the therapists' interpretation of the client's needs and the context the clients belonged to, such as the organization which referred them.

Based on the goals set, the means to achieve the goals were designed. The intervention strategies included techniques of various kinds: preparation, theme based, relaxation and reflecting techniques. Specific to the use of arts in therapy was the use of metaphor as a technique to glue the session together and gain deeper meaning from the symbolic responses that emerged within the session.

Once the expected outcome was achieved and autonomy was gained, the therapeutic relationship was terminated. The duration for this outcome to occur could be fixed by the therapists' from their experience and understanding of the process and/or it could depend on the individual's needs. However, most therapists talked of a maturity period where they felt that a particular number of sessions were required for changes to be seen.

Since the therapeutic process involved expression using various symbols, methods to document the same varied from verbal therapy. In case of art work such as painting or sculptures, the therapists either stored them or took pictures of the work done. Observation notes that were reflective of the nuances of the art form were kept; some instances were when dance therapists observed and documented the movements and facial expressions of the clients; when music therapists had audio CDs or videos of the work done. The documentation helped the therapist and client gain an insight into the process as it could be reviewed at any time, alongside, it fulfilled certain criteria established by the organization the therapists worked with (if any) as well as provided material for research in the field.

While the above stated therapeutic processes were used in the session, the manner in which they were operationalized in therapy flowed in a step wise fashion. Before the session began, clients approached the therapists either through an organization which was in touch with the therapist or through information they had received via websites owned by the therapists, or through 'word of mouth'. Before the client and the therapist interacted, the therapist prepared himself or herself for the therapeutic encounter. Preparation involved the self, the space, and the session. The therapists used themselves as the 'instrument for change' (Bor and Palmer 2001) and felt the need to bring in a particular mindset and energy into the session so that they could act as the catalysts for change. In CAT, therapists used resources such as art materials, music, physical space for movement and the like, the space and materials used had to be given equal attention. Depending on the activities and the needs of the clients, the space and the materials were prepared so that the therapeutic encounter was further enhanced. The therapists had to enter the session with an 'intention', thus, mentally orienting oneself to the session and having an idea of the outcome of the session helped in structuring and providing a *therapeutic experience* for the client(s).

The therapeutic encounter took place in three parts—warm up, theme building and closure. Warm up involved the initial interactions between the therapist and the client, which could involve small talk, to build rapport, in assessment, and problem clarification. During theme building in the middle phase of the session, intensive activities directly addressing the client's issues were used. Closure was the final phase of the session where the therapist and the client reflected on the session and prepared to refocus on their normal lives. Rituals were used to bring the client(s) down to a more regular state of being as expressing through art forms could result in an altered state of mind (Atkins and Williams 2007).

The study indicated that there were similarities and differences in practice among therapists in each modality. Further research can explore each modality in detail so that deeper insight can be gained into the therapist and the therapeutic process. The study looked only at self-identified therapists using CAT; there are therapists in the field who use arts in their therapeutic work but do not carry the CAT label. Exploring the practices of the therapists specific to use of arts modalities, examining their pool of knowledge as well as the coexistence of other therapies could be explored.

This study has explored the therapists' perspective; the experience of the client in CAT could give an idea of the effects the arts have on an individual seeking therapy. A perception of other health professionals is an important domain in this field, as it lies parallel to other healthcare professionals who have greater acceptance in mainstream therapy. The process of therapy when using the art form stands in contrast to verbal therapy—importance given to materials used, symbolic expression are some of the features that are unique to this practice. Exploring the effects that these special features can have in therapy can help highlight the areas and issues in which CAT could be beneficial.

The arts are inherent to a person's being. Thinking in terms of images, movement, and enjoyment of music or telling stories are a part of every culture. They are not unique to a person but are more ancient and universal than verbal language. While words are given to a person, images, sounds and movements are more natural. They provide more clarity and give a more authentic expression of the person within.

Engaging in the arts taps into the more aesthetic elements of being, along with the deeper mind of the individual. It nurtures the innate creativity every individual possesses, and can result in deeper insight (Rogers 2010). The act of engaging in creating something of personal relevance can be therapeutic. Creativity as a tool for healing is a concept that therapists using CAT have brought into the therapeutic setting which can be developed and adopted as counselling is a creative endeavour by nature (Gladding 2011).

Using CAT was seen as an *alternate* therapy—one that was tried when all else failed. The creative arts complement the existing practices in therapy and provide a new dimension for therapists and clients to work. To promote individuals who are interested in working in this area as well as professionals who are already practising CAT, training centres, research in the field, registration bodies, ethical guidelines and other forms of organizing the profession must be encouraged. This will help build the profession, validate and standardize their practices as well as allow greater accessibility to those individuals who require these services.

References

Arts Therapy London. (2015, December 24). Retrieved from http://artstherapylondon.co.uk/anthroposophical-art-therapy.

Ashley, F. B., & Crenan, M. (1993). Dance: The movement activity for the elderly. *Nursing Homes, 42*, 50–51.

Atkins, S., & Williams, L.D. (2007). (Eds.). *Sourcebook in expressive arts therapies*. Boone, NC: Parkway Publishers.

Beier, E. G., & Young, D. M. (1998). *The silent language of psychotherapy: social reinforcement of unconscious processes* (3rd ed.). New York: Transaction Publishers.

Benenzon, R. (1981). *Music therapy manual*. Illinois: Charles C Thomas Pub Ltd.

Bor, R., & Palmer, S. (2001). *Beginner's guide to training in counselling and psychotherapy*. London: Sage Publications Ltd.

Casson, J. W. (2004). *Drama, Psychotherapy and Psychosis: Drama therapy and psychodrama with people who hear voices*. London: Routledge.

Cevasco, A. M., Kennedy, R., & Generally, N. R. (2005). Comparison of movement-to-music, rhythmic activities, and competitive games on depression, stress, anxiety, and anger of females in substance abuse. *Journal of Music Therapy, 42*(1), 64–80.

Chang, M. Y., Chung, H. C., & Kuo F. (2008). Effect of music therapy on psychological health of women during pregnancy. *Journal of Clinical Nursing and Special Issues-Complementary and alternate medicine*, 2580–2587.

Chasen, L. R. (2011). *Social skills, emotional growth and drama therapy: Inspiring connection on the autism spectrum*. New Jersey: Jessica Kingsley Publishers.

Chesner, A. (1995). *Drama therapy for people with learning disabilities: A world of difference*. New Jersey: Jessica Kingsley Publishers.

Corbett, B. A., Gunther, J. R., Comins, D., Price, J., Ryan, N., Simon, D.,… Rios, T. (2011). Brief report: Theatre as therapy for children with autism spectrum disorder. *Journal of Autism and Developmental Disorders, 41*(4), 505–511. doi:http://dx.doi.org/10.1007%2Fs10803-010-1064-1.

Cormier, L. S., & Hackney, H. (1987). *The professional counselor–A process guide to helping*. New Jersey: Prentice Hall Inc.

Cresswell, J. (2009). *Research designs*. California: Sage Publications.

Dingle, G. A., Gleadhill, L., & Baker, F. A. (2007). Can music therapy engage patients in group cognitive behaviour therapy for substance abuse treatment? *Journal of Music Therapy, 27*(2), 190–196.

Dryden, W., & Reeves, A. (2008). *Key issues for counselling in action*. London: Sage Publications Ltd.

Emunah, R. (1990). Expression and expansion in adolescence: The significance of creative arts therapy. *Arts in Psychotherapy, 17*, 101–107.

Flick, U. (2010). *An introduction to qualitative research* (4th ed.). New Delhi: Sage Publications India Pvt Ltd.
Freud, S. (1923). *The ego and the Id*. London: Hogarth Press and the Institute of Psycho-analysis.
Geldard, K., & Geldard, D. (2009). *Counselling adolescents: The proactive approach for young people*. London: Sage Publications.
Gibbs, G., & Gibbs, G. R. (2008). *Analyzing qualitative data*. Yorkshire: Sage Publications Ltd.
Gladding, S. T. (2011). *The creative arts in counseling* (4th ed.). Alexandria: American Counseling Association.
Grayer, E. (2005). Story of Alex- an improvisational drama. *Clinical Social Work Journal, 33*(1), 21–36.
Hendricks, C. B. (2001). A study of the use of music therapy techniques in a group for the treatment of adolescent depression. *Dissertation Abstracts International*, 62-2A.
James, M., & Johnson, D. (1996). Drama therapy in the treatment of combat related posttraumatic stress disorder. *Arts in Psychotherapy, 23*, 383–395.
Kashyap, T. (2005). *My body, my wisdom*. New Delhi: Penguin.
Kiran, D. (2011). Expressive art therapy-Creative movement/dance. Retrieved from http://deepakiran.in/Documents/UGC_FinalDraft.pdf.
Knill, P. J., Barba, H., & Fuchs, M. N. (1995). *Minstrels of soul: Intermodal expressive therapy*. Toronto: Palmerston Press.
Laungani, P. (2004). *Asian perspectives in counselling and psychotherapy*. New York: Brunner Routledge.
Loue, S. (2008). *The transformative power of metaphor in therapy*. New York: Springer Publishing Company.
Mace, C. (1995). *The art and science of assessment in psychotherapy*. London: Routledge.
Machado, N., Kaur, A. & Pant, N. (2005). Education infrastructure for complementary health practice in India. *The World Centre for Creative Learning Foundation*. Retrieved from http://wcclf.org/Education%20Infrastructure%20for%20Complementary%20Health%20Practice%20in%20India.pdf.
Mackay, B. (1989). Drama therapy with female victims of assault. *Arts in Psychotherapy, 16*, 293–300.
Malchiodi, C. A. (2007). *Expressive therapies*. New York: Guilford Press.
Manthei, R. J. (1997). *Counselling: The skills of finding solutions to problems*. New York: Routledge.
Mcleod, J. (2003). *Doing counselling research* (2nd ed.). London: Sage Publications Ltd.
Meekums, B. (2000). *Creative group therapy for women survivors of child sexual abuse*. London: Jessica Kingsley.
Menen, R. (2002). *The miracle of music therapy*. Mumbai: Pustak Mahal.
Menon, R. R. (1998). *Indian music: The magic of the raga*. New Delhi: Somaiya Pub.
Montello, L. M., & Coons, E. E. (1998). Effect of active versus passive group music therapy on preadolescents with emotional, learning, and behavioral disorders. *Journal of Music Therapy, 35*, 49–67.
Moon, B. L. (2007). *The role of metaphor in art therapy: Theory, method and experience*. Springfield, IL: Charles C Thomas.
Moursund, J. (1985). *The process of counseling and therapy*. New Jersey: Prentice Hall Inc.
Mulky, M. (2004). Recreating Masculinity: Drama therapy with male survivors of sexual assault. *Arts in Psychotherapy, 31*, 19–38.
National Coalition of Creative Arts Therapies Association. 2011. Retrieved September 3, 2011 from http://www.nccata.org/.
Pavlicevic, M., Trevarthen, C., & Duncan, J. (1994). Improvisational music therapy and the rehabilitation of patients suffering from schizophrenia. *Journal of Music Therapy, 31*(2), 86–104.
Payne, H. (1993). *Handbook of inquiries in the arts therapies: one river, many currents*. London: Jessica Kingsley Publishers.
Pratt, R. R. (2004). Art, dance and music therapy. *Physical Medicine and Rehabilitation of North America, 15*, 827–841.

Ranade, F., & Ranade, S. (2004). *Ayurveda, nature's medicine*. Delhi: Motilala Banarasidass Publications.

RASA centre for theatre arts and special needs. (2007). Retrieved August 4, 2010 from http://www.rasaindia.org/rasa/theatre_story.htm.

Rogers, N. (2010). *Person centred expressive arts therapies*. Retrieved from http://www.nrogers.com/PCExArtsArticle.pdf.

Schonmann, S. (2011). *Key concepts in theatre of drama education*. Boston: Sense Publishers.

Schwalbe, A. (2014). http://www.annetteschwalbe.co.uk/. Retrieved August 10, 2015, from Body Mapping: http://www.annetteschwalbe.co.uk/body-mapping/.

Silverman, M. J. (2003). The influence of music on the symptoms of psychosis: A meta-analysis. *Journal of Music Therapy, 40*(1), 27–40.

Slayton, S., D'Archer, J., & Kaplan, F. (2010). Outcome studies on the efficacy of art therapy: A review of findings. *Art Therapy: Journal of the American Art Therapy Association, 27*(3), 108–118.

Tang, W., Yao, X., & Zheng, Z. (1994). Rehabilitative effect of music therapy for residual schizophrenia: A one-month randomised controlled trial in Shanghai. *British Journal of Psychiatry, 165*, 38–44.

The British Association of Art Therapists. (2011). Retrieved from http://www.baat.org/art_therapy.html.

Voracek, M., Wilgram, T. & Gold, C. (2004). Effects of music therapy for children and adolescents with psychopathology: A meta-analysis. *Journal of Child Psychology and Psychiatry*, 1054–1063.

Wadeson, H. (2010). *Art psychotherapy*. New Jersey: John Wiley and Sons.

Wilson, C. A. (2011). *Healing power beyond medicine*. Washington DC: O Books.

World Centre for Creative Learning Foundation. (2010). Retrieved December 22, 2011 from http://wcclf.org/about.htm.

Chapter 9
The Role of a School Counsellor

Sindhura Tammana

Abstract When I first thought of what school counselling entailed, I envisioned a process that focused on the intra-psychic processes of the child. I imagined the role of a school counsellor to be limited to just interacting with the child and addressing the emotional needs/issues of the child. My field work experience as well as the theory classes helped me broaden my perspective to the plethora of responsibilities that a school counsellor has to undertake and juggle with. This paper is a narration of that journey. Conveying what a counsellor's role in the school setting is and working through building rapport with children, not offending the teachers and administrators, assessing the classroom needs, planning and implementing individual and group sessions for children and providing counselling and guidance for parents formed the challenges of the multiple roles. The entire journey has also been placed in the light of literature in the field.

Keywords School counselling · Counsellor role

Today's schools face a unique set of demands. They are expected to provide an education in basic skills to a large student population while at the same time preparing technologically sophisticated professionals. Schools are expected to compensate for the changes in societal patterns, such as (a) the change from the traditional worker–homemaker family structure to that of either a two-worker or a single-parent family structure; (b) the growing incidence of poverty and economic instability experienced by families; (c) the increased incidence of family transience and violence; and (d) the growth of commercialism, consumerism, violence and sexualized behaviour depicted in popular culture. Additionally, as a result of the significant increase in school size experienced throughout the country, schools now educate children in a more impersonal social context, often far removed from the student's family and community.

Sindhura Tammana (✉)
Inner Space Counselling and Assessment Centre, Mumbai, India
e-mail: sindhura.tammana@gmail.com

S. Sriram (ed.), *Counselling in India*, DOI 10.1007/978-981-10-0584-8_9

9.1 The Role of the School Counsellor

One wonders where exactly the school counsellor fits within the larger ecosystem of the school. But the main question of whether referrals derive predominantly from the school or from students themselves is important to think about, in conjunction with what is supposed to be the principal purpose of a counselling service—to support individuals in need of help, or to enable schools in dealing with what they see as problematic behaviour of the students?

In literature, there are varying notions of what a school counsellor's role is supposed to be. But we do observe that from a very narrow definition of a school counsellor's role, gradually the scope for the responsibilities along with the demands for a school counsellor has been increasing. Much of the literature on school counselling and the role of the school counsellor is derived from studies done in various parts of the world other than India. Many of the studies referred to here have been done in the developed world, and not in developing countries.

Some authors (Bemak 2000) have described school counsellors as being instrumental in the integration of community-wide mental health services. Other authors such as House and Martin (1998) have suggested that the school counsellor plays a powerful role in (a) promoting student advocacy, (b) developing higher educational and career aspirations in students, (c) eradicating educational practices such as student tracking that inadvertently maintain inequities among disadvantaged student groups and stratify opportunities and (d) using data to identify educational practices that may help or hinder student progress.

McLaughlin (1993) argues that counselling in schools has three elements: an *educative* function, i.e. to develop students personally and socially in the context of the school; a *reflective* function, which is the exploration of the possible impact of and contribution to personal and social development and mental health of practices in the classroom and other aspects of the school community; and a *welfare* function, which is the responsibility to plan for and react to issues which impact on students' welfare. Hamblin (1978) wrote: 'The counsellor's job is to help a pupil find more effective ways of using what he has already got in terms of aptitudes, ability and personal in a truly satisfying way… More of the good that exists rather than a creation of a different person' (Hamblin 1978, p. 5).

In India, counselling emerged as a labelled activity in schools in the 1970s. The counsellor training courses for teachers which appeared at that time largely adopted the American model of specialist school counsellors, based on the client or person-centred approach of Carl Rogers and others. Many local education authorities employed school counsellors. Often, these were teachers who went on to train in counselling after some experience in schools.

In the 1980s, there was an increasing emphasis on counselling skills and this approach drew from the person-centred, behavioural and cognitive approaches, and was developed alongside to adapt with work in school counselling. It promoted the idea that all teachers should have basic counselling skills; i.e. should be able to listen to pupils and to react to and respond in the emotional domain.

There was also a focus on pupil–teacher interactions and the promotion of good relationships. The second level of counselling was seen as the school's ability to provide continuity of care: it focused on systems of early detection, provision of co-ordinated approaches and links with other agencies. The third level was seen as a more specialist activity where a teacher or counsellor worked with a group or an individual in greater depth.

In the 1980s there were also numerous initiatives that enhanced and were improved by the development of counselling skills. Changes in in-service education, which gave schools control over the agenda and the funding for in-service education, meant that there was growth in counselling skills training for teachers. One could argue that counselling skills were becoming more generalized and more widespread in their application. In addition, there was a growing body of work in the field of pastoral care and personal education.

Given the work being done by the BCSCA (British Columbia School Counsellors Association) on behalf of all school counsellors in British Columbia, it is important to be aware of the role description contained in the Ministry document Special Education Services: A Manual of Policies, Procedures and Guidelines. According to the role description contained in this manual, (Section D, p. 5, 1998) school counselling functions include individual, group and class work. The focus of school counselling is to provide both an intervention and a prevention service, enhancing the students' development, assisting with the development of an enabling school culture and empowering students toward positive change.

The counsellor:

- *supports* personal and social development appropriate to developmental level
- *counsels* students, their families and the community to foster growth in the students' self-esteem individual responsibility, and in skills such as decision making and social skills
- *ameliorates* factors which may precipitate problems for students
- *enhances* students' educational achievement through goal setting, assisting with the development of SLPs, individualized education plans and activities such as promotion of effective work and study habits
- *provides* appropriate interventions to assist students with school related problems and issue
- *facilitates* the goals of career education by assisting students and their families to explore and clarify the student's career options, through developmental activities that stress decision making, personal planning and career awareness (Manual of Policies, Procedures and Guidelines, Section D, p. 5, 1998).

In a study titled, 'Changing Schools, Changing Counsellors: A Qualitative Study of School Administrators' Conceptions of the School Counsellor Role' (Amatea and Clark 2005), the authors wished to generate a description of administrators' role conceptions of school counsellors, and hoped to achieve a greater understanding of the possible role options counsellors might have. They hoped that their findings might (a) provide clearer guidance to counsellors in their selection of appropriate school environments and professional development goals, and (b) generate substantive ideas for improving the design of school counsellor preparation programmes. Analysis of the data collected from school administrators and teachers over a period of 2 years, produced descriptions of four distinctive types of counsellor role conceptions with particular valued work activities and styles of relating that were clearly describable and differentiated from one another. The four role conceptions are organized historically from the most contemporary version of the counsellor role to the most traditional.

9.1.1 *The Innovative School Leader*

To implement this role, administrators described their counsellors as 'seeking out the perspectives of all the school stakeholders—the students, parents, staff, and community members'. As a result, they believed that the counsellors often had a 'bigger picture of the needs of the school than other staff members'. In addition, they saw their counsellors 'as taking responsibility for working with staff and introducing skills to them', which allowed teachers to change how they work with students, their families, and each other.

9.1.2 *The Collaborative Case Consultant*

In this role, the counsellor was expected to have specialized knowledge about the social, psychological, and academic needs of students and about appropriate intervention strategies that parents and teachers could use to respond to individual students. Although the administrators also expected counsellors to be knowledgeable about and to intervene directly with students, and to manage necessary school procedures and paperwork, these administrators believed that the most effective use of the counsellor's time would be to work with the key adults in a student's life-teachers and parents.

9.1.3 *The Responsive Direct Service Provider*

These administrators viewed their counsellors as having distinctive expertise in meeting the needs of individual students either by providing a preventative programme of psychoeducational activities and educational and career guidance or by helping students resolve problems or crises.

9.1.4 The Administrative Team Player

This role of the school counsellor was characterized by viewing him/her primarily as a member of the administrative team whom they expected to fulfil administrative needs and goals. Rather than viewing their counsellors as having specialized psychological knowledge or expertise in psychological interventions, these administrators viewed them as 'another pair of hands' responsible for implementing administrative goals. Common activities that these administrators described relying upon counsellors to perform were class scheduling, coordination of the standardized testing programme, coordination of the special education staffing and placement process, referral of students for outside services, and 'pinch hitting' as a disciplinarian, substitute teacher.

The innovative school leader role is the most contemporary of the four groupings and is emphasized in the ASCA (American School Counsellors' Association) National Model (2003), yet it is the one that was least described by administrators in the study ($N = 3$) as a preference for their counsellors. Several implications could be drawn from Amatea and Clark's study. First, the typology can help school counsellors re-examine their existing roles in the context of current school change and reform efforts. To do this, counsellors might wish to consider the following questions: Which of these four roles are they currently enacting in their school? Which of these roles seems to be expected or supported by their school administrators, and which do they believe to be the most effective in carrying out their mission and that of the school? In addition, counsellors must ask themselves whether they are willing to move outside their comfort zones and develop dramatically different roles in their schools. What resources are needed and what obstacles are in the way of change?

9.2 School Counselling in India

In the Indian context, school counselling is a relatively young profession. The first school mental health clinic was set up at Nair hospital in Mumbai in 1979. The secondary education department, and the secondary and senior sections in Central Schools in India, run by the Kendriya Vidyalaya Sangathan have mandated the presence of a school counsellor to deal with academic and non-academic issues in school from 2014. The need for counselling in schools in India is seen to be on the rise, with an increase in the number of suicides of school children, incidences of bullying, drug abuse and other issues of concern (Kodad and Kazi 2014).

Despite the role played by the family, schools and the educational system play an important role in the lives of children, especially in the context of the twenty-first century. School counselling in India is often subsumed as guidance; with guidance being offered for careers and vocations. Counselling, which has a facilitative and curative function needs to be distinct from guidance. Both guidance and counselling are necessary in Indian schools today (Kodad and Kazi 2014;

Ramakrishnan and Jalajakumari 2013; Sinha 2006). Sinha (2006) refers to the role of the school counsellor extending beyond school students to parents of students, who may feel the need of availing of counselling services to deal with issues stemming from their role as socialization agents.

In a study to investigate knowledge, attitudes and practices related to mental health carried out in five states in India, the researchers found that teachers and counsellors were important sources of information on mental health. Teachers and counsellors were found to be influential in their ability to affect and encourage help-seeking behaviour. This finding is vital to the development of a community mental health programme, where there is a convergence between mental health services and education programmes (Gaiha et al. 2014).

In the following section, I will discuss my own understanding of the role of the school counsellor, with respect to my experiences in the field as well as by readings of literature.

9.3 My Understanding of the Role of the School Counsellor

9.3.1 An Emphasis on the Systemic Perspective

In this section, I will present my abstracted understanding of the role of the school counsellor, based on my experiences at working as a school counsellor at a school in Govandi,[1] Mumbai and by corroborating it with relevant research. I worked in the school setting for about three and a half months, twice a week, under the guidance of a faculty supervisor. The school was situated in a poor neighbourhood and catered to children belonging to low socio-economic groups; some of my learning was specific to this context. I choose to look at the role of the school counsellor, by placing her in various levels of the ecosystem of the child, which I have explained in detail below.

9.3.2 The Ecosystem of the Child and the School Counsellor

My main learning was that the school counsellor cannot view the child and his/her issues in isolation. The counsellor must take into account the different factors playing a role in the child's life and development, at various levels of his/her ecosystem. This was especially true in the school that I was placed at, where a number of issues arose not from within the child, but from the child's ecosystem. Therefore, as a counsellor, it becomes important not only to work with the child,

[1]Govandi is a suburban neighbourhood of eastern Mumbai.

but also with the child's environment. This would require the counsellor to take on a more proactive role, rather than a passive one and requires much more commitment. This is how I conceptualize a child's ecosystem, in which he/she is embedded and the various levels at which the School Counsellor can work for the child are: with the Child, with the Family, with the School and with the Community (Kodad and Kazi 2014; Sinha 2006).

9.4 Child in the Community

9.4.1 Role of the School Counsellor

The macrosystem of the child refers to the larger culture that the child belonged to and in my experience at the school; I viewed poverty as being an important part of the child's macrosystem, at the level of the community. In this context, several issues of children emerged from being in an impoverished home and neighbourhood.

Psychological investigations into the impact of poverty on early childhood development have shown general cognitive impairments to be positively correlated with lower socioeconomic status. Anjali and Sinha (2000) for example have documented significantly lower opportunities for linguistic stimulation among low socio-economic status 2 year olds when compared to age peers from middle and higher income backgrounds in an urban setting.

Reviewing available Indian studies, Misra and Mohanty (2000) indicate that poverty has an impact on several other cognitive functions such as visual-motor coordination, immediate memory and concept formation. Interestingly however, mere nutritional supplementation does not seem to have an adequate counteracting influence on impaired cognitive functioning. Instead it is high quality stimulation (for example through preschools) that has a positive impact on the child's cognitive development (Jachuck and Chatterjee 1989). Thus, counsellors could help provide this stimulation as well as train teachers and parents to be the providers of such intellectual stimulation. An important target for psychological interventions by counsellors would be to focus on enhancing the quality of the teaching–learning environment that the child in poverty is a victim of and build up his/her learning skills.

A number of studies have reported positive correlations between socio-economic status and adolescent self-esteem and indicate that adolescents in poverty consistently score lower on measures of self-esteem (Bharsakle and Srivastava 1991; Kapur 1991). Characteristic differences are also seen in motivational patterns. Lower socio-economic status adolescents demonstrate low internal and higher external control orientation with a higher reliance on significant others, God and luck for success (Sinha 1994). The school counsellor in such a setting then, pays special attention to issues of self-esteem and would consider working in groups as well as individually, with children to help them build their self-esteem, help them regain their sense of control as well as to motivate them to pursue their goals.

Disadvantaged adolescents tend to have low and stagnant levels of aspiration coupled with low achievement needs (Pareek 1994). Studies of attribution found that adolescents from higher socio-economic backgrounds were more likely to attribute failure to luck, while disadvantaged individuals were more likely to attribute success to luck and assume greater personal responsibility for failure (Misra and Misra 1986). An interesting and useful finding is with relation to the impact of socio-economic status on the adolescent's time orientation. Findings indicate that low socio-economic status adolescents are characterized by a short-term orientation to the future. Finally, studies examining the impact of poverty on adaptive behaviour have pointed to a lack of self-direction amongst disadvantaged adolescents (Gunthey and Sinha 1983) with lower levels of task persistence, a higher tendency to give up the task more quickly and higher expressions of helplessness (Srivastava and Lalnunmawii 1989).

Taken together, these studies indicate that a typical psychological profile appears to differentiate the disadvantaged child and adolescent from those who are more privileged. It seems possible that underlying cognitive structures, beliefs and attitudes, together with reduced social mobility and difficulties with status enhancements could lie at the heart of issues faced by adolescents hailing from lower SES conditions. The role of the school counsellor is to work with these issues, especially when working in a school where children largely come from a low-socio-economic status, as was the case with the school I was placed in. Since the environment is impoverished, the role of the counsellor in a child's all-round development becomes all the more pronounced and necessary.

9.5 The Child in the Family

9.5.1 Role of the School Counsellor

The parents of most of the children coming to this school were occupied with the task of making both ends meet, which left them little time to attend to the emotional needs of their children, or get involved with the academic achievement. Almost all children in the school went for tuition classes, as well as for learning Arabic,[2] which created a tightly packed schedule for children. Whenever, there was any free time, the children would be largely unsupervised which could contribute to issues of limit-setting. Also given the limitations of space in the home and a lack of proper open areas to play; it appeared that their energies were hardly used, and instead, often ended up in outbursts of aggressive behaviour. This was also evident as most children were referred to the counsellor for issues of aggression and externalizing problems.

---

[2]Many of the children came from Muslim families, and needed to learn Arabic in order to read the Koran.

Issues emerged from the fact that parents hardly had time for their children, leaving them without any scope to share their concerns with them. Both parents were often engaged in working to provide for basic needs of shelter, food and clothing; meeting emotional and psychological needs were considered a luxury, not available for the poor. What emerged to an observer from the outside was that there was a lack of exposure to appropriate role models of social behaviour and emotional expression, especially anger and frustration. Such a system, would give rise to externalizing issues, especially aggression, lack of self-regulation skills and a deprivation of emotional needs, especially care and attention which was then sought for, by unhealthy means.

9.6 The Child in the School: The Role of the School Counsellor

9.6.1 The School Environment and Culture

The school culture itself, including its philosophy, its disciplining methods, the infrastructure, etc. were all potential sources of psychosocial issues that impacted the child's development and well-being. The primary means of discipline used by teachers and other adults in the school towards any misdemeanour of the children was corporal punishment in the form of beating. This gave rise to fear and anxiety among many of the children; almost every child who came for individual counselling sessions mentioned feeling scared of teachers and authority figures (even on days when their work had been completed).

Given that the teacher–student ratio was imbalanced, with one teacher managing a class of 70 students, consequences of being unsupervised arose as well. One teacher would find it difficult to manage such a large classroom; as a result, many children who needed more help with academics, did not receive the necessary assistance. Such children were often not able to engage in the classroom and then, ended up feeling restless, and were labelled by the teachers as 'distracting the classes'. This initiated spanking on the part of the teachers as a short-term quick fix solution to 'wrong' behaviour, which in turn perpetuated the cycle. This cycle churned out academic problems, problems with attention and concentration, fear of teachers or school, anxieties, negative emotional impact of harsh punishment (such as reduced self-esteem), etc.

Another common issue was the conflict experienced by counsellors between personal values and the ethics and policies of the school. When major decisions pertaining to the students had to be made, the counsellors could see themselves playing a valuable part in the consultation process between the principal, administrative staff, the student and the student's parents or caregivers. Counsellors could advocate for a more student-centric approach in these decision-making processes (Kodad and Kazi 2014; Sinha 2006).

Confidentiality and trust, from the client's point of view, that confidentiality would be maintained, are at the heart of the relationship between counsellor and client. However, in school more than in private practice, the counsellor is constrained by legalities and ethics governing the context and by professional relationships with school staff and those working with schools, and with parents, as well as with the clients themselves. Counsellors could feel torn between keeping confidentiality and the demands of principals and teachers who felt they had a right to know what was bothering particular students.

In the school setting where I worked, teachers would feel curious about what exactly went on during the counselling sessions; but instead of approaching the counsellors, they would question the children about the session. In several meetings with teachers, we tried to give them some glimpse into what happened in a typical counselling session and at the same time, helped them understand that it was not the best idea to make a child reveal the details of the counselling session.

Issues of confidentiality also came up when it came to teachers making student referrals. Despite repeated attempts to make teachers aware of the impact of labelling and stigmatizing children in the classroom and about confidentiality issues, children would be referred for counselling in front of the entire classroom along with a reiteration of the 'complaints' about him/her. A more effective way to make referrals would be for teachers and counsellors to meet the counsellors separately, discuss the referrals and then to leave it to the counsellor to pull the children out of the classrooms. Conversely, it can be said that school was an excellent place for counselling because children would not have to be accompanied by parents/adults and without much ado, the problem could be addressed (Kodad and Kazi 2014; Sinha 2006).

An understanding of these issues was important to put the child's concerns in perspective and not view them as emerging completely from within the child, but appreciating the role of these larger systemic factors, and as far as possible, working with these factors simultaneously, as one works to empower the child.

9.7 Working with Teachers

9.7.1 Teacher Attitudes: Prejudices and Beliefs

India being a land of diversity, the socio-cultural differences sometimes become sources of prejudices and biases. The school being located in a poor neighbourhood, the teachers had different kinds of beliefs about the children and their families; which in turn influenced their approach to teaching and interacting with children as well as their parents. Many of the teachers believed that the children coming to the school hardly had any value for education and did not care much for academics; the same belief was attributed to the families as well. Hence, they admitted that they were not motivated to put in much effort towards the children, and their learning, since it was anyway 'of no use'.

This reminded me of the concept of learned helplessness—wherein the teachers had learned to feel helpless about the children's situations and backgrounds, by attributing problem behaviours and the inability to learn to their environment, and being passively unable to do anything about it. The teachers were unaware of the possibility of the school, where children spent a significant amount, becoming an important medium of socialization. The role of teachers functioning as facilitators, who had immense opportunities to work with children and aid their development to overcome the limitations in their home environments, was hardly considered. Teachers, it seemed had completely stopped trying to make a difference in the lives of children and went about their regular teaching, in a routine, pedantic fashion, without considering the need to modify strategies or content in keeping with the context of the children and the school. The counsellor's role included challenging these negative assumptions and helping teachers recognize that such attitudes impeded a child's progress and mental well-being.

In the context of the school on Govandi, the teachers showed little awareness about the counselling aspect of their role. The teachers were not willing to take responsibility of any role apart from the purely academic role transacting information in the classroom. Many of the teachers located the problems and the solutions to pupil misbehaviour, outside the school: 'Put problem children into problem schools—it is a government problem; they are not helping'. They felt powerless to address the issue. These findings are similar to those of the study by McLaughlin (1993) in the United Kingdom, wherein teachers were uncomfortable with the counselling role, and preferred to externalize pupil problems and misbehaviour.

9.7.2 Labelling

Another issue where a school counsellor can work is that of labelling. The school counsellor can emphasize the damaging effect that labelling could have on children—when they were referred to as 'mischief-makers' or 'lazy' or 'dumb' over and over again by teachers and administrators. The counsellor has to bring to fore the role that the self-fulfilling prophecy could play when teachers operated from such labels when addressing children or by demonstrating them through their interactions with and in expectations from children.

Values such as unconditional positive regard, a non-judgemental attitude and the importance of listening, guide the approach as well as the process of counselling. Overall in addressing the above issues, I strongly feel that these values must not stay limited to just counselling, and in fact, need to be practised by various human service professionals, and in this case, especially by teachers and principals of schools. The role of the counsellor lies in illustrating the importance of these values as well as training teachers to practise these values in classroom with children, in dealing with parents, as well as with each other.

In McLaughlin's (1993) study, students talked about the desire to be heard in school about their feelings and school experiences. They demonstrated a depth of feeling about not being heard, feeling lost or trapped in the system, being unclear about expectations, feeling isolated, and not being treated with respect. They wanted to feel their opinions mattered, despite differences in ideas or outlook:

> Students did want to talk about problems at home but they had no real expectations of staff being able to solve them. On the whole, they just needed to air them. They did have the opinion, however, that staff were in a position to help them to sort out in-school problems. (McLaughlin 1993, p. 46)

9.7.3 The Student–Teacher and the Student–Counsellor Relationship

There were differences in the relationship that the counsellor shared with the children in school and the relationship that the teachers shared with the children. Most teachers found the nature of the interaction of the counsellors with the children to be unacceptable. The time taken by the counsellors in listening to the views of the children was considered in a disparaging manner. They interpreted the mode of relating to children as 'pampering' and 'spoiling' them. During a group session with five boys (who were referred to the counsellor for being disruptive in class), the teacher peeped into the session several times and made statements such as, 'It's no use talking to them like that and pampering them! They'll never learn a thing! You need to be stricter with them'. The statement reflected the teacher's beliefs about disciplining children, and at the same time, brought to fore her scepticism and disapproval of the way in which the counsellor engaged with children. There were hints made that the teachers, with more experience, were better equipped to 'handle' the children than the counsellor. The role of the school counsellor had to be clarified to the teachers, along with differentiating the counsellor–student relationship from the relationship between a teacher and a pupil, without belittling the latter or threatening its importance.

This raised the problem of introducing the new values through counselling to children who lived in an environment that did not understand or encourage these values. The most common example of this was emotional expression. As school counsellors, we have always emphasized to children, the importance of expressing one's emotions in an assertive way, rather than bottling them up. This emotional expression and assertive style of communication is often misinterpreted by teachers and other authorities in Indian culture as either being 'disrespectful to elders' or 'self-centred'. At such times, the school counsellor had to strike a delicate balance, where he/she without hurting cultural sentiments and without threatening existing value structures, introduced new values to the children, as well as to professionals working with children and with families, so that the child felt encouraged to practise newly learned behaviours.

9.7.4 Clarifying Misconceptions

There were a considerable number of misconceptions about the 'results of counselling. Teachers often expected to see results immediately after a child was sent for counselling. When we were working on behaviour modification for a child of six who was referred for hyperactivity, we were told that since the time he had been going for counselling sessions, his hyperactivity had increased! I was stunned because I could see improvements during the session—in terms of his attention span and ability to sit for longer durations of time. But at the same time, I was able to see where the teachers were coming from. They were expecting drastic changes in the child's behaviour and the fact that he was receiving counselling, put him on the spotlight, which made his behaviours seem more conspicuous. It prevailed upon us, as school counsellors, to explain that counselling did not offer quick-fix solutions, and that changes in behaviour happened gradually and in small ways, over a period of time, rather than overnight.

Teachers' Perceptions of School Counsellors

As counsellors, we sometimes felt that our role and presence was personally threatening to other school staff and in some cases, parents. In schools where counselling was not seen as integral, many school counsellors spent considerable time and energy justifying their role to other school staff and marketing their services to school personnel and to the students.

Previous research indicates that teachers do not have a universally positive view of counselling. Montgomery (2003), for instance, found a climate of scepticism towards counselling in one of the five schools that she studied, where teachers did not feel that such work was appropriate to an educational environment. Montgomery suggested that in the school where he worked, teachers had to deal with high levels of aggression from pupils, they did not see why pupils, 'should have an easy comfy seat to sit on and the space to talk about their problems' (Montgomery 2003, p. 68).

Ellis (2002), writing in The Guardian, suggested that some teachers did not appreciate a counsellor's intervention. He quotes one counsellor as claiming, 'Some teachers feel we should be able to wave a magic wand. They want to see a child cured after a few sessions. But often a child's problems may have gone on for years and are not simply solved' (p. 23). One way forward is to continue to keep the dialogue open between counsellors and teachers and to build on the more positive outcomes that appear to be generated, the longer the counselling service is in place.

Black and William (1998) show that counselling skills and processes have a part to play in learning as well as in developing the school as a guidance community. They say;

> Learning is driven by what teachers and pupils do in classrooms. Here, teachers do have to manage complicated and demanding situations, channelling the personal, emotional and social pressures amongst a group of 30 or so youngsters in order to help them to learn now and to become better learners in the future. Standards can only be raised if teachers can tackle this task more effectively what is missing from policies is any direct help with this task. (p. 1)

Black and William detail the evidence for involving students in processes of formative assessment: processes which draw on similar skills to counselling skills, i.e.

the skills of listening, giving feedback and asking appropriate questions. They detail the relationship of these processes to motivation and self-esteem. The evidence seems to be that we need to develop the role, skills and pedagogy of counselling, not to restrict it. The needs of young people in the context of a personally and socially complex society, which is aiming to become a learning society, require us to develop and integrate counselling theory and skills into the role of all teachers, not compartmentalize it.

9.8 The Child: Role of the School Counsellor

9.8.1 Identifying

Identification of children requiring counselling becomes an integral part of the school counsellor's job (Kodad and Kazi 2014; Sinha 2006). The school counsellor must be aware that though children with externalizing problems will be prominent and can be easily identified, there will be children with internalizing problems and it is a challenge to identify such children as easily. Children who were isolated, rejected, withdrawn, emotionally volatile, frequently angry, quick to anger, cry easily, frequently complain, saw things negatively, or who were exhibiting sad moods must be identified, and interventions must be provided for them.

9.8.2 Assessing

Ideally, skills that were required often in a school setting would include sharing, accepting criticism, giving and receiving compliments, complying to certain rules, understanding others' feelings, listening, perspective taking, controlling anger, turn-taking, managing conflict, giving others personal space, etc. A child may have deficits in one or more of these skills and may be adept at others. Assessment would entail an analysis of such information.

Observations during unstructured school period (recess, cafeteria, corridors) and observations during small group activities (cooperative learning, work groups, teamwork) were rich contexts for determining social skills weaknesses.

The role of the counsellor would require him/her to be aware of the different situations or problems that a child comes across in different contexts within the school that would call for emotion regulation abilities. This could also be accomplished by direct observation of settings within the school, such as the classroom, the corridors, the playground, the canteen, etc. Situations encountered by such observation could help the counsellor plan appropriate intervention, serve as practice examples during training, as well as facilitate transfer of learning.

This would also help formulate a functional behavioural assessment for the child and help gauge the child's sense of control over his/her environment. For individual interventions, such observation would also help formulate a functional behavioural assessment for the child and help gauge the child's sense of control over his/her environment. Given the amount of research showing the heavy influence of parents and the family on a child's emotion regulatory abilities, it would be imperative to include family history and to look at parenting styles and practices as part of the assessment process.

Working with Individuals and Groups

From how I see it, I believe the goal of counselling is to empower the client, and speaking specifically of working with a child, the goal of the school counsellor would be to facilitate a child's process of bringing out his/her own inner resources, building on them not just to cope, but also to grow and develop. The school counsellor facilitates self-awareness of the child and initiates the child to engage in much reflection—a skill that the child could use at any point in his/her life.

In working with children, the school counsellor is at an advantage since she also has the opportunity to work with groups, rather than just with individuals. Typical issues pertaining to different developmental stages can be addressed in groups of children, such as the psychosocial issues pertaining to puberty, issues of bullying, assertiveness, gender stereotyping, etc. The group process could be made interactive and could be used as an opportunity for children to practise empathizing with each other.

One of the responses to bullying in schools has been to involve students in the detection, analysis and response to the problem. This is based on a view of the student as a partner and contains different views of the power and authority relationship between pupils and teachers. Rudduck et al. (1996) argue that these processes should be adopted more widely in schools and should be an essential feature of school improvement in the future. The school counsellor must always think on her feet on the field, because she is interacting with children- who are themselves very spontaneous. She must apply her creativity to deal with situations like having limited resources or when planned methodologies fail.

Working with Biases

I believe that the school counsellor in a country like India has the added social responsibility of addressing issues of gender bias and prejudice rampant in the culture. In the school that I worked, children at the age of nine, had strong ideas about the segregation of labour, believing strongly that it was 'shameful' for a boy to have to help a mother clean the house, and that girls should rather stay at home and help out with household chores. I took it up as a task to address these biases and attempted to restructure them to form more healthy beliefs that resided on premises of equality of gender—in terms of dignity as well as making opportunities available (Sinha 2006).

Limit-Setting

As counsellors, when we interacted with children in huge classrooms, we had to establish certain basic ground rules in order to make the process more effective. Engaging in such limit-setting became an important part of our work there, as children were new to this concept and were used to engaging in improper classroom behaviour and then used to get spanked, which was all a part of their daily routine. The spanking did little to serve to 'correct' or prevent inappropriate classroom behaviour. Limit-setting without having to use the stick, was a concept which was very new to them. As counsellors, we did not do a dictatorial limit-setting, but instead involved the children in it, negotiated with them the nature of the limits and the consequences of flouting them. Inviting this involvement communicated that we respected their interests and being a part of the process made them feel more attached to and motivated to follow the rules. As counsellors, we had to take on the responsibility of demonstrating to children an attitude of fairness through negotiation as well as the value of treating everyone with respect and dignity—on a larger scale. More specifically, we had to restructure the way in which classrooms were managed and inculcate new methods.

Marshall (1996) argued that attitudes to power informed discussions of exclusion: 'The main reason for exclusion given by schools to parents and children… is 'disobedience in various forms' which consists primarily of insolence, disruption and uncooperative behaviour rather than violence' (p. 93). She argued that this invokes:

> … an expectation of children as normally obedient to the natural authority of teachers and schools and in which children may be understood as actors only when disobedient. Children themselves were not understood as sharing in adult authority, and issues of power do not figure in the discussions unless an abuse of adult power is thought to have occurred. (Marshall 1996, p. 92)

She argued that this excluded the child from the educational partnership, since the partnership was understood to be between the teacher and the parent, and not with the child. This was a feature of thinking that underpinned changes in the classroom.

This view of power and obedience runs counter to many developments in the field of counselling in schools. Developments in school counselling have emphasized listening to and involving students in the processes of schooling and problem-solving (Rudduck et al. 1996).

9.9 Raising Awareness About the Nature and the Need for Counselling

Children in this school, just like the teachers had no idea about what counselling entailed and what a counsellor did. In some ways, this was an advantage because they did not have any previous notions or biases against counselling or against children who were referred for counselling. This gave me a chance to start afresh, in building their ideas about what counselling was all about. I started out by introducing myself to all the students and to make myself approachable. I did this by conducting fun group activities in classrooms—which helped break the ice and helped me in building rapport with the children. It was through such activities that I gradually began talking about my role in the school and how I could help them. Subsequently, when children were asked to go see the counsellor, they did not feel threatened or scared, and instead, looked forward to seeing me.

At the same time, neither did the other children look down upon the child who was sent for counselling; as the concept of the counsellor, and going to the counsellor, had more positive connotations for the children. In order to build rapport with each child and to make myself seem approachable, I conducted needs assessment for children in the classrooms. Here, I had short sessions with children, where I spoke with each child individually, in private, and told him/her about what counselling was about, and what my role was, and then had them talk about any issue that bothered him/her. I had a long list of issues that bothered the children; however, I could see many recurrent themes—which helped me locate some of their issues as emerging from their context—the school as well as the home. Additionally, these sessions helped build rapport with each child as well as to give the child an idea of what counselling actually was by really experiencing it, and to clarify any misconceptions about it, if any.

9.10 Mapping the Way Forward

I wish to conclude the discussion on my understanding of the role of the school counsellor by presenting Kapur's (2011) ideas on working with children in schools that coincides with my ideas of working from the systemic approach. In her book, *Counselling Children with Psychological Problems*, Kapur (2011) stressed the importance of intervention at the community level, especially in the context of developing countries. According to Kapur (2011), an effective school mental health programme had the following components and it was evident that the school counsellor played an important role in each of these components:

- Takes into account the relationship between the school and the community environment, as well as any unique cultural values and identities
- Identifies the socio-political conditions and processes likely to be associated with the establishment and survival of a comprehensive mental health programme in school
- Involves families and community members as active partners in planning, implementation and on-going evaluation
- Intervenes at multiple levels
- Focuses on teacher and parent training
- Evaluates effectiveness and utilizes this information in programme modification.

The school counsellor straddles the space between the school, the family, the community, and most importantly the child. He or she plays the role of an intermediary, ensuring that the best interests of the child are kept in the forefront while appreciating the context in the backdrop.

References

Amatea, E. S. & Clark, M. A. (2005). Changing schools, changing counsellors: A qualitative study of school administrators' conceptions of the school counsellor role. *American Counseling Association.* Retrieved from http://www.redorbit.com/news/education/284790/changing_schools_changing_counsellors_a_qualitative_study_of_school_administrators/.

American School Counsellor Association. (2003). *The ASCA national model: A framework for school counseling programs.* Alexandria, VA: Author. Retrieved from http://www.schoolcounselor.org/files/6-3-170%20Sc%C3%A0wallie-Giddis.pdf.

Anjali, & Sinha, D. (2000). *Social class and language development.*

Bemak, F. (2000). Transforming the role of the counsellor to provide leadership in educational reform through collaboration. *Professional School Counseling, 3*, 323–331. Retrieved from http://www.eric.ed.gov.

Bharsakle, S., & Srivastava, R. P. (1991). Self-image as related to socio-economic status in scheduled caste and non-scheduled caste college students. *Indian Journal of Management* (pp. 118–128). Retrieved from http://www.indianjournalofmanagement.com/.

Black, P., & William, D. (1998). *Inside the black box: Raising standards through classroom assessment.* London: King's College, University of London.

British Columbia School Counsellors Association [BCSCA] (1998). *Special education services: A manual of policies, procedures and guidelines.* Retrieved from http://bctf.ca/bcsca/role.htm.

Ellis, P. (2002). Can teachers be counsellors too? *The guardian*, p. 23. Retrieved from http://www.guardian.co.uk/.

Gaiha, S. M., Sunil, G. A., Kumar, R., & Menon, S. (2014). Enhancing mental health literacy in India to reduce stigma: The fountainhead to improve health-seeking behaviour. *Journal of Public Mental Health, 13*(3), 146–158. doi:10.1108/JPMH-06-2013-0043.

Gunthey, R. K., & Sinha, P. (1983). Socioeconomic status as a determinant of anxiety, adjustment and affiliation in teenagers. *Indian Psychological-Review, 24*(4), 1–6.

Hamblin, D. (1978). *The teacher and pastoral care.* London: Basil Blackwell.

House, R. M., & Martin, P. J. (1998). Advocating for better futures for all students: A new vision for school counsellors. *Education, 119*, 284–291. Retrieved from http://www.questia.com.

Jachuck, K., & Chatterjee, R. (1989). Effect of preschool education on cognitive abilities of high and low caste children. *Indian Psychologist, 6*, 79–84.

Kapur, M. (2011). *Counselling children with psychological problems.* India: New Delhi.

Kapur, M. (1991). *Mental health of Indian children.* New Delhi, India: Sage.

Kodad, H., & Kazi, S. (2014). Emerging area of counselling in schools in India. *International Research Journal of Social Sciences, 3*(3), 44–47.

Marshall, W. (1996). Professionals, children and power. In E. Blyth &, J. Milner (Eds), *Exclusions FROM School: Inter-professional issues for policy and practice.* London: Routledge.

McLaughlin (1993). Counselling in a secondary setting: Developing policy and practice. In K. Bovair and McLaughlin, J. (Eds.) *Counselling in schools: A reader.* London: David Fulton.

Misra, G., & Misra, S. (1986). Effect of socio-economic background on pupil's attributions. *Indian Journal of Current Psychological Research. 1*(2), 77–88.

Misra, G., & Mohanty, K. A. (2000). Consequences of poverty and disadvantage: a review of Indian studies. In K. A. Mohanty & G. Misra (Eds.), *Psychology of poverty and disadvantage* (pp. 121–148). New Delhi: Concept Publishing Company.

Montgomery, S. (2003). *Person-centred working and young people*. Birmingham: The University of Hull.

Pareek, U. (1994). Interventions to deal with poverty. In Pareek, U. (Ed.), *Beyond psychology* (Vol. 66, No. (1–4), pp. 61–70).

Ramakrishnan, V. K., & Jalajakumari, V. (2013, September). Significance of imparting guidance and counselling programmes for adolescent students. *Asia Pacific Journal of Research, 2* (9), 102–112.

Rudduck, J., Chaplain, R., & Wallace, G. (1996). *School improvement: what pupils can tell us?*. London: David Fulton.

Sinha, D. (1994). Some cognitive consequences of deprivational environment and their policy and action implications. *Trends in Social Science Research, 1*, 43–57.

Sinha, V. K. (2006). Counselling in schools. *Indian Journal of Social Psychiatry, 22*(3–4), 82–83.

Srivastava, A. K., & Lalnunmawii. (1989). Cooperative-competitive behaviour and conflict resolution style among Mizo children: A cultural perspective. *Psychology and Developing Societies, 1*, 191–205.

Chapter 10
Marital Counselling in India: Perspectives from Family Court Counsellors

Sujata Sriram and Chetna Duggal

Abstract At a national convention organized to commemorate the 25th anniversary of the establishment of the Family Court in Mumbai, 98 family court marriage counsellors from 14 states in India discussed issues connected to the Family Courts Act of 1984. Matters relating to the setting up and functioning of the courts, nature of cases, challenges encountered and good practice models were deliberated on. There was little parity across states on how the Act was implemented. Kerala and Maharashtra emerged as model states, wherein rules and processes were in place and enforced. Problems arising from occupying dual roles of advocate or judge with marriage counsellor were illustrated. There was agreement that the nature of cases seen across states was similar, with an increase in cases of maintenance, dowry and family violence. Interference by advocates and family members was expressed as a challenge that counsellors had to deal with on a daily basis. Counsellors brought up work-related issues such as high case load, involuntary clients, stagnation in the work role and lack of support from the system, coupled with inadequate training. Suggestions were made on the need for periodic training, accreditation and licensing of marriage and family counsellors. Systematization of procedures and processes in the court through the development of manuals and guidelines was emphasized.

Keywords Family courts act · Marriage counsellors · Marital counselling

The Family Courts Act, 1984, and its subsequent Amendment in 1991, was passed to promote conciliation in, and speedy settlement of disputes related to marriage and family affairs. Under the purview of the Act, family courts were set up in various states of India, dealing with family related matters and domestic relations. Family courts in India cover issues of marriage, divorce, adoption or surrogacy,

S. Sriram (✉) · Chetna Duggal
School of Human Ecology, TISS, Mumbai, India
e-mail: sujatasriram@gmail.com

S. Sriram (ed.), *Counselling in India*, DOI 10.1007/978-981-10-0584-8_10

property settlements, child custody, juvenile adjudication, paternity testing, etc. Family courts come under the category of District and Sessions courts and are subordinate to the high courts in the respective states. Family courts were a part of the legal procedures to ensure the welfare of women, facilitating the resolution of familial disputes in a manner in keeping with the dignity of women (National Commission for Women 2002). The idea for the family courts, and for the provision of marital counselling by trained professionals within the setting, came from Durgabai Deshmukh after her visit to China in 1953. Subsequently, in 1974, the National Law Commission recommended the setting up of special courts that could simplify the procedures involved in familial and marital disputes. The Family Courts Act was passed in 1984, and came into effect from September 1984 (Gazette of India 1984). The establishment of the family courts in India was indication that India had made the shift from 'legalism to welfarism' (Nagasaila 1992) on the subject of family law.

10.1 The Implementation of the Family Courts Act, 1984

Family courts over the world fall into two main categories; courts from countries such as the United States of America, Australia and Hong Kong follow a model that focuses on legal matters that relate primarily to families and children. Pre-trial mediation programmes are not an integral part of the legal processes.

> By contrast, in Japan and India family courts not only deal with family matters but are also cast as informal, comfortable spaces where litigants frame their own issues before judges or counsellors (paralegal mediators) and where conciliatory rather than adversarial practices are to be employed. (Basu 2012, p. 474)

The passing of the Family Courts Act can be seen as the outcome of the efforts of the women's movement in India, wherein familial and marital disputes were withdrawn from the congested, intimidating and overbearing atmosphere of the Civil Courts, and discussed and settled in a more amicable, sympathetic and women-friendly environment (Family Court Mumbai 2015; Basu 2012). A major concern arising from the patriarchal cultural context in India was to ensure that women received a fair hearing in the judicial system, which tended to favour the interests of men. Yet another intention of the Central Government of India in the setting up of the family courts was to provide an inexpensive remedy for family disputes and problems. According to Basu, the delay in setting up the family courts in India was in part due to resistance from lawyers and advocate bodies (Basu 2012). The first state to set up a court under the Family Courts Act was Rajasthan in 1986, followed by states such as Tamil Nadu, Maharashtra, Kerala and Bihar (EKTA Resource Center for Women 2008).

According to the 1984 Family Courts Act, the family courts in India were set up "with a view to promote conciliation in, and secure speedy settlement of disputes related to marriage and family affairs" (Gazette of India 1984). The term conciliation is a form of alternative dispute resolution, which is a contrast to the adversarial legal procedures commonly followed in the courtroom. However, most practitioners in the family court—lawyers, counsellors and judges consider conciliation to be more akin to reconciliation or efforts to patch up a marriage. The language of the Act speaks of preserving the institution of marriage, and promoting the welfare of children within the institution of the family.

According to clause 3 (1) (a) of the Family Courts Act, 1984, provisions have been made through which the state government, after consultation with the high court of the state, can establish a family court for every city or town in the state, whose population exceeds one million (10 lakhs) (Gazette of India 1984). The jurisdiction of the area served by the family court would be determined and specified by the state or union territory. Apart from such million-plus agglomerations, state governments have the freedom to establish family courts in parts of the state, if there is a need felt. Expansion in terms of an increase in the number of family courts, according to this provision, is important. Data from the Department of Justice in the Ministry of Law and Justice show that there are 410 functional family courts in India, as of 31 October 2014. Among the states of India, Uttar Pradesh reportedly has 75 functional family courts, followed by Bihar with 33 Courts, Madhya Pradesh, with 31 courts, and Rajasthan and Kerala with 28 courts (Department of Justice 2014).

The Family Courts Act allows for the family courts in each state to formulate and institutionalize their sets of procedures and rules. Apart from prescribing the requirements for the appointment of judges in the family courts, the Department of Justice, under the Ministry of Law and Justice has little or no role to play in the administration of the Act. This has led to significant differences between states on the effective implementation of the Act. The Family Courts Act attempts to loosen the shackles of the conventional legal system by bypassing the lawyers and advocates; the Act stipulates that litigants are not entitled to have a lawyer present, unless specifically allowed to do so by the court. In practice, however, this requirement is rarely adhered to (National Commission for Women 2002).

10.1.1 Marriage Counsellors in the Family Court

The post of Marriage Counsellor was created, enacted, legalized and introduced by the Family Courts Act, 1984, in India and provisions were made to conduct independent proceedings of therapeutic counselling before the marriage counsellor to attempt to settle matters between families and couples amicably before initiating trial in the court (Gazette of India 1984). The intention was to dispense with the lawyers and advocates in the process of litigating family disputes. The presence of lawyers was perceived to increase the time taken for the litigation, along with increasing the cost for the litigants. Additionally, it was felt that for family disputes, a venue separate from that of the civil courts was preferable, as family matters required a separate expertise and experience. After the establishment of the family courts at Mumbai in 1989, all matrimonial disputes from city civil courts were transferred to the family court and counsellors in the city civil courts were appointed as marriage counsellors in the family court at Bandra, Mumbai.

The marriage counsellor is the mandatory first point of contact for all parties entering the family court. Under the counsellor's jurisdiction, each party is given the opportunity to voice their concerns wholly. During the course of the counselling sessions, the counsellor identifies the detrimental emotional, social and physical effects caused due to strains in personal affairs. The marriage counsellor, over three to five sessions attempts to assist towards a reconciliation of the parties involved, without the presence of any advocates. If reconciliation fails, the marriage counsellor works towards an amicable settlement of the issue, with mutual consent (EKTA Resource Center for Women 2008; National Commission for Women 2002). The marriage counsellor begins the interaction with the client through an intake sheet. This intake sheet contains the demographic background of the parties involved, and also elucidates basic reasons for approaching the legal system. Further, the counsellor documents the subsequent interactions with the parties involved, thus providing a rich source of processes and conclusions to all cases. While the Family Courts Act, 1984, recommends that suitable trained and qualified marriage counsellors be appointed to provide the necessary therapeutic inputs, in practice, most states have not done so. Even in states where there are counsellors in places, procedures and rules have not been laid down (Basu 2012; EKTA Resource Center for Women 2008).

The National Convention of Family Court Counsellors

The Family Court, Mumbai, celebrated its silver jubilee in October 2014. In 1989, five family courts were initially set up in Mumbai, and by 1995, there were seven courts in operation. In 2014, there were seven courts functioning in Mumbai in the Bandra-Kurla Complex, and one court in the adjacent Thane district. On the occasion of 25 years of the establishment of the Family Court, Mumbai, the Department of Marriage Counselling, Family Court, Mumbai, and the Centre for Human Ecology, Tata Institute of Social Sciences (TISS), Mumbai organized a national convention titled 'Counselling couples in India: Perspectives from family court counsellors', during 11–12 October 2014. TISS played a crucial role in the setting up of the Department of Marriage and Counselling in the Family Court in Mumbai, first as an experimental project, and then as a permanent establishment (Agnes 2001).

The national convention provided an opportunity to bring together counsellors, activists, judges and other individuals who play the role of mediation in the family courts in India. The event allowed for a collective discussion relating to the implementation and setting up of family courts in various states, the nature of issues placed before the courts, techniques and practices of the counsellors, challenges arising for counsellors in practice, and suggestions for ensuring synergy and continuity in family court practice. The scope of further growth and development of the counsellors was debated.

The participants for the discussions were 98 individuals, from fourteen states and one union territory in India,[1] who played the role of marriage counsellor, in their state family courts. While most of the participants were designated marriage counsellors, two states that did not have the post of marriage counsellors, had family court judges who participated in the proceedings.

10.2 Themes that Emerged

The deliberations of the marriage counsellors have been drawn up under the various areas in which the discussion took place. This convention was the first opportunity that marriage counsellors had of coming together to debate on issues that were common across states in India. The convention provided an opportunity for counsellors to discuss issues pertinent to their practice, and to identify possible solutions for the same.

10.2.1 The Implementation of the Family Courts Act

The discussions among the counsellors amplified the differences between the various participant states on the interpretation and implementation of the Act, and the actual setting up of the courts. There was considerable variation that emerged across states with regard to recruitment, eligibility requirement and composition of workforce in family courts across states. These variations across states have been brought out by many of the earlier reports on family courts functioning in India (Basu 2012; EKTA Resource Center for Women 2008; National Commission for Women 2002; Agnes 2001; Jamwal 1999).

The timeline for setting up the family courts in the states varied; the earliest report came from Tamil Nadu, where the first court was set up in 1988. Maharashtra and Kerala followed suit in 1989. Bihar reported the setting up of family courts in 1992, while in states such as Manipur, Tripura and Chhattisgarh, the courts were set up as late as 2004.

While Maharashtra and Kerala had rules and procedures in place, and had appointed marriage counsellors as state government employees, there was considerable variation in this regard. As already mentioned, two of the states participating in the convention—Punjab and Haryana and Bihar, did not have marriage counsellors in place, and in their lieu the Principal Judge from the family courts attended the event. States such as West Bengal had only two functioning family courts, with

[1]The States represented at the convention for the discussions were Maharashtra, Kerala, Tamil Nadu, Pondicherry (UT), Karnataka, Telengana, Andhra Pradesh, Madhya Pradesh, Chhattisgarh, Uttar Pradesh, Punjab and Haryana, Manipur, West Bengal, Bihar and Tripura.

very few counsellors available. It was only in Maharashtra that all litigants coming to the family court went to the marriage counsellor prior to approaching the Bench, having to mandatorily attend at least three sessions with the counsellor. In all other states, litigants were directed to the counsellor or towards mediation at the discretion of the judge. It was a mere handful of cases that were referred to the counsellors, and the number of counselling sessions varied.

While marriage counsellors in Maharashtra were Grade I state government employees, in Kerala, they were only Grade II employees. In Kerala, the principal marriage counsellors in the court were supported by contractual employees, who were hired at the discretion of the judge. The states of Maharashtra and Kerala were the only two represented herein, where trained social workers and psychologists with therapeutic experience of working with families were employed. According to Basu (2012), counsellors in the family courts in Kolkata were appointed because of their connections with the Communist Party of India (Marxist), which was in power in West Bengal at the time appointments were being made (Basu 2012). In most other states, the counsellors were employed on contract basis, for a certain fixed number of cases. The remuneration in most cases was low, offered as an honorarium instead of a salary, and was not paid on time, adding to the frustration of the counsellor's role. In states where advocates and judges played the role of mediator and counsellor, conflict arising from the dual roles was clearly seen. This situation was considered as problematic and avoidable.

There was consensus among the participants about the fact that the number of courts dealing with family and marriage-related cases was far less than the optimum number required, and additionally, there was a paucity of counsellors present in family courts, with the requisite skills of working with families and couples. This resulted in work overload for both the legal service authorities and the counsellors. There has been considerable delay in the establishment of new courts. As a case in point, the city of Mumbai, with a population of 20.7 million residents as per the 2011 Census of India has only seven courts, with 14 marriage counsellors, to serve the entire population, as against the recommendation of one court for a million population. This has led to overcrowding of the court premises, and delay and pendency of cases.

Another issue arising from the discussion was the low numbers of female judges in the family court system. The original Act mentioned the need to increase the number of female judges over time. The counsellors taking part in the discussions felt that many of the judges who were in the family court did not have the necessary sensitivity or skill to deal with the needs of families and women.[2] A suggestion of appointing separate judges to hear family related disputes was made; this was because criminal cases were of a different nature and required a different set of skills on the part of the advocates and judges dealing with such cases. In

[2]Judges in the family court are drawn from the pool of judges in the states, who can be transferred from civil courts, which deal with criminal matters.

contrast, a custody battle or a case concerned with domestic violence would require different skills to deal with a child-related or woman-related legal issue with the necessary sensitivity.

A recent report published in Bangalore indicated that there were more than 8,600 cases pending at the Bangalore family courts (Mukherjee 2014). While we might not have detailed data for all family courts, the anecdotal evidence from the marriage counsellors attending the event confirmed that high workload and the attendant backlog of cases was indeed a pressing concern.

10.2.2 Nature of Issues and Types of Cases Handled

One of the aspects of the discussion related to the types of cases seen in the various courts. There was an agreement between the group members on the broad nature of issues arising. Across states, counsellors reported that the aim of the counselling was more towards reconciliation of the dispute. It was only when reconciliation was seen to fail that separation was addressed. The aim of marriage counsellors, as seen by them was to ensure that reconciliation should be considered as the first alternative in the case of marital disputes.

Most of the issues related to marital discord and custody, maintenance, property and restitution of conjugal rights. Dowry-related issues were mentioned across the board. In cases where dowry issues were conflated with domestic violence issues, the problems escalated and the chances of reconciliation became more remote. Many counsellors hinted at an increase in the number of cases where there was a criminal case also registered under section 498A of the Indian Penal Code.[3] One of the participants maintained that women were misusing the law, and using it as leverage against their in-laws. This was echoed by participants from other states as well. Basu (2012) mentions how the simultaneous filing of a case under section 498A was indicative of a deliberate damage of the marriage, and embarrassment of her spouse and his family by the woman. Data from the National Crime Report Bureau report of 2012 underscored that the number of 498A cases were 106,527 in 2012, 21.1 % higher than the average of the past 5 years indicating that crimes against women were on the rise (National Crime Records Bureau 2012). The figures for 2013 for cases filed under section 498A of the IPC stand at 118,866; with an increase of 11.6 % over the 2012 figures (National Crime Records Bureau 2014).

The nature of cases mentioned by the counsellors reflected the changes that were taking place in India as a result of changes in social beliefs, norms and mores. Marital conflicts arising due to clashes with the extended family were

[3]Section 498A of the Indian Penal Code was introduced in 1983 to protect a woman from her husband or her husband's family where there are claims for illegal dowry demands. An offence filed under section 498A of the IPC is a non-bailable, cognizable offence, carrying a prison term of up to 3 years, and a fine.

mentioned by many of the counsellors. Counsellors mentioned that the number of cases that mentioned homosexuality in one of the partners was on the rise. Cases being filed for maintenance were seen more often. Many of the counsellors indicated that they saw an increase in the number of live-in relationships, and problems arising from the dissolution of live-in relationships were important to consider. Issues related to complications arising out of alcohol abuse were seen increasingly among either partner. Difficulties stemming from out of marriage relationships were indicated as being on the rise. Problems arising due to one of the partners not wanting to have children were mentioned. Yet another increasingly seen phenomenon was conflict arising due to infertility in a partner. Some of the newer concerns that were mentioned related to the use of technology in the form of mobile phones and Internet, which was mentioned as an increasing cause for problems in couples. In Kerala, access to Internet and mobile phones, referred to as the social consumption of technology has contributed to an increase in out-of-marriage relationships (Thomas 2013).

Many of the issues mentioned above, raised by the counsellors, were themes that were cross-cutting, with relevance for counsellors from all the states represented at the convention. Alongside were issues that were specific to the context that the particular counsellors came from. Counsellors from Maharashtra and Kerala made reference to the increase in mutual consent divorces over the past few years. In cases of mutual consent divorce, there was little scope for any counselling to be done.

In cities such as Mumbai, it was observed that many of the conflicts seen were a result of out-of-marriage relationships of either of the partners. It was felt that couples were very career oriented, which affected their relationship negatively. In such a scenario, family and familial responsibilities were not the most important priorities for these couples. One participant from Mumbai reflected that women were sometimes so absorbed by their careers that they were willing to give away custody of their children. The problem of extramarital involvement of spouses was aggravated in the case of states such as Kerala, where it was common for a spouse (usually a husband) to be working overseas for extended periods of time. When there was a delay in the return of the spouse, the probability for out-of-marriage involvement increased.

In tribal areas such as Chhattisgarh, the problem of polygamy was mentioned. The first wife was sometimes abandoned by the husband, who then took a second wife. The issue faced by the counsellors was to ensure maintenance for the first wife and for the children, if any.

In states such as Kerala and Maharashtra, counsellors mentioned that there was an increase in the number of litigants from the Muslim community who were opting to file for divorce in the court. The legal approach was seen in addition to the traditional religious methods of obtaining divorce. The reason for this was attributed to the documentation that the courts provided, which was demanded as evidence indicating dissolution of a marriage.

Desai and Bhujbal (2004) analysed the reasons for couples seeking separation and found that most couples stated temperamental differences, financial issues, family interference, dowry and adultery as reasons. A decade later, there seem to be additional aspects that are influencing couple relationships in India and there is a need to review these changes.

10.2.3 Good Practice Models—Techniques and Practices

The Family Courts Act places emphasis on reconciliation. Bringing about an understanding and preserving the sanctity of the institution of marriage is at the core of the Act, and many counsellors work with reconciliation of couples as their primary task (Basu 2012; EKTA Resource Center for Women 2008; National Commission for Women 2002; Nagasaila 1992). The emphasis on reconciliation, based on the belief that marriage is to be preserved at all costs, is accompanied by the certainty that the best environment for caring for children is the family. Neither of these beliefs hold actuality in the context of the twenty-first century, where much of the violence against women and children takes place within the milieu of the family.

When counsellors were asked about the counselling process and the techniques used while working with couples and families, there was broad consensus seen in the process of counselling being followed. The importance of confidentiality, empathy, objectivity and non-judgementality as the hallmarks of professional behaviour for counsellors was emphasized. Rapport formation with the clients was given importance, and the counsellors reported using multiple methods to develop rapport with the couple and the families who came to their chamber. Processes such as establishing ground rules that did not allow for brow-beating of any of the members, taking turns to speak, assuring the litigants of a fair hearing, were some of the methods commonly used. Many counsellors claimed to know in the first meeting with the couple whether reconciliation would be possible or not.

Differences emerged between counsellors who were trained as professional social workers and psychologists and the advocates and judges who were playing the role of counsellor. The advocates and judges followed a more directive approach of counselling, going so far as to tell the client about their opinions and offering solutions to the issues at hand. The difference in counselling styles and practice between the trained counsellors, and social workers and the lawyers, judges and activists who had embraced the counselling role was clearly demonstrated. The professionally trained counsellors and social workers had a more professional, non-directive approach of helping the couple identify strengths and weaknesses and looking for possible solutions to the conflicts. Counsellor neutrality was emphasized by the counsellors who had some professional training. The practice of using para-professionals such as activists from women's organizations has been questioned in critiques of the functioning of the family courts (Nagasaila 1992).

While counsellors from states such as Kerala indicated that they were trained in therapeutic skills, the opportunities of using these skills were limited in the context of the court setting. The heavy caseloads often precluded the use of any therapeutic procedures apart from active listening and providing options for the issues raised. Many of the counsellors opined that by the time the couples came to the court, and were referred to the counsellors for counselling, matters had also gone too far, and there was limited scope for counselling.

The counselling format most commonly used by the counsellors consisted of an individual session with the petitioner, followed by an individual session with the respondent, and then a joint session with both parties. The individual sessions were when the detailed history of the couple was taken. If necessary, counsellors asked other family members to come for a session. In most circumstances, efforts were made to ensure that a particular case was followed up, from start to closure, by the same counsellor, to ensure continuity of process. In many states there was a ceiling on the number of sessions a counsellor could have with a case; most states allowed a maximum of three to four sessions per case. It was only in exceptional circumstances that more than four sessions were allowed.

States such as Kerala and Maharashtra had detailed intake forms, with specific questions that were asked and the answers to the same were recorded. The filled intake sheets were filed by the counsellor for further reference. The recommendations of the counsellor for the case were recorded alongside, to ensure some degree of continuity in case the counsellor was transferred to another court before the case had been dismissed. The individual and joint sessions were used to help the counsellor understand the case and help the couple arrive at their desired goal. After the first session, the couple was sometimes advised to carry out some homework exercises and to consider their decision for divorce. There was usually a time period of about 3–6 months that elapsed between two sessions with a couple. However, such detailed procedures were not uniformly practiced by all counsellors across the states. Additionally, the extended time frames did not allow for enough scope to recapitulate what was done in the earlier sessions, both for the couples concerned and for the counsellors.

Some states followed the practice of calling in family members, or other influential community members, in order to help with settlement of the case. This was especially so in cases when both parties had different goals and expectations from each other. In such cases, time was set aside to summon the families to come to meet the counsellor and help break the deadlock. In such situations, the counsellors said that they laid out the ground rules to the families at the outset, and did not hesitate to call in the security if there was discord. Counsellors from states such as Maharashtra played an active role in psycho-educating the families and the couple in order to help them in the future. According to one of the counsellors, it was important to get couples to understand and accept what had gone wrong in the relationship and to learn from the mistakes in order to ensure that the same errors were not committed again.

While client confidentiality was an important value that was recognized by the social workers and psychologists, it was felt that confidentiality was difficult to maintain in the court setting. Most clients preferred to have their lawyers with them while discussions were in progress. This was despite the fact that lawyers were not necessary to the process of counselling in the court. Apart from the lawyers, the case had to be discussed with the judges, which again led to breach in confidentiality. The problems of client confidentiality as a result of the infrastructure and interference by lawyers and advocates have been discussed in a later section.

Many states had a provision for home visits by the counsellors. The home visits were decided upon in consultation with the judge. Home visits were considered as particularly important when custody cases were to be decided. Additionally, if there was a demand for restitution of conjugal rights, a visit to the conjugal home was necessary, in order to ascertain that the safety of the woman would be ensured.

In states such as Maharashtra and Kerala, where children's complexes were available at the court premises, the counsellor was the mediator of the interactions of the children with the non-custodial parent. The counsellors spoke to and observed children who were caught in custody battles, to ensure that the best interests of the children were kept in mind.

Formats for reporting of the cases and the process followed with the case varied from state to state. States such as Maharashtra and Kerala had defined formats and procedures for every step of the counselling process, which were followed by the counsellor. There was consensus among participants that such standard procedures and formats should be laid down and followed.

Referrals were made to other professionals if the need was perceived. Referrals could be for further therapy or for assessment if there was a psychiatric issue seen. Referrals to various voluntary organizations were also made, especially for women who needed shelter and rehabilitation as a result of domestic violence.

10.2.4 Challenges Faced by Counsellors

There were certain systemic issues mentioned by the counsellors with regard to the functioning in the court. These issues ranged from problems in the infrastructure, to problems in attitude among the stakeholders, to counsellor-related personal issues. EKTA's study of the family courts in Tamil Nadu in 2008 highlighted several of these challenges (EKTA Resource Center for Women 2008). Basu (2012) in an ethnographic study of the family court complex in Kolkata mentions the lack of privacy in the counsellor's room, where the room was divided into assortments of furniture, and the noise from one counselling session often interfered and threatened to drown out the sound of the adjacent sessions (Basu 2012).

Infrastructural Issues

Infrastructural problems were identified repeatedly by the counsellors. Difficulties related to lack of space for counselling, inadequate seating arrangements for the counsellors and the clients, no separate space for working with children, and poor toilet facilities hampered the functioning of counsellors across states. The lack of space and privacy for counselling meant that client confidentiality could not be maintained. In many states, counsellors mentioned having to 'counsel' individuals and couples in a large common space, where lawyers, other couples and children were all present. At times, the space was demarcated by a curtain, which gave an illusion of privacy. Situations such as this resulted in loss of privacy and breach of client confidentiality. The problems of infrastructure were mentioned by counsellors from all states.

Other infrastructural issues related to inadequate and insufficient secretarial support. Caseloads of the counsellors varied; in Kerala and Maharashtra, counsellors saw as many as 12–15 cases in a day. With a heavy caseload, it was difficult for the counsellors to ensure that the records were up to date, without any undue backlog. This was in contrast to states like Chhattisgarh, Manipur and UP where the counsellors were not allowed to see more than three cases in a day.

Payment for cases was mentioned as a problem by counsellors. Many states only paid an honorarium to the counsellors for the cases seen by them. This amount varied across states, and was not commensurate with the work that was carried out by the counsellors. The low salary paid to the counsellors further contributed to their low status in the court hierarchy in many of the states.

In states such as Maharashtra, technological facilities in the form of computer support were felt to be inadequate. Many clients asked for sessions by video and teleconferencing, or by Skype. This scenario was becoming more common when one litigant was in India, while the other lived abroad, and could not be present for the meetings with the counsellor. These sessions often took a long time to set up and did not always work efficiently due to various technical problems and inadequate technical know-how and backup.

Problems of security and safety for the counsellors and the families of the counsellors were mentioned as a factor that needed attention. In Naxal-prone areas such as Chhattisgarh and Madhya Pradesh, counsellors mentioned that the safety of the female counsellors and their family was at risk. They had to deal with threats from families of clients, where there was a perception that the counsellor had favoured one party over the other.

Lack of Awareness About Counselling

A major challenge faced by the counsellors in the court related to a general ignorance about the nature, process and benefits of counselling among multiple stakeholders in the system, from the judges, the advocates, the clients and the family members of the clients. This resulted in reluctance of the clients to approach the counsellor and speak openly on issues that needed to be addressed. The general perception among people in the court was that going to the counsellor was a waste of time, and only resulted in the process being drawn out, and having to come to meet the counsellor for extended meetings.

Judges and advocates were poorly informed about the counselling process, and as a result did not see the necessity for all cases to be mandatorily seen by the counsellor. Additionally, this resulted in poor access of the counsellors to the judges to discuss sensitive cases. A counsellor from Uttar Pradesh remarked that one family court judge was not aware about the presence of marriage counsellors in the court. Within the court system, there was a hierarchy operating, which privileged the judges and the advocates over the counsellors. In some states, counsellors mentioned that they faced verbal abuse from the judges and advocates. Often advocates and lawyers barged in on a counselling session, or demanded to see the files and the notes made by the counsellors. In some states, such as Tripura and Andhra Pradesh, there was a mediation centre run by lawyers and advocates which had a similar function as the marriage counsellors of ensuring reconciliation. Marriage counsellors mentioned that after they had done the hard work involved with the family, the credit if the couple reconciled would be taken by the mediators from the mediation centre.

These problems related to judges and advocates were mentioned more by counsellors from states other than Maharashtra. Judges from Maharashtra were seen as being more sympathetic and aware about counsellors and counselling needs, as compared to the judiciary from other states.

Attitude to Women's Issues

Many counsellors expressed that judges and advocates were insensitive about women's issues. Many judges emphasized reconciliation rather than separation; which could be deleterious to the women in the cases; this has been discussed at length by previous reports on family courts in India as well (Basu 2012; Nagasaila 1992). There were very few women judges, which added to the problem. Reports on family courts functioning have emphasized a need to evolve a pro-woman framework for marriage counselling to be adopted by the marriage counsellors. According to Agnes (2001), considering the patriarchal nature of Indian society, a neutral stand by the counsellors could get translated into an anti-woman posture; and there was a requirement for periodic training to evolve gender sensitive, women-oriented counselling in the family court.

The case of Uttar Pradesh was brought up specifically during the discussion. Due to the existing patriarchal ethos in the state, the plight of women was deplorable. Since very often the husbands were responsible for paying the legal fees, their demands were given preference in the court over the women's rights. Gender sensitization was crucial for advocates and lawyers, having to fight such women-related issues or dealing with social evils such as dowry deaths and with victims of domestic violence and physical and emotional abuse.

Interference by Advocates and Family Members

One of the challenges expressed by counsellors across the board related to the role of the advocates and family members. The role of the advocate was seen as a major hindrance to the process of counselling. Though the Act negated the role of the advocate, in actuality, it was difficult to keep the advocates out of the counselling chamber. In cases where the advocate played the role of the counsellor, the problem became worse; the obligations to the client became difficult to fulfil.

Counsellors reported that advocates were poorly informed about the counselling process and the need for counselling, and often gave wrong information to the clients about how speaking openly to the counsellor would result in delays in the case. Mohan Raj (2014) has illustrated at length how the interference from lawyers in the family courts impacted the work of the marriage counsellors in Kerala. While counselling and family court practice in Kerala was relatively advanced compared to many other states, this interference by advocates was a challenge that had to be dealt with by the counsellors.

Cases of advocates misinforming clients were mentioned by many of the counsellors. The misuse of section 498A of the IPC, and combining it with the Domestic Violence Act of 2005 was mentioned as problematic. Often, women were wrongly advised by their advocate to file a case under section 498A, irrespective of whether it was warranted or not.

The counsellors gave examples of family members and advocates barging into the counsellor's room and disrupting the proceedings. This was a problem mentioned across states. The counsellors emphasized that there was a need for better coordination and communication between lawyers, advocates and counsellors, which would in turn lead to better understanding of the roles played by each of the stakeholders in the legal system. This would ensure better service for the client in the long run.

Client-Related Issues

The problem of dealing with involuntary clients was repeatedly brought up. The court procedure required the session with the counsellor. Counsellors felt inadequately prepared to deal with such reluctant clients. In cases of mutual consent divorce, the client was not required to make any disclosures. This was felt to obstruct the process of counselling, limiting the scope for probing by the counsellor.

Counsellor-Related Issues

Various issues pertaining to the skill, awareness and training of the counsellors were broached. Many counsellors felt inadequately prepared to deal with some of the issues that they saw in their chamber, such as homosexuality, sexual problems, mental illness and superstitions. Many of these cases needed to be referred to outside agencies and experts. Here again, it is important to differentiate between professionally trained social workers and counsellors, and the activists and lawyers who were playing the role of counsellor; with the former being better equipped to handle the cases as compared to the latter. Counsellors from Maharashtra mentioned the mandatory in-service training for counsellors during the year. Counsellors mentioned the need to maintain and update referral lists.

Job-related problems such as stagnation caused by poor scope for promotions were mentioned as an issue that had to be dealt with. There was a lack of initiative among the counsellors due to poor scope of growth in the profession both in terms of salary and a career ladder that assured progress. Counsellors were not promoted on the basis of their seniority. Their remuneration or pay scale was not based on or determined by years of experience in their field and their educational qualifications. Unlike judges, lawyers and advocates whose pay scales were based on seniority, in most states, counsellors did not have a pay scale, and were paid on a case-by-case basis.

While some states had a transfer policy in place, most counsellors resented the transfers which disrupted their family life.

10.2.5 Future Directions

The Maharashtra family court model was felt to be the model that all other states should adopt and follow. There were rules in place, which specified the procedures for the counselling process, and for the recruitment of functionaries. The counsellors emphasized the need for synergy and uniformity across states on family court practice. It was felt that counselling should be mandatory for all litigants, and not be left to the discretion of the judges, as was the practice in most courts across the country.

There was a need for increasing the number of courts and judges handling marriage and family related cases, which were felt to be inadequate given the increase in the population and the number of cases being filed. Alongside was the necessity for having trained counsellors who could function in the courts. It was felt that there should be appointment of separate judges to hear family related disputes. The reasoning behind this was that criminal cases were of a different nature, compared to those heard in the family court, and therefore required a different set of skills, compared to a custody battle or a case concerned with domestic violence.

Efforts should be made by family courts to ensure that additional counsellors were appointed, such that the caseload was not disproportionate. Alongside, the need to establish some uniform standards and criteria with regard to the qualifications of the marriage counsellors across states was clearly expressed. It was necessary to bring about uniformity in the job profile and description of a counsellor, which would help in establishing consistency across states on service conditions, remuneration and infrastructural requirements. There was a need for developing a code of conduct or manual with prescribed rules and regulations to be followed by all the states. Better coordination and communication was important to establish between the judges, lawyers, advocates and counsellors.

Referring cases to marriage counsellors outside the court system is not currently in place. While cases are referred to hospitals for psychiatric assessment if necessary, there is seldom referral made to family therapists outside the court. This referral can help families that need the marital and couple therapy that goes beyond the limited number of sessions offered by the court. The three sessions offered by the marriage counsellors in the family court may provide the initial assessment and hypothesis building about the issues confronting the family or the couple. Intervention may require more time, as compared to what the three sessions can provide.

Systems of centralized accreditation and licensing of the marriage counsellors would be beneficial for the regulation and growth of the profession. At present, apart from Kerala and Maharashtra, there are no prescribed requirements in place about who can be a marriage counsellor. The professional development of the field necessitates the setting up of a cadre of specialists, who have the requisite training and skills for providing marital counselling in the court system. Rules pertaining to educational and professional qualifications for counsellors have to be laid down and adhered to by the courts. For the continuing development of the counsellors, there have to be regular in-service training programmes, through collaborations with academic institutions. Refresher courses and exchange programmes and visits to courts in other states would help counsellors orient themselves about the best practices being followed elsewhere. Training for gender sensitization was a felt need expressed for training for all court functionaries—counsellors, lawyers and judges.

The need for premarital counselling was raised as an issue wherein the counsellors could provide inputs. While some form of premarital counselling did take place among Christian communities, the need to develop modules for the same was raised by the counsellors. Marriage counsellors from Kerala and Maharashtra mentioned the increase in the number of couples who had been married for 5 years or less seeking divorce. Data from courts in India have shown that while divorce rates are relatively low, the number of couples divorcing within the first year was increasing (Dutt 2015). The reasons cited for divorce in many of these cases were considered to be due to problems of incompatibility and inability to adjust or make compromises. Premarital counselling on issues, responsibilities and expectations related to marriage could help in preserving the union, especially in cases when couples had been married for brief periods.

Research in various aspects of practice and content was identified as a necessity for the development of the profession. Currently, most of the counsellors did not go back to analyse the data obtained in the sessions held. Analysis of the data would provide useful insights at a regional level about important psychosocial issues pertaining to families in the Indian context, which are currently not easily available. The resultant research could be disseminated through in-house journals, or through seminars and conferences.

Awareness and sensitization on local and regional cultural issues was considered as important, and needed to be done on a regular basis. Understanding the changing psychosocial contexts with the needs, situations and dilemmas confronting families was important for the counsellors.

Establishing a network of marriage counsellors and having regular conferences would go a long way in allowing for discussions on practice across settings. This would afford valuable opportunities for sharing and learning. Organizing an event like the present National Convention could be done on an annual basis, in different locations.

10.3 Looking Ahead

In the 30 years since the Family Courts Act was passed in India, there has been considerable growth in the number of family courts in the country. However, this growth has been scattered and inconsistent. While the Family Courts Act is a Central Act, its implementation and administration is at the state level. This has resulted in considerable differences and variations in the interpretation and implementation of the Act. At present, there are about 410 functional family courts in the country, which is much less than what is required, given the population size. While the central government provides incentives for the setting up of courts, not all states are taking the requisite measures for such establishment. Setting up of additional courts is a priority.

While some states such as Maharashtra and Kerala have rules and regulations in place for the various functionaries in the court system along with clearly defined processes in place for the counselling process, this is not so in most of the other states in the country. The lacunae arising from the lack of uniform rules and procedures have been illustrated at length. Even if some of the suggestions coming from the marriage counsellors are considered for action, there is substantial scope for improvement in the implementation and administration of the Act.

The marriage counsellor, who was envisioned as being central to the process of administration of the Act, has not received the attention necessary for the growth of the profession. If the Family Courts Act has to have its desired effect across the country to resolve family disputes in a harmonious fashion, there is much that needs to be done with regard to the training, roles and responsibilities of the counsellors serving in the various family courts in the country. The separation of roles of the various functionaries in the family court will be essential if marital counselling is to actually take place. Marriage counsellors in the family courts in India are more involved in marital mediation, rather than marital counselling. Marriage and couple counselling in its truest sense is not really taking place within the court system. Much of what transpires as 'counselling' is akin to giving advice and attempting to maintain the status quo.

Acknowledgments This chapter is drawn from the National Convention on '*Changing Scenario of Marriage and Family in India: Perspectives from Family Court Marriage Counsellors*' held at the Tata Institute of Social Sciences (TISS), Mumbai on 11 and 12 October 2014. The convention was organized by the two authors, and sponsored by the Indian Council of Social Science Research and TISS. The authors would like to thank all the counsellors who attended the convention.

References

Agnes, F. (2001). *Family law (volume II): Marriage, divorce, and matrimonial litigation*. Delhi: Oxford University Press.

Basu, S. (2012). Judges of normality: mediating marriage in the family courts of Kolkata, India. *Signs, 37*(2), 469–492. Retrieved May 30, 2015, from http://www.jstor.org/stable/10.1086/661712.

Department of Justice. (2014, December 5). *The family courts act*. Retrieved from Number of Family Courts Functional, October 31, 2014. http://doj.gov.in/sites/default/files/userfiles/fc_fuctional.pdf.

Desai, M., & Bhujbal, S. (2004). Pratibimb (Maharashtra Family Courts Magazine).

Dutt, A. (2015, January 4). How and why number of young Indian couples getting divorced has risen sharply. *Hindustan Times*. Retrieved from http://www.hindustantimes.com/sexandrelationships/why-number-of-young-indian-couples-getting-divorced-has-risen-sharply/article1-1303204.aspx.

EKTA Resource Center for Women. (2008). *A study of family courts Tamil Nadu*. Madurai: EKTA. Retrieved May 25, 2015, from http://ektamadurai.org/wp-content/uploads/2011/pdf/Family_Court_Study_Book_let.pdf.

Family Court Mumbai. (2015, May 25). Retrieved from Maharashtra Family Courts. http://ecourts.gov.in/mumbai/family.

Gazette of India. (1984). *The family courts act*. Delhi: Government of India. Retrieved December 5, 2014, from http://doj.gov.in/sites/default/files/family-courts-act.pdf.

Jamwal, N. S. (1999). Have Family Courts lived up to Expectations? *Mainstream Weekly*.

Mohan Raj, J. (2014). Counselling practice in family courts: conflicting interests among key persons. *Changing scenario of marriage and family in India: Perspectives from family court marriage counsellors*. Mumbai.

Mukherjee, S. (2014, August 25). 8,600 cases pending in family court. *Times of India*. Retrieved from http://timesofindia.indiatimes.com/city/bengaluru/8600-cases-pending-in-family-court/articleshow/40861495.cms.

Nagasaila, D. (1992, August 15). Family courts: A critique. *Economic and Political Weekly*, 1735–1737.

National Commission for Women. (2002). *Family courts: Report on working of family courts and model family courts*. New Delhi: National Commission for Women.

National Crime Records Bureau. (2012). *Crime in India, 2012 statistics*. Delhi: Ministry of Home Affairs. Retrieved December 5, 2014, from http://ncrb.nic.in/CD-CII2012/Statistics2012.pdf.

National Crime Records Bureau. (2014). *Crime in India, 2013, compendium*. New Delhi: Ministry of Home Affairs. Retrieved from http://ncrb.nic.in/CD-CII2013/compendium%20 2013.pdf.

Thomas, C. S. (2013, July 15). Seeking the Forbidden Fruit. *The New Indian Express*. Retrieved from http://www.newindianexpress.com/cities/thiruvananthapuram/Seeking-the-forbidden-fruit/2013/07/15/article1684594.ece.

Chapter 11
Telephone Counselling in India: Lessons from iCALL

Sujata Sriram, Aparna Joshi and Paras Sharma

Abstract Delivery of mental health services to clients has been profoundly impacted by the advent of technology. Across the globe, the telephone has been a medium of providing counselling for many years; with services being provided by trained volunteers and also by mental health professionals. Helplines run by professionals have begun to supplement the delivery of mental health services in many countries, including India. There is a growing body of literature that suggests that telephone helplines are efficacious in dealing with a range of mental health issues. In developing countries such as India, individuals in need of mental health services remain unserved and unattended, owing to the lack of trained and qualified mental health professionals. Telephone helplines ensure easy accessibility and immediate assistance to people in need. iCALL—The Psychosocial Helpline was set up by the Tata Institute of Social Sciences to address the psychosocial needs of individuals in need of mental health services in India, offering counselling by telephone and by email. This paper examines how telephone counselling is carried out and offers insights into the experience of providing counselling through a distance mode. Many of the process skills required for effective face-to-face counselling are required in telephone interaction as well.

Keywords Telemedicine · Mental health · Helplines · Telephone counselling · Empathy

The use of the telephone for counselling has been prevalent for a number of years. The term telemedicine has been used to refer to the delivery of medicine using the mechanism of information and communication technology (ICT). The American

S. Sriram (✉) · Aparna Joshi
School of Human Ecology, TISS, Mumbai, India
e-mail: sujatasriram@gmail.com

Paras Sharma
iCALL Psychosocial Helpline, TISS, Mumbai, India

S. Sriram (ed.), *Counselling in India*, DOI 10.1007/978-981-10-0584-8_11

Telemedicine Association has used the term telemental health as ‘an intentionally broad term referring to the provision of mental health care from a distance’ (American Telemedicine Association 2009, p. 6), which encompasses mental health assessment, treatment, collaboration and education. Telemental health can be provided by a range of service providers such as counsellors, psychiatrists, social workers, nurses, primary health providers and others. The term ‘telepsychiatry’ has been used to refer to the delivery of psychiatry services by such ICT devices (Scarf India 2015; Malhotra et al. 2013), and can be considered as a component of telemental health.

Changes in technology have resulted in changes in the ways in which mental health services are being provided to clients. While the telephone was the first means of providing telemental health, the internet has given rise to a multitude of new ways of providing and accessing support through computer mediated communication—through email, chat rooms, and other such methods (Fukkink and Hermanns 2009).

This paper examines the process of telephone counselling as offered through one helpline service in Mumbai, India, that provides counselling both online through email, and through the telephone.

11.1 Mental Health in India

In a country like India with a scarcity of mental health professionals, helplines can be seen as effective means of providing services for populations who may not have ready access. Data about the state of mental health services and professionals in India indicates the scarcity of resources. Though mental illness accounts for about a sixth of all health related concerns in India, the means of addressing these problems is not increasing in a commensurate manner (Kumar 2011). Kumar (2011) in his paper on mental health concerns in India cites figures from WHO (2005) to indicate that the number of psychiatrists serving the total population in India actually fell between the years 2001–2005. According to Malhotra et al. (2013), only 29 % of the mental health needs in India could be met with the existing number of mental health professionals.

Thara et al. (2004) lament the scarce budgetary provisions from the Government of India, along with a scarcity of professionals, compounded by stigma to deal with problems of mental illness (Thara et al. 2004). According to Pathare, less than 1 % of the health budget in India was spent on mental health, despite increasing mental health concerns in the country (Pathare 2005). While the National Mental Health Programme was initiated in 1982, and implemented from 1984, with the intention of integrating mental health with existing primary health care services, the on-ground implementation remains weak and inefficient; the District Mental Health Programme (DMHP) is operational only in 125 out of the 626 districts in the country (Kumar 2011). The DMHP, initiated in 1996, went beyond the identification and treatment of mental illness. The emphasis is on promotive and preventive mental health, with services for schools, colleges and workplaces, apart from suicide prevention work. According to the 2014–15 report of the Department of Health and Family Welfare, of the Ministry of Health and Family Welfare, India, the coverage of the DMHP has extended to 241 districts in the country (Department of Health and Family Welfare 2015). While there is some provision of mental health services in the urban areas of the country, the rural masses of India stay unserved and unattended.

Non-governmental and voluntary agencies have stepped in to augment the scarce mental health resources provided by the government. There are a number of voluntary organizations in different parts of the country who have set up services for people with mental illnesses and their families. The Schizophrenia Research Foundation, Chennai, and the Richmond Fellowship Society, Bangalore and Delhi provide specialized care for people with chronic mental illness. Sneha in Chennai works with people with suicidal ideation. The Alzheimer's and Related Disorders Society of India (ARDSI) has chapters in several states of the country for elderly people suffering from Alzheimer's and dementia. Sangath, in Goa, works on issues of children and adolescent health and mental health (Thara et al. 2004; Patel and Thara 2003). Many of these voluntary organizations help and support people with mental illness. Individuals and their families are assisted to come together to form support groups and self-help groups.

11.2 Telephone Counselling—The Origin and History

Telephone counselling does not necessarily come under the realm of telepsychiatry, but is definitely considered under the scope of telemental health. The nature of telephone counselling can vary depending on the objectives of the service, the type of service providers, and their level of training. Telephone helpline services operated by professionals would have different outcomes and objectives as compared to those manned by volunteers, though there may be an overlap with regard to the clientele.

Provisioning mental health through the telephone services arose in the middle of the twentieth century through the services provided by The Samaritans in the United Kingdom. The Samaritans helpline, and other similar helplines that have opened in countries all over the world are focused on providing emotional support for those in need, more specifically to help deal with crisis situations such as suicide. The services provided by organizations such as The Samaritans are through trained volunteers. Volunteer-run helplines do not use the term counselling for the services provided, though the emotional support provided uses many of the tenets and skills of counselling. The reach of Samaritans internationally to countries such as India is through the services of Befriender's Worldwide. In India, there are eleven helplines located in the cities of Kolkata, Calicut, Mumbai, New Delhi, Secunderabad, Ahmedabad, Chennai, Jamshedpur and Kochi that are members of the Befriender's Worldwide network (Befrienders Worldwide 2015).

In 2002, there was an agreement between Befriender's Worldwide, Lifeline International and the International Federation of Telephone Emergency Services (IFOTES) to together form the Volunteer Emotional Support Helplines (VESH), which work together to provide services for people in emotional distress, and not just crisis intervention. In 2015, a new alliance called the World Alliance of Crisis Helplines (WACH) was formed by IFOTES, Life Line International, Befrienders Worldwide, Lifeline Australia, De Leo Fund and the National Suicide Prevention Lifeline. The aim of the network is to improve access to emotional support, to provide an advocacy mechanism for such services, to develop and share best practices and training for volunteers, and to cooperate with other organizations working with similar aims (IFOTES 2015).

Telephone helplines have been set up world over with differing orientations and objectives. In many countries, telephone counselling helplines run by professionals have been set up to supplement the delivery of mental health services. In countries like Australia, telephone helplines offer mental health services to people located in remote parts of the country, where resources are scarce. Helpline counselling in these cases acts as an adjunct service to individual and group therapy. The popularity of helpline counselling is attributed to low cost, ease of access for remote locations, and immediacy of assistance.

A review of 14 studies by Leach and Christiansen (2006) indicated that telephone administered therapy was effective in reducing symptoms of mental illness. Telephone interventions have been effective in reducing depression, anxiety, eating disorders, alcohol use and rehospitalization for schizophrenia (Leach and Christensen 2006; King et al. 2006; Reese et al. 2002). Telephone helplines have been found to be particularly efficacious in dealing with issues pertaining to children and adolescence (Christogiorgos et al. 2010; Fukkink and Hermanns 2009). The telephone is recognized today as a medium for multiple therapeutic endeavours, from suicide to hypnosis (Henden 2008; Rosenfield 1997; Shepard 1987).

Data indicate that even professionals who primarily use a face-to-face mode for therapy, have begun to use technology to provide services. A survey carried out in 2008 on psychology health services providers by the American Psychological Association (APA) indicated that the telephone was the technology most widely used to provide health services, with 85 % of the respondents stating their preference for the telephone. Of the 85 %, about 35 % used the telephone at least once a week or more. There has also been an increase in the number of practitioners using email in their clinical practice; with 45 % of the respondents reporting the use of email for health provision (Jacobsen and Kohout 2010).

11.3 Telephone Counselling in India

Research from countries such as Australia, Canada, the United Kingdom, Greece and the Netherlands, indicates the efficacy of mental health services provided over the telephone. In India as well, telephone helplines have been set up to extend scarce mental resources to a wider population, and to cover a wider area.

Telephone counselling in India began in the latter part of the twentieth century. Many of the early helplines used the model of 'befriending', providing emotional support and assistance, especially in crisis situations. Many of the early helplines in India were run by volunteers and lay counsellors, who were trained to provide the emotional support required by callers. Sanjivini Society for Mental Health in New Delhi has been providing volunteer run face to face, telephone and email based emotional support for crisis situations. While Sanjivini was originally set up in 1976 to provide face-to-face assistance in crisis situations, the service grew to include telephone support and then to other modes as well (Sanjivini Society for Mental Health 2015). Similarly, Sneha in Chennai set up services for people with suicidal ideation in 1986, offering emotional support face to face, by telephone, and by email (Sneha India 2015).

Helpline services in India provide a range of services; from information, referrals, emotional support, befriending and psychotherapeutic interventions. Some helplines are government run, e.g. Childline which was the first toll-free helpline for children in need of care and protection, bringing together various government agencies, along with voluntary organizations, corporate houses, community organizations and academic institutions. Other government-run helplines include 1091 for women in distress, 103 for violence against women in Maharashtra. Since 2010, there have been helplines set up through public private partnerships between state governments and emergency medical service providers. One such helpline is the 181 Abhayam Women's helpline in Gujarat, which is a toll-free number for women in distress, run in partnership between the Government of Gujarat and GVK EMRI (Emergency Management and Research Institute).

Apart from the government-run helplines, there are helplines run by voluntary organizations, such as Sneha and Sanjivini. Many of the voluntary organizations such as the Schizophrenia Research Foundation, Chennai, and the Richmond Fellowship Society, Bangalore and Delhi augment scarce mental health resources by offering services through distance modes, including telephone helplines.

11.4 iCALL—The Psychosocial Helpline

In 2012, iCALL,[1] the Psychosocial Helpline was set up as a field action project of the then Centre for Human Ecology at the Tata Institute of Social Sciences (TISS) Mumbai in order to demonstrate an innovative intervention model to address the psychosocial needs of individuals. Since its inception in 1936, TISS has been recognized as an institute of higher education with a difference. Innovative programmes such as the Childline helpline were incubated as field action projects at TISS. The Centre for Human Ecology (CHE) was already training counsellors and psychologists through the MA in Counselling programme. Setting up of the

[1]iCALL stands for Initiating Concern for ALL, a name given by an alum of TISS.

iCALL helpline was the means of extending counselling services to the community at large, to people in distress. Given the scarcity of trained mental health professionals in India, an attempt to provide a centralized nodal professional counselling service that could reach out to serve populations in various parts of the country was considered as the next step in the extension of mental health services in the Indian context by CHE and TISS.

iCALL is a telephonic counselling service for addressing the psychosocial needs of people in distress in a gender sensitive manner. It caters to individuals across all age groups, with a special emphasis on vulnerable groups such as children, adolescents, women and the elderly. It operates for 6 days a week, from Monday to Saturday, from 8.00 a.m. to 10.00 p.m., with the ultimate aim of providing services in a 24 * 7 mode. The helpline provides information, emotional support and referral linkages. It is managed by trained counsellors with educational qualifications of a Masters' degree in psychology. The counsellors actively and supportively listen to the individuals' disclosures of emotional distress, and attempt to provide a safe and holding environment along with other assistance needed by the callers. Counsellors also offer email counselling services to those who wish to communicate that way. Though initially conceptualized as a service to provide psychosocial and legal counselling and guidance, the current mandate of iCALL is to provide psychosocial assistance by telephone and email. Counselling services are provided in English, Hindi, Marathi, Gujarati, Tamil, Malayalam, and Punjabi. Counsellors who are fluent in at least one Indian language, other than Hindi, are given preference during the selection of counsellors (iCALL Annual Report 2013).

At its inception, iCALL was fully funded by TISS as a field action project. After the first year of functioning, the helpline has moved to a model of funding, whereby it is financed through a series of collaborations with organizations, such as corporate bodies, government agencies and voluntary organizations, whereby iCALL provides counselling and consultancy services for a fee. This model has resulted in the subsidizing of the cost of calls to the general public through these paid services (iCALL Report 2015).

The service addresses a range of issues; from crisis-oriented needs to more long term emotional needs. It covers relational concerns, work-related matters and concerns, parenting and child rearing issues, mental health and distress, substance abuse and addiction, senior citizens problems, violence-related problems, etc. The services of iCALL are backed up by an extensive referral list consisting of agencies spanning across the country; this includes Government organizations, voluntary and community based organizations, hospitals, mental health professionals and legal aid services. The referral list includes contact details of helplines dedicated to issues of mental health, suicide prevention, sexuality, violence against women, disability, substance abuse and children and senior citizens in distress. As a policy, iCALL always makes the first referral to government hospitals and services; this was done in order to avoid association with any private practitioner or service, for profit motives. It was only if callers expressed problems accessing these government services that private practitioners and services were given as reference (iCALL Annual Report 2013).

11.4.1 Laying the Foundation for iCALL

Prior to the initiation of the helpline's services, a 1-day National Level Consultative Meet of representatives from helplines across the country was convened. The meeting was attended by ten representatives from various organizations such as Sneha Helpline from Chennai, Tamil Nadu; the IPH Maitra Helpline from Thane, Maharashtra; Yuva Maitra Helpline by MAVA from Mumbai, Maharashtra; the Nana Palkar Smruti Samiti from Mumbai, Maharashtra; Parivarthan from Bengaluru, Karnataka; LABIA from Mumbai, Maharashtra; TARSHI from Delhi, and Vandrewala Foundation Helpline from Mumbai, Maharashtra and ten representatives from the Tata Institute of Social Sciences (iCALL Annual Report 2013).

The Consultative Meeting of Helplines in India was intended to help identify the best practices on a wide range of issues from the wealth of experience of the organizations invited for the meeting. Many of the decisions relating to the everyday functioning of iCALL were clarified at this meeting. Some of these decisions related to issues such as using the helpline as a paid service, and not as a toll-free service.[2] Data from helplines in India indicates that the use of a toll-free number results in misuse of the service by prank and nuisance callers, who use the helpline for sexual gratification (Shrivastava et al. 2013).

While many of the participants for the Consultative Meeting used volunteer services for running their helplines, the decision taken by iCALL was to use professional, trained counsellors. It was opined that the helpline should initially begin with full-time employees as it may be difficult to get a project off the ground on the strength of volunteers alone, given that there are restrictions on the number of hours volunteers can clock in (iCALL Annual Report 2013).

Issues of confidentiality were discussed. It was important to clarify that the helpline would have a policy of shared confidentiality. Confidentiality and anonymity would be breached only if there was a possibility of harm to self, or harm to others. Technology in telecommunications has made complete anonymity difficult. This is because sophisticated EPBAX systems capture telephone numbers of callers. Many software packages and systems track callers by the telephone number. Complete anonymity was not possible with the caller identification system; while the telephone number was captured, the name and identity of the caller was not required. At iCALL, the policy followed is that the number is not used for any purpose which would breach the confidentiality of the caller, except for the predefined reasons of harm to self and harm to others.

The principle of two-way anonymity was followed—anonymity of the caller, and of the counsellor. All counsellors were identified by pseudonyms that were used to ensure safety of the counsellors who had little control over the nature of the call and the caller who made the call. Calls received by iCALL are documented using a customized MIS that has been extensively field-tested. No

[2]Each call to iCALL is billed to the caller. The service is not free for the caller, as the number is not a toll-free number.

audio-recording of calls takes place, to ensure client anonymity and confidentiality (iCALL Annual Report 2013; iCALL Report 2015).

In order to avoid caller dependency, the policy was to encourage callers to speak to the counsellor who took the call, rather than wait to speak to a specific counsellor. Over time, this policy has been adhered to, though a few exceptions have arisen, wherein a caller, identified as a follow-up caller, or a repeat caller wanted to continue discussion on an issue previously raised with a counsellor. However, these cases are few, and are decided on a case to case basis.

Protocols on how to receive calls and call flow were defined and practices are laid down in a training manual, which is used for internal circulation among the counsellors.

11.4.2 Training of Counsellors

Training of telephone counsellors is important, because most counselling training in India does not have a component on telephone counselling. It is necessary for counsellors who have been trained in face-to-face counselling to extend their skills to counselling on the helpline. At iCALL, there is a training period of about 4 weeks during which the trainee counsellor is only allowed to observe the counselling process. There is a rigorous training procedure that is followed, before any counsellor is allowed to take calls.

The training begins with an orientation about the philosophy of TISS and iCALL, along with the objectives and the journey of the helpline from inception. This is followed by modules on skills for telephone counselling, with role plays, mock calls and case discussions. Much of the training is experiential; the senior counsellors from the helpline play an active role in the training. Once the basic skills are provided, more specific training is imparted on areas such as suicide prevention, violence against women, sexual and reproductive health topics, substance abuse and addiction related matters, relationship concerns, problems of the queer community, and legal issues (iCALL Report 2015).

During training, counsellors are trained on how to deal with sexual callers and prank callers. As a policy, the counsellors at iCALL do not terminate any call, unless the client turns abusive or threatening towards a counsellor. In such cases, the caller is told politely and firmly that the service is meant for any emotional or psychological difficulties they may be facing and that any requests or offers of a sexual nature will not be entertained. iCALL does not block or filter out any clients as it believes that even a client who may regularly make such calls, may eventually come up with a genuine issue, at which time the service should remain available. The policy is one of containment.

Additional information on the process of call documentation is provided during the training period. All counsellors are familiarized with the custom-made MIS software that is used for call documentation. The process of entering the call data after each call is rigorously followed.

11.5 The Telephone Counselling Process

Telephone-based helpline services operate on the principle that the first call may be the last call; as a result it becomes important to ensure operating principles that maximize the efficiency of the service for the caller (Rosenfield 1997; Shepard 1987). All helplines, irrespective of whether they are serviced by volunteers, or by professional counsellors and mental health personnel, work on some common principles. A call comes in from a caller, is received by a telephone counsellor, who then proceeds to extend the service that is asked for. In general, there is some institutional information that is provided by the counsellor to the caller, which could take the form of a greeting, followed by a query (Danby et al. 2009; Fukkink and Hermanns 2009).

Each call to iCALL is responded within a minimum of two rings of the telephone, or a maximum of six rings. When a caller first calls a helpline number there is an uncertainty about whether they have reached the correct service, who will answer the call, whether that person is an operator or an expert, whether they have to start talking on their own or whether the person answering the call will ask a set of questions, whether identifying information needs to be provided, etc. An effective opening serves to effectively dispel such doubts at the very outset. Counsellors at iCALL usually open calls with phrases such as: 'Good morning/afternoon/evening iCALL Psychosocial Helpline. You are speaking to Counsellor _____. How may I assist you? What would you like to discuss?' If, at this point the caller has queries about the nature of iCALL's services and the help offered, they are answered.

The caller could present a problem and a reason for calling. Once the reason for the call has been obtained by the counsellor, the actual assessment of the client concerns and problems begins. Callers are often not clear about what they can discuss on the helpline. The policy at iCALL is to assure callers that they can discuss any issue, however trivial they may feel it to be. The skill of 'normalizing' can be effectively used to reduce the anxiety for the caller, wherein the counsellor helps the caller realize that the disquiet is appropriate for the situation, and the response is normal. Normalization attempts to reframe client problem situations as being understood as human. The normalization statement also contains the counsellor's implicit acceptance of the client (Henden 2008). Statements such as 'It is OK to feel that way'; 'There are other callers who call with similar issues. It's OK', help in reducing anxiety for the caller, and paves the way for an alliance to be developed with the counsellor.

If the caller requests for information, once the information is provided, the counsellor may sense openings pertaining to other issues. Often, the stance of asking 'Is there anything else I can help you with?' after the information sought is given, provides space for the caller to talk further (Rosenfield 1997).

Often, concerns about confidentiality may be raised by the caller. In iCALL, assurance is given to the caller at the start of the call about the policy of confidentiality. Phrases such as 'Everything we speak during this conversation will remain between the helpline and you', and 'Your details will not be shared with anybody else' are used to communicate confidentiality.

One of the strengths of telephone counselling reposes in the control that is in the hands of the caller. The caller is free to hang up, and end the call if they choose to do so (Christogiorgos et al. 2010; Danby et al. 2009; Shepard 1987). Most telephone helplines do not call back unless they have been given consent by the caller, which is to ensure safety for the caller (Sneha India 2015). In iCALL, counsellors call back only in the case of apprehension of harm to self or harm to others. In such cases, care is taken to ascertain client consent prior to calling back. The policy at iCALL requires counsellors to obtain a safe number and time prior to calling back.

There is a process of turn taking, proceeding by stops and starts, between the caller and the counsellor, wherein the counsellor uses prompts and questions to determine the nature of the call, and the pertinent issue with which the caller has approached the helpline. Active listening, which is a core skill in counselling is demonstrated through minimal responses such as *mm, hmm, okay, right*, followed by paraphrasing and summarizing what was said in order to ascertain if the counsellor had correctly understood the caller. Active listening helps in engaging the caller, and encourages them to feel comfortable enough to continue discussing their problem, forming the therapeutic alliance (Danby et al. 2009; Reese et al. 2002; Christogiorgos et al. 2010).

While active listening is easy enough to identify in a face-to-face interaction, it is more difficult to do so in a telephone interaction, and still more difficult in an online counselling session. While face-to-face communication allows for social-relational information to be drawn from visual, para-lingual and verbal cues, telephone counsellors only have access to verbal and para-lingual cues to work with (Fukkink and Hermanns 2009; Danby et al. 2009). The lack of visual cues makes it difficult for the counsellor to ascertain the truth value of what is being spoken about. It is not possible to challenge what is being said, without the risk of the caller hanging up.

One of the skills required by a telephone counsellor is to recognize and respond to the feelings of the caller, using only the verbal and the para-lingual cues. This requires sensitivity to silence, sighs, pauses, hesitations, along with changes in pitch and tone of voice. The feelings need to be responded to appropriately, so that the caller does not feel rushed. Phrases such as 'It's okay… Take your time', may be the telephonic equivalent of providing a tissue to a client in a face-to-face session. At iCALL counsellors are trained not to interrupt the flow of emotion, but to provide reassurance that they are available and present, and the caller does not have to apologize for the display of emotion.

For effective reflection of feeling, counsellors need to have a robust emotional vocabulary that can help them give specific, rather than broad labels to the different kinds of positive, negative, and at times ambivalent feelings that are expressed by clients. However, counsellors must be careful not to reflect their own reactions or what they feel that the caller would probably feel or ought to feel in a given situation, or mimic a client's feelings as it may achieve the opposite of the desired outcome (Rosenfield 1997; Shepard 1987).

The counsellor can offer formulations, which demonstrate active listening, and whether what has been previously said is clearly understood, and offers the scope for elaboration or continuation of that. Formulations allow the counsellor to pick up on, or ignore, aspects of the clients' narrative, or recast what has been said, in such a way that the client can either agree or disagree with them (Hutchby 2007). In other words, formulations summarize and paraphrase what the counsellor considers relevant or what the client has just described in terms of their emotions or a description of events. The idea is to simultaneously communicate to the client that the counsellor has not only been listening to everything she has been saying but has also understood it well enough, and has developed a sense of which parts of the narrative are most important (Danby et al. 2009).

Exploration of the problem using open-ended questions helps identify previously tried solutions, narratives about what worked and what did not work, the resources that are available for the caller in terms of the internal reserves (strengths and coping mechanisms), or the external sources available (family, social circle, supportive organizations etc.), the areas of life that have been affected by the problem, i.e. the physical, psychological, social and professional consequences of the problem, all of which help in prioritizing and goal-setting. Often the client may provide a whole gamut of issues that have been unearthed through the exploration process. This may lead to both counsellor and client feeling completely swamped by the problem story. The counsellor helps the client arrive at the most important aspects of the problem, and if possible establish an order of importance amongst these issues identified. Beyond this, it may become extremely difficult to provide any direction to the intervention being planned. For each of the areas ascertained, the counsellor helps the client arrive at specific, time-bound goals.

After identifying the focus areas and the specific goals for each of the areas, the counsellor may give the client homework exercises that are smaller steps to achieve the larger goals that have been agreed upon, which need to be completed by the next call. The feasibility of the exercises given, along with any possible obstacles expected is discussed in the conversation. The objective behind providing homework is to translate talk into action and to encourage the client to start working hands-on towards achieving their goals. Homework allows the client to practically test what was agreed on during counselling and see what works and what does not.

The counsellor uses summarization to remind the client about the things discussed during the session and what needs to be done further, and also demonstrate the progress from the start of the call to the end. The counsellor may ask the client to rate their feelings at the start of the call in comparison to the end of the call in order to see the change over the duration of the call. Yet another effective strategy used by counsellors at iCALL is to ask the client to summarize the session rather than the counsellor doing so.

While helplines operate on the 'first call is the last call' principle, it is important to encourage the client to call back after having worked on the issues discussed during the call. When a client makes this follow-up call, it suggests that something about the conversation worked for the client, making them call back. At iCALL, clients are asked to provide feedback about the call and their important takeaways from the session. Clients are also asked where they heard of the helpline, which serves to guide future publicity efforts.

11.5.1 Call Duration

In a face-to-face therapeutic interaction, session durations are predetermined, and are agreed upon by the therapist and the client. In telephone counselling, it is more difficult to pre-judge a therapeutic session. Most telephone helplines in the world which provide emotional support do not have delineated time limits for call duration or for frequency of calls. Call duration could last from a few minutes to several hours, often dependent on the nature of the issue with which the caller originally called the helpline (Young 2009). According to Rosenfield (1997) professional telephone counselling can be done effectively in the 50 minute hour as used by face-to-face counsellors. She recommends that the call duration be established and communicated to the caller, rather than leave this as an open-ended option. Many professional helplines do not advocate call length of more than 20–30 min in order to avoid calls becoming unproductive and repetitive (Rosenfield 1997).

In iCALL, there is no fixed time that is allotted for a call. Generally, it has been seen that the average call duration is 15–20 min per call. Examination of call data indicates that follow-up calls are longer than first calls. While the first call may be for about 15 min, the follow-up call may take 20 min. For repeat calls, there is exploration about what has happened between the calls, how the caller has responded to the suggestions and the homework given, and planning for the future. It has been seen that over the last 3 years, call duration has stabilised at about 20 min. Crisis calls can extend for longer periods of time, extending into several hours, and requiring support from multiple counsellors.

11.5.2 Supervision

Supervision is available for all the counsellors at iCALL, both in individual and group formats. For new counsellors, all calls answered are debriefed by the senior counsellors and by the coordinator. Regular debriefing, case discussions and case presentations are facilitated by the coordinator and advisors in order to continually enhance the skills of the counsellors. The debriefing provides inputs into how the call developed, if the counsellor experienced any problems during the call, and what additional interventions could be possible. In the case of difficult calls, sexual calls, and nuisance calls, debriefing plays an important role in allowing counsellors to vent their feelings and emotions related to these calls in a supportive manner. Debriefing ensures that counsellors have resolved any issues relating to their work, besides providing them the opportunity to discuss their feelings related to the calls. Debriefing plays a supportive role for the counsellor, ensuring that they do not feel pressured and under threat during or after taking a call (iCALL Annual Report 2013; Child Helpline International 2013; Rosenfield 1997). Counsellors who are not given a chance to vent their feelings related to difficult calls, sexual calls and other nuisance calls are more prone to burnout.

Apart from the debriefing that takes place on a daily basis, case conferences are organized periodically to bring out the linkages between theory and practice that would otherwise be lost. Case conferences provide additional inputs on call handling and other possible interventions and theoretical frameworks for the same.

11.6 Data Handling and Storage

While maintaining an audio and/or a detailed written transcript is a standard practice in face-to-face counselling, which clients are usually aware and accepting of, the same does not apply to telephonic counselling. Maintaining audio transcripts for a helpline pertaining to psychological and emotional issues is at odds with the ethics of telephone-based counselling. However, it is quite important to maintain a detailed account of each call from the point of view of accountability and quality assurance.

At iCALL, a detailed typed transcript of the call is maintained for each call received. Verbatim quotes as far as possible are transcribed during the call, and the counsellors' interventions, reflections, referrals (if any), along with any demographic data available for the caller, are fed in after the call. Each counsellor feeds in this information into a customized MIS software. The master document allows caller information to be pulled up by any of the counsellors, even if they have not previously spoken to the client, which is important for repeat callers who do not have to go over the entire history of the earlier call. Identifying details includes variables such as the telephone number, age, gender, marital status and language spoken by the client. Names (or pseudonyms) are recorded only when provided by the clients.

Given the extremely sensitive nature of the information discussed on calls on a helpline, data security is a matter of paramount importance. The data entered on the MIS is stored in encrypted form in the cloud. The MIS can only be accessed by the counsellors who have been registered with a service provider who generates a one-time password. While the counsellors can view the data entered by all counsellors, they cannot edit or delete data that has been entered by others. The data received by iCALL is used for dissemination, research and training. Care is taken to ensure that the identity of the callers is changed and the narratives are edited sufficiently to hide any identifiable details (iCALL Annual Report 2013).

11.6.1 Analysis of Call Data

Analysis of call data is done using the code book that evolved over the first 6 months of operation of iCALL. The core issues discussed by the callers are coded using a code book that was created for categorization and data analysis of the calls. There are twenty-two different categories of calls that have been identified in the code book. The code for each call has been determined on the basis of the call transcripts and the core issues identified by the counsellor who had received the call. Based on this, the call was categorized into three categories (Primary, Secondary and Tertiary, based upon the centrality of the issue). This categorization has been done keeping in mind how calls start with a particular issue, and during the process of exploration, other themes begin to emerge as well. The primary, secondary and tertiary categories, therefore, do not just mention which issue was addressed first, but also which issue was jointly determined as the highest priority by the caller and the counsellor. For example, calls primarily pertaining to any kind of substance abuse were classified under 'Addiction'. Further, if the addiction had led to discord in the marital relationship, the secondary code was 'Relationship Issues—Marital'. Lastly, if the addiction had hampered work performance leading to the possibility of job-loss, 'Workplace concerns' was considered as the tertiary code (iCALL Annual Report 2013).

11.7 The Journey of iCALL—Challenges and Growth

From 2012, when iCALL was launched till 2015, over a period of 3 years, the helpline has received over a thousand calls a month, along with about a hundred emails. The calls have emanated from all parts of India, with a preponderance being from Maharashtra, the state where the helpline is located. Many of the calls are from urban centres, though the hinterland is also represented. The helpline received calls from individuals from the ages 8 years to 80 years. The median age for the callers was 28 years. While the services of iCALL are open to individuals of all age groups, it would seem that the services are preferred by adolescents and young adults, with over 45 % of the total calls to the helpline being made by callers aged 11 years to 30 years, (with more callers between the 21–30 years age bracket than in the 11–20 years age bracket). Academic Concerns, Emotional Distress, Health (Mental, Physical, Sexual and Reproductive Health), Relationship Concerns and Work-Life Concerns were the main themes for which calls were received (iCALL Report 2015; iCALL Annual Report 2013).

The call flow to iCALL has steadily increased from the inception of the service, indicating its visibility in the public domain. The second year of operations of iCALL has resulted in the development of a service that has moved beyond the geographies of Mumbai and Maharashtra, to being a pan-India facility. There has been a steady flow of media features which helped in maintaining the flow of calls and emails, indicating the potential to handle higher volumes of calls and emails with the existing staff strength. The optimal utilization of the given staff strength is a challenge that can be met by a mass-media campaign at a professional scale. Future collaborations would need to account for ways to not just keep the project financially viable but also to increase the visibility of the service.

Social media and the Internet have proved to be a great avenue to increase the visibility of iCALL. Efforts are being made to develop user-friendly online resources such as self-help newsletters and articles in order to keep the conversation on social media active. Publicity for iCALL has predominantly been in the English language media, though there have been a number of stories in regional newspapers.

Being promoted on the internet by public interest television shows such as *Satyamev Jayate*[3] gave a great boost to iCALL's image as a mental health service.

Professional development and personal well-being of counsellors continues to be a great concern. iCALL engages in regular dialogue with its team of counsellors to keep burnout at bay. The helpline has set aside a portion of its funds towards mental health needs of its team. A major challenge for iCALL, which is experienced by other helplines in India is attrition of the workforce. Telephone counselling as a profession for a trained counsellor is considered as being lower in stature as compared to the face-to-face format of counselling. Though counsellors consider the experience at iCALL to be rewarding professionally, there is a desire to move to the more conventional face-to-face format of counselling.

11.8 Conclusion

Telephone counselling has to be recognized as an attractive alternative to face-to-face-counselling. In a country as starved of mental health resources as India, it provides a viable alternative that needs to be strengthened. It is cheap, it is convenient, and it offers anonymity and confidentiality to the caller along with control. The telephone counsellor plays an influential role in the progress of the counselling relationship. According to Rosenbaum (1974, p. 484), 'The ringing of the telephone symbolizes the crying of a baby and there is an immediate response, especially as the voice of the counsellor corresponds to the immediate response of the mother' (Rosenbaum 1974, cited in Christogiorgos et al. 2010).

References

American Telemedicine Association. (2009). *Evidence-based practice for telemental health.* Washington D.C.: American Telemedicine Association. Retrieved September 20, 2015, from http://www.americantelemed.org/docs/default-source/standards/evidence-based-practice-for-telemental-health.pdf?sfvrsn=4.

Befrienders Worldwide. (2015, September 27). *Befrienders worldwide*. Retrieved from Befrienders Worldwide: http://www.befrienders.org/.

Child Helpline International. (2013). *Counselling practice guide.* Child Helpline International.

Christogiorgos, S., Vassilopoulou, V., Florou, A., Xydou, V., Douvou, M., & Tsiantis, J. (2010). Telephone counselling with adolescents and counter-transference phenomena: particularities and challenges. *British Journal of Guidance & Counselling, 38*(3), 313–325. doi:10.1080/03069885.2010.482394.

Danby, S. J., Butler, C., & Emmison, M. (2009). When 'listeners can't talk': Comparing active listening in opening sequences of telephone and online counselling. *Australian Journal of Communication, 36*(2). Retrieved from http://eprints.qut.edu.au/.

[3]*Satyamev Jayate* is a widely viewed television show anchored and created by the film star Aamir Khan. The show focuses on sensitive social issues in India, such as rape, child sexual abuse, domestic violence, and substance abuse.

Department of Health & Family Welfare. (2015). *Annual report 2014–15*. New Delhi: Ministry of Health and Family Welfare, Govt. of India. Retrieved from http://www.mohfw.nic.in/.

Fukkink, R., & Hermanns, J. (2009). Counselling children at a helpline: Chatting or calling. *Journal of Community Psychology, 37*(8), 939–948. doi:10.1002/jcop.20340.

Henden, J. (2008). *Preventing suicide: The solution focused approach*. Chichester, UK: Wiley.

Hutchby, J. (2007). *The discourse of child counselling*. Amsterdam/Philadelphia: John Benjamins Publishing Company.

iCALL Annual Report. (2013). *iCALL annual report 2012–13*. Mumbai: Tata Institute of Social Sciences.

iCALL Report. (2015). *iCALL report September 2013–March 2015*. Mumbai: Tata Institute of Social Sciences.

IFOTES. (2015, September 28). *IFOTES*. Retrieved from IFOTES.org: http://www.ifotes.org/members/world-alliance-of-crisis-helplines-wach.

Jacobsen, T., & Kohout, J. (2010). *2008 APA survey of psychology health service providers: Telepsychology, medication and collaboration*. APA Center for Workforce Studies. Washington D.C.: American Psychological Association. Retrieved October 14, 2015, from http://www.apa.org/workforce/publications/08-hsp/telepsychology/report.pdf.

King, R., Bambling, M., Reid, W., & Thomas, I. (2006). Telephone and online counselling for young people: A naturalistic comparison of session outcome, session impact and therapeutic alliance. *Counselling and Psychotherapy Research, 6*(3), 1405–1746. doi:10.1080/14733140600874084.

Kumar, A. (2011). Mental health services in rural India: Challenges and prospects. *Health, 3*(12), 757–761. doi:10.4236/health.2011.312126.

Leach, L., & Christensen, H. (2006). A systematic review of telephone-based interventions for mental disorders. *Journal of Telemedicine and Telecare, 12*(3), 122–129.

Malhotra, S., Chakrabarti, S., & Shah, R. (2013). Telepsychiatry—promise, potential and challenges. *Indian Journal of Psychiatry, 55*(1), 3–11. Retrieved September 20, 2015, from http://www.indianjpsychiatry.org/article.asp?issn=0019-5545;year=2013;volume=55;issue=1;spage=3;epage=11;aulast=Malhotra.

Patel, V., & Thara, R. (2003). *Meeting the mental health needs of developing countries: NGO innovations in India*. New Delhi: Sage Publications.

Pathare, S. (2005, June). *InfoChange India news and features*. Retrieved September 27, 2015, from Infochange India website: http://infochangeindia.org/agenda/access-denied/less-than-1-of-our-health-budget-is-spent-on-mental-health.html.

Reese, R. J., Conoley, C. W., & Brossart, D. F. (2002). Effectiveness of telephone counseling: A Field-based investigation. *Journal of Counseling Psychology, 49*(2), 233–242. doi:10.1037//0022-0167.49.2.233.

Rosenfield, M. (1997). *Counselling by telephone*. London: Sage Publications.

Sanjivini Society for Mental Health. (2015, September 27). *Sanjivini*. Retrieved from sanjivini.org: http://sanjivinisociety.org/aboutus.php.

Shepard, P. (1987). Telephone therapy: The alternative to isolation. *Clinical Social Work Journal, 15*(1).

Shrivastava, A. K., Johnston, M., Stitt, L., Thakar, M., Iyer, S., Shah, N., & lester, D. (2013). Suicidal ideation in callers to a crisis hotline in Mumbai, India. *Journal of Public Health and Epiedemiology, 5*(7), 305–308. doi:10.5897/JPHE2012.0487.

Sneha India. (2015, September 27). *Sneha India*. Retrieved from SnehaIndia.org: http://www.snehaindia.org/index.php.

Thara, R., Padmavati, R., & Srinivasan, T. (2004). Focus on psychiatry in India. *British Journal of Psychiatry, 184*(4), 363–373. doi:10.1192/bjp.184.4.366.

www.scarfindia.org. (2015, September 20). *Schizophrenia Research Foundation*. Retrieved from scarfindia.org: http://www.scarfindia.org/tele-medicine/.

Young, H. R. (2009). *Exploring the dynamics of telephone counselling: A qualitative study of lifeline, Melbourne (unpublished doctoral dissertation)*. Victoria, Victoria University, Australia: Faculty of Arts, Education and Human Development, School of Psychology. Retrieved October 15, 2015, from http://vuir.vu.edu.au/15508/1/young2010.pdf.

Chapter 12
The Road Ahead: Conclusion and Directions for Future Research

Sujata Sriram

Abstract This volume has brought together a set of papers that examine the process of counselling as practiced by counsellors and therapists in India. Challenges faced by therapists due to poor mental health literacy have been illustrated. Inadequacies arising from training and supervision, due to variations in academic curricula and expectations have been identified. The scope of counselling as a profession, along with ethical dilemmas arising out of practice has been examined. The impact of the profession on the personal and professional self of the therapist, and the motivational factors and values of the counsellor are propositions that need consideration. Implications for research, training and outreach have emerged from the studies.

Keywords Counselling · Counselling process · Challenges · Training needs · Motivating factors · Personal and professional self

> Becoming a therapist offers the promise that one can have a sense of feeling real, to be alive, creative, spontaneous, and playful…. Realness is something that one brings to being a therapist or that one discovers in one's own therapeutic journey. Realness is not the "payment" one receives for becoming a therapist, since achieving the capacities depends upon specific relationships that may not be part of the therapist's experience within the therapist/client relationship. (Hamman 2001, p. 354)

The research studies that have been included in the present volume titled 'Counselling in India: Reflections on the Process' disseminate research findings from studies carried out with practicing counsellors and therapists in India. This is a body of work that contributes to research on the process of counselling in India. The counselling process examines what happens during the psychotherapy sessions, the interactions between the client and the therapist. The studies draw on primary research done with therapists and counsellors in different parts of

S. Sriram (✉)
School of Human Ecology, Tata Institute of Social Sciences, Mumbai, India
e-mail: sujatasriram@gmail.com

S. Sriram (ed.), *Counselling in India*, DOI 10.1007/978-981-10-0584-8_12

the country, and offer insights and perspectives on the current state of the art of a contested profession in the Indian context. In India, counselling has not been the sole prerogative of psychologists and psychiatrists. The studies in this volume illustrate that the terms 'counsellor' or psychotherapist is indeed a fuzzy category (Bhola et al. 2012). The term 'counselling' itself is a disputed one; in India it is used in contexts other than those intended for dealing with mental health issues. In this volume, the term counselling has been used interchangeably with psychotherapy, though they do not necessarily mean the same thing.

Counselling in India, as identified by papers in this volume, is a career that is slowly gaining recognition. However, it is still a profession relegated to urban areas of the country, catering to the mental health needs of the middle classes. The need for counselling is yet to percolate to the hinterland and to the lower socioeconomic strata. While the profession is being acknowledged as playing a role in attending to the mental health needs of the population, it is still underpaid and poorly remunerated, especially in the early stages of the career. While the awareness about what a counsellor does is slowly gaining ground, there is still considerable confusion about how a counsellor's role is distinct and different from that of a social worker. While counsellors can be found in multiple settings, their roles and responsibilities are still ambiguous. It is hoped that over time, as the profession gains credibility, this ambiguity will be overcome; allowing the full potential of counsellors to address mental health issues to be met.

Data from the studies indicates that counselling in India is a gendered field. All the studies included in this volume have samples with a preponderance of women over men. Counselling in India is a female dominated profession, with few men seeking entry. This gender disparity can be partly accounted for by the fact that many colleges offering under-graduate education in psychology in cities such as Delhi are colleges only for women. This then limits the number of students eligible to enter into post-graduate training in disciplines such as counselling and clinical psychology. While effective training of counsellors can help women counsellors to deal with a range of issues, male clients often indicate a preference for male counsellors and therapists; this preference can only be met if more men enter the profession.

The gender disparity in psychotherapy is not unique to India; it is something that is seen in other countries as well. Diamond (2012), Carey (2011) and Willyard (2011) all write about the feminization of mental health and psychotherapy in the United States of America. Willyard (2011) asserts that three times the number of women earn doctoral degrees in psychology as compared to men. The dominance of women over men in psychotherapy is likely to have an impact on the issues being dealt with in therapy and also the process of therapy itself. In the interests of the profession, the perspectives of men need to come to the forefront.

According to Carey (2011), psychiatry, a male dominated profession, has been turning more towards medication for treatment of mental illness; and women were more drawn to psychotherapy in its various forms. While Carey asserts that gender of the therapist does not matter in therapy, he goes on to say that there are certain issues that are best discussed within gender; sex and aggression are just two of them. According to Diamond (2012), men left the field of psychotherapy due to financial reasons. While psychotherapy was a lucrative profession at one time, over time it has become less profitable. He goes on to say that the profession has decreased in power and prestige over the last two decades particularly, unlike psychiatry. The preference for medication over therapy comes from the greater ease for reimbursements for medication, over talk and other methods, from health insurance companies. The difference between the professions has been attributed to the dependence and the ability to prescribe psychotropic medicines by the psychiatrists, which may result in many adult Americans consuming medication that may be unnecessary, and which may not work (Diamond 2012; Smith 2012; Carey 2011). In India too, there is a preference for a quick acting 'silver bullet' in the form of medication, either in tablet or injection, over a long drawn out therapeutic session with a counsellor. The understanding of the relationship between counselling and medication needs to develop over time, along with the recognition that dependence on medication alone may not serve to treat mental health issues.

The role ambiguity faced by counsellors becomes acute in settings wherein they work alongside medical professionals. Often the term counsellor attracts less respect as compared to that of 'doctor'. Many counsellors working in such medical settings have appropriated the term 'doctor' to refer to themselves, often in an effort to gain respectability and credibility in the eyes of the clients. Counsellors and therapists are dependent on doctors to refer cases that the medical professional feels could benefit from counselling. This referral is not consistent; and could result in clients not receiving the benefits from counselling services.

While many urban schools have begun to recognize the need for a school counsellor, the understanding of what a counsellor does in a school setting has been slow to come about. The role of a counsellor often gets confused with that of a special educator; both have distinct roles and responsibilities that schools need to recognize and accept. This is more so in schools that cater to the lower income groups, with scarcity of human resources. The school counsellor has to often play multiple roles that only tangentially address the mental health needs of the children in the schools. Teachers and the school administrators often co-opt the services of the counsellor to serve the agenda of the school, which may not be in accordance with the needs of the community, and is detrimental to the profession of counselling.

The full potential of what a counsellor can do in a school setting has rarely been explored. School counsellors can play an effective role in working with multiple stakeholders in the school system, apart from the students. Often the role of the school counsellor is confined to that of career guidance, or for dealing with 'problem' children. The role and scope of the school counsellor can extend far beyond this limited perspective. Counsellors can help identify children with potential developmental issues so that necessary early intervention can take place. Though the value of the school counsellor has been recognized in the Indian context, there is much that needs to be done at the policy level to legitimize the post of school counsellors. The counsellor in a school can play a vital role in the mental health of students and families in India (Kapur 2011). Gaiha et al. (2014) in a study on knowledge, attitudes and practices related to mental health in India found that teachers and counsellors were considered as important sources of information on mental health. They were considered to be important change agents for bringing about help-seeking behaviour. In the context of mental health literacy in India, teachers and counsellors can play a vital role in integrating the mental health services with the education system at the secondary and high school levels. In order to increase the effectiveness of the school counsellor, the awareness about counselling for students, parents, teachers and school administrators needs to occur. This would imply a shift away from the current paradigm of one counsellor working with all children in a single school, which contributes to heavy workload and unrealistic expectations. The stigma attached with going to the counsellor needs to be corrected over time.

Some of the common features obtained from this series of papers relates to the fact that counsellors in India are drawn from varied backgrounds and disciplines, ranging from social workers, to clinical and counselling psychologists, to psychiatrists. Each discipline emphasizes different aspects of counselling in the training offered. While process skills are uniformly acquired in the basic academic training, the emphasis on therapeutic skills varies. Many counsellors augment the skills acquired during basic academic training by attending further skill-based programmes, often offered by practicing therapists. The need to continually update oneself and the skills employed has been emphasized in all the studies covered in this volume.

Lacunae in training have been identified by participants. It has to be recognized that inadequate training is detrimental for novice counsellors, and for the field as a whole (Ridley and Mollen 2011). Most of the counselling training offered in India does not draw on the use of technology for counsellor training. Additionally, most of the resources available are western textbooks on therapy, augmented by journal articles many of which are also from Western sources (Arulmani 2007; Kapur et al. 1996; Varma 1982). While the importance of experiential, skill-based training is considered as vital for the development of effective counsellors, in practice much of the training is theoretical and does not incorporate adequate supervised fieldwork. The textual material that describes Indian experiences is sparse and not readily available. It is left to individual trainers to try and develop a contextual understanding which is relevant. While all trainers and counsellors recognize the importance of supervision for trainee counsellors, supervision is not always available or adequate. The multilingual nature of clients, trainees and trainers in the Indian context makes the process of supervision cumbersome and not entirely effective.

The research studies have all indicated the importance of self-work for counsellors. Counselling is a profession wherein the self of the counsellor is an important therapeutic aid in determining the process and the outcomes of counselling. This necessitates the counsellor to do intense self-reflection and introspection on individual motivations, values, beliefs, assumptions and prejudices about clients and client groups. In India, unlike many other parts of the world, it is not necessary for trainee counsellors to go through counselling or therapy themselves, to experience what it is like to be a client, before they begin to work as counsellors. This is accompanied by inadequate supervision, during training and during the early phase of career development, which can lead to intense distress, feelings of inadequacy and incompetence, and inability to apply what is learnt in theory to practice for novice counsellors. Burnout of novice counsellors can be high when there is a heavy workload coupled with inadequate supervision.

Self-care practices are important for counsellors to acquire, which helps in the prevention of burnout, exhaustion and compassion fatigue. Figley (2002) talks about the importance for therapists in today's context to acquire self-soothing and stress management techniques in order to deal with distress and to continue working with empathy and compassion. He goes on to mention the need for therapists to support each other in order to deal with the compassion fatigue through the development of a suitable desensitization programme. Burnout according to Ray et al. (2013) consists of three components: 'emotional exhaustion, cynicism and personal efficacy. However, emotional exhaustion is considered the central element of burnout resulting in cynicism about one's work and low efficacy.' (p. 256) Burnout can result from a mismatch between expectations and the job on six areas of work-life. The six areas have been identified by Ray et al. (2013) as:

> Workload (job demands placed on an employee given a specified amount of time and resources), Control (opportunity for employees to make important decisions about their work, as well as their range of professional autonomy and ability to gain access to resources necessary to do their job effectively), Rewards (recognition for work contributions, i.e., financial, social, and/or internal), Community (quality of the social context in which one works, including relationships with managers, colleagues, and subordinates), Fairness (the extent that openness and respect are present in the organization and the decision-making process), and Values (represent the congruence between the organization's priorities and values and those of the employee). (p. 256)

Compassion fatigue and burnout are determined not just by personal factors, but by macro systemic factors as well. Prevention of burnout would require stronger relationships between colleagues, more supervision from peers and superiors, awareness about own and others' emotions, and a balanced workload. The studies included in this volume indicate that while relationships with colleagues are positive, supervision for entry level counsellors is not always available. Balancing workload is problematic, with a scarcity of trained counsellors, especially for entry level counsellors in the early stage of their career. It is over time that counsellors learn to leave the stresses of challenging cases at work, rather than taking them home.

Supportive networks of counsellors such as the Counsellors' Association of India Association of Indian School Counsellors and Allied Professionals, and the Indian Association of Clinical Psychologists, and the Yahoo Psychologists' group are available for conferences, meetings, that allow exchange of information and for discussion of issues that are of concern. Groups that allow for supervision are also available in some cities in the country, which are useful for counsellors to access. Other self-care methods such as mindfulness training, exercise and yoga have been beneficial for counsellors.

Research has shown that most of the training available for counsellors in India is carried out in English. If we consider the linguistic diversity of the country, this monolingual training of counsellors does not prepare them adequately to deal with clients in other languages. Often the lexicon of emotional terms that counselling students and novice counsellors have access to are inadequate to allow for effective counselling practice. Supervision can resolve issues emerging from working with clients from varied linguistic and cultural backgrounds; however, training material and literature in languages other than English is scarce. There has been a hegemony of English speaking counsellors, without adequately recognizing the needs of populations other than middle-class English speaking groups. There is a pressing need for counsellors in the vernacular medium.

In the United States of America, the United Kingdom, and in some countries in Europe programmes have been specifically developed to train supervisors. Developing the skills and practice for supervision is integral to the development of the profession of counselling. According to Holloway and Carroll (1999), specific training for supervision has come to the forefront only since the 1980s. Prior to this, the belief was that the training to become a good counsellor would suffice to develop effective supervisors. The developmental model and the social role systems model of supervision have contributed to the awareness of the need for separate training for supervision (Holloway and Carroll 1999). In India, there is no formal training for becoming a supervisor. While the importance of supervision has been reiterated in the papers in this volume, and in research, one of the issues besetting counsellors in the early stage of the career is the lack of adequate supervision. Training for supervision may help in providing supervisors better equipped to provide supervision to counsellors at various stages of the career.

The importance of creative arts therapy to augment regular therapeutic processes is important to consider. Creative art therapies have just begun to find a place in the therapeutic landscape in India, with therapists acknowledging their utility. However, they are still regarded as alternative therapy methods and not as complementary to existing therapy. Often creative arts in therapy are resorted to when nothing else works; rather than being seen as an experiential method that can tap into aspects not accessed in talk therapy. Training in creative art therapy, and its use in mental health services, needs to be included in the battery of skills that a therapist has to deal with clients. Creative art therapies can be used with clients of all ages with different problems.

Most of the training in counselling and therapy in India focuses only on the face to face mode of counselling. Most university training programmes in counselling in India do not have a component on distance modes. This is despite the evidence from research on the effectiveness of telephone counselling from multiple international sources (Jacobsen and Kohout 2010; Henden 2008; Leach and Christensen 2006; King et al. 2006; Reese et al. 2002). Organizations that set up distance counselling programmes provide on the job training to equip counsellors trained in the face-to-face mode to work with clients in a distance mode. While many of the process skills may be the same, training at the university level for online counselling may erode the hegemony that face-to-face counselling enjoys in comparison to other modes. In a country with scarcity in resource allocation for mental health, and a paucity of trained professionals, telemedicine and telemental health offer a viable means of providing mental health services to the hitherto unserved and unreached masses. There is little research on online counselling in India, by telephone, email, chat rooms and other online mediums.

Data from the family court indicates that problems faced by families is on the rise. Counselling as provided by the marriage counsellors in the family courts is either aimed at reconciliation, or to ensure that the separation process is as amicable and fair to all parties as possible. Rarely is there any counselling provided to help families adjust to divorce. Given the heavy workloads of counsellors in the family court, the counselling that is provided is problem-focused, rarely bringing in any theoretical framework or techniques that could be used with families and couples. While some of the family courts in the country have trained social workers and psychologists working as marriage counsellors, there are lacunae in others. If the promise of marriage counselling has to be met in the family court, counsellors trained in working with families and couples need to be in place.

Additionally, the theoretical perspectives emphasized in most university training programmes in counselling in India is on individual psychotherapy. The common models and theoretical perspectives that are taught to students are those of behaviour therapy, cognitive behaviour therapy, rational emotive behaviour therapy, client-centred therapy, and an orientation is given to psychoanalytic and psychodynamic approaches. Apart from this, there is some training given on group therapy for organizing and running groups. At the masters' level, there is little or no orientation given to systemic approaches and therapies for working with families and couples. Globalization has resulted in a number of relational issues for families and couples in India; however, there is a shortage of trained professionals to work with these issues using a systemic perspective which has been proven as having positive impacts in other cultural contexts (Carson et al. 2009). In the Indian milieu the family plays an important role in determining the process and outcome of therapy. Research on how to integrate the family into the process and outcome of research is crucial for the Indian contextual reality.

While counselling in India is today emerging as a recognized profession, it is still to acquire a regulatory body. All the research studies included in this volume have brought up the issue of lack of regulation of the profession, which has oftentimes resulted in inadequately qualified individuals entering the field, and working with clients. This can result in breach of ethical practice, harm being done to the client, along with client dissatisfaction with the services provided; these factors are not conducive to the development of the profession. A regulatory body that controls the entry of professionals into the field is mandatory. Mechanisms such as licensing come within the purview of the regulatory body. Licensing of the profession can be one of the means of addressing the lack of standardization of education and training for counselling; this can ensure that all trained, licensed counsellors will have a minimum skill set, drawn on theory and practice. Ethical codes of conduct that are currently absent can be established and enforced. The absence of a code of ethical conduct for Indian counsellors has led to some counsellors perforce using codes already established in other countries and cultural contexts. For the development of the profession in India, a culturally relevant code of ethical conduct has to be developed and disseminated.

Research in the field of counselling should be encouraged. Counsellors and therapists who are practitioners rarely document their practice. Involvement and inclusion of practitioners in training, supervision and academic instruction is a possible method for increasing the disciplinary rigour of the field. Both research and documentation of practice can augment the sparse data that is currently available, for training and for further research. This can also contribute to the documentation and discussion of cases and practice that will allow for a culturally appropriate model of counselling and therapy.

This volume is a compilation of studies done on counsellors and the counselling process. The studies have been carried out in some cities in the country. It would be pertinent to have similar research studies carried out in other parts of the country, to understand the challenges, experiences, and issues of counsellors and therapists. This volume has studies on novice counsellors, and on experienced counsellors. Research carried out at each of the phases of therapist development will provide insights into the challenges confronted by therapists.

In the Indian context, there are few studies which examine the use of specific therapeutic models and their impact on clients. For the sustained growth of the profession of counselling, research on the use of particular therapeutic models on clients of different age groups in specific settings will provide useful insights that can contribute to a contextually relevant field of practice. Similarly, sustained research with practitioners in different work situations will help in integrating practice about how western models of therapy are being adapted for clients with very different expectations and experience.

The voice of male therapists is rarely heard. Research that captures the perspectives of male therapists, their experiences, and their narratives would yield valuable inputs for the profession. Research output based on the experience of male therapists may result in more men joining the profession.

The studies in this volume examine the psychotherapy process from the perspective of the therapist. For a true understanding of the process of psychotherapy, client views need to be obtained. Client perspectives on the various aspects of the process need to be integrated into the perspectives obtained from the practitioners. If the therapeutic relationship is to be truly seen as a partnership, the perspectives of the client have to be obtained. Research into client perspectives on various aspects of the therapy process can contribute to better service delivery. Research on client perspectives will offer insights on what aspects or ingredients of the therapy process work best for clients. Difference in perspectives between clients and the therapists may provide more accurate interpretations about what works in therapy, and how the components of the therapeutic process come together (Gordon 2000; Llewelyn 1988).

Psychotherapy and counselling in India are forms of treatment that need to be integrated into the local and cultural understanding of mental health and illness. There is limited research in India about ethno-theories of illness, wellness and healing. Research at multiple levels of these issues can only serve to inform those who work in the mental health sector more meaningfully. Furthermore, it is necessary to examine how folk beliefs and practices can be integrated along with models of counselling and therapy, for holistic development and treatment of the individual.

Counselling is a profession wherein the self of the therapist plays a major role. Research that examines various aspects of the counsellor and therapist, such as the values and belief systems and their influence on practice and their interactions with clients is another possible avenue to be explored. The religious beliefs and practices of the therapist and their influence on therapeutic practice is another aspect that requires in-depth study. Ethical standards and codes of conduct followed by counsellors and therapists is another area that requires investigation. At present, some counsellors follow the code of ethics and standards as laid down by the organizations, such as the American Psychological Association, or the British Association of Counselling and Psychotherapy, to name a few. Having an ethical code or standard based on Indian reality would be necessary for training, and for regulating practice. While there is Western literature that examines counsellor ethics, there is little sustained work done in the Indian context.

In terms of methods of research, the studies included in this volume use the qualitative approach and methods thereof, which are applicable to a deeper understanding of the profession. The qualitative exploratory studies can serve to inform quantitative research that can cover larger numbers of therapists and counsellors to allow for a more generalized understanding of the profession. However, this does not preclude detailed qualitative research into aspects of practice that can then serve to increase the disciplinary rigour. Researchers can explore other qualitative methods for data collection and analysis, such as the grounded theory, phenomenological approaches, and ethnomethodology. The scope for new mixed methods in research as discussed by Lutz and Hill (2009) would yield fresh perspectives to the field.

Just as process of research can be studied, it is important to study the outcomes of therapy. There is limited research in India on outcomes of therapy. For the development of the profession, it is imperative to study from client groups what aspects of therapy were effective and what contributed to the effectiveness. Outcome research of this nature will help in the development of indigenous models of therapy that are informed by what is culturally relevant and appropriate.

References

Arulmani, G. (2007). Counselling psychology in India: At the confluence of two traditions. *Applied Psychology: An International Issue, 56*(1), 69–82.

Bhola, P., Kumaria, S., & Orlinsky, D. E. (2012, July 5). Looking within: Sel-perceived professional strengths and weaknesses among psychotherapists in India. *Asia Pacific Journal of Counselling and Psychotherapy*, 1–14. doi:10.1080/21507686.2012.703957.

Carey, B. (2011, May 21). Need therapy? A good man is hard to find. *The New York Times*. Retrieved November 09, 2015, from http://www.nytimes.com/2011/05/22/health/22therapists.html?_r=2&hp.

Carson, D. K., Jain, S., & Ramirez, S. (2009). Counseling and family therapy in India: Evolving professions in a rapidly developing nation. *International Journal for the Advancement of Counselling, 31*, 45–56. doi:10.1007/s10447-008-9067-8.

Diamond, S. A. (2012, October 5). End of men: The "feminization" of psychotherapy. *Psychology Today*. Retrieved November 9, 2015, from https://www.psychologytoday.com/blog/evil-deeds/201210/end-men-the-feminization-psychotherapy.

Figley, C. R. (2002). Compassion fatigue: Psychotherapists' chronic lack of self care. *Journal of Clinical Psychology, 58*(11), 1433–1441. doi:10.1002/jclp.10090.

Gaiha, S. M., Sunil, G. A., Kumar, R., & Menon, S. (2014). Enhancing mental health literacy in India to reduce stigma: The fountainhead to improve health-seeking behaviour. *Journal of Public Mental Health, 13*(3), 146–158. doi:10.1108/JPMH-06-2013-0043.

Gordon, N. S. (2000). Researching psychotherapy, the importance of the client's view: A methodological challenge. *The Qualitative Report, 4*(3 & 4). Retrieved November 4, 2015, from (http://www.nova.edu/ssss/QR/QR4-3/gordon.html).

Hamman, J. J. (2001). The search to be real: Why psychotherapists become therapists. *Journal of Religion and Health, 40*(3), 343–357.

Henden, J. (2008). *Preventing suicide: The solution focused approach*. Chichester, UK: Wiley.

Holloway, E., & Carroll, M. (1999). Introduction. In E. Holloway & M. Carroll (Eds.), *Training counselling supervisors* (pp. 1–7). London: Sage Publications.

Jacobsen, T., & Kohout, J. (2010). *2008 APA survey of psychology health service providers: Telepsychology, medication and collaboration.* APA Center for Workforce Studies. Washington D.C.: American Psychological Association. Retrieved October 14, 2015, from http://www.apa.org/workforce/publications/08-hsp/telepsychology/report.pdf.

Kapur, M. (2011). *Counselling Children with Psychological Problems*. New Delhi.

Kapur, M., Shamasundar, C., & Bhatti, R. (1996). *Psychotherapy training in India*. Bangalore: NIMHANS.

King, R., Bambling, M., Reid, W., & Thomas, I. (2006). Telephone and online counselling for young people: A naturalistic comparison of session outcome, session impact and therapeutic alliance. *Counselling and Psychotherapy Research, 6*(3), 1405–1746. doi:10.1080/14733140600874084.

Leach, L., & Christensen, H. (2006). A systematic review of telephone-based interventions for mental disorders. *Journal of Telemedicine and Telecare, 12*(3), 122–129.

Llewelyn, S. (1988). Psyhcological therapy as viewed by clients and therapists. *British Journal of Clinical Psychology, 27*, 223–237.

Lutz, W., & Hill, C. E. (2009). Quantitative and qualitative methods for psychotherapy research: Introduction to special section. *Psychotherapy Research, 19*(4), 369–373. doi:10.1080/10503300902948053.

Ray, S. L., Wong, C., White, D., & Heaslip, K. (2013). Compassion satisfaction, compassion fatigue, work life conditions, and burnout among frontline mental health care professionals. *Traumatology, 19*(4), 255–267. doi:10.1177/1534765612471144.

Reese, R. J., Conoley, C. W., & Brossart, D. F. (2002). Effectiveness of telephone counseling: A field-based investigation. *Journal of Counseling Psychology, 49*(2), 233–242. doi:10.1037//0022-0167.49.2.233.

Ridley, C. R., & Mollen, D. (2011). Training in counseling psychology: An introduction to the major contribution. *The Counseling Psychologist, 39*(6), 793–799. doi:10.1177/0011000010377664.

Smith, B. L. (2012). Inappropriate prescribing. *Monitor on Psychology, 43*(4). Retreived January 5, 2016, from http://www.apa.org/monitor/2012/06/prescribing.aspx.

Varma, V. K. (1982). Present state of psychotherapy in India. *Indian Journal of Psychiatry, 24*(3), 209–226.

Willyard, C. (2011). Men: A growing minority? *gradPSYCH*, 40. Retrieved November 9, 2015, from http://www.apa.org/gradpsych/2011/01/cover-men.aspx.

MIX
Papier aus verantwortungsvollen Quellen
Paper from responsible sources
FSC® C105338

If you have any concerns about our products,
you can contact us on
ProductSafety@springernature.com

In case Publisher is established outside the EU,
the EU authorized representative is:
Springer Nature Customer Service Center GmbH
Europaplatz 3, 69115 Heidelberg, Germany

Printed by Libri Plureos GmbH
in Hamburg, Germany